The

7

Minute

Solution

FREE PRESS
New York ■ London ■ Toronto
Sydney ■ New Delhi

Free Press
A Division of Simon & Schuster, Inc.
1230 Avenue of the Americas
New York, NY 10020

First Free Press hardcover edition January 2012

FREE PRESS and colophon are trademarks of Simon & Schuster, Inc.

For information about special discounts for bulk purchases, please contact Simon & Schuster
Special Sales at 1-866-506-1949 or business@simonandschuster.com.

The Simon & Schuster Speakers Bureau can bring authors to your live event.
For more information or to book an event, contact the Simon & Schuster Speakers
Bureau at 1-866-248-3049 or visit our website at www.simonspeakers.com.

DESIGNED BY KATY RIEGEL

Manufactured in the United States of America

10 9 8 7 6 5 4 3 2 1

Library of Congress Cataloging-in-Publication Data

Lewis, Allyson.
    The 7 minute solution : creating a life with meaning 7 minutes at a time / by Allyson Lewis.
        p.   cm.
    (hbk. : alk. paper)
    1. Time management.   2. Self-management (Psychology)   3. Values.
4. Self-actualization (Psychology)   5. Self-realization.   I. Title.   II. Title: Seven minute
solution.
    BF637.T5L49 2012
    158.1—dc23   2011039471

ISBN 978-1-4516-2822-7
ISBN 978-1-4516-2824-1 (ebook)

Allyson Lewis

Creating

a Life with Meaning

7 Minutes at a Time

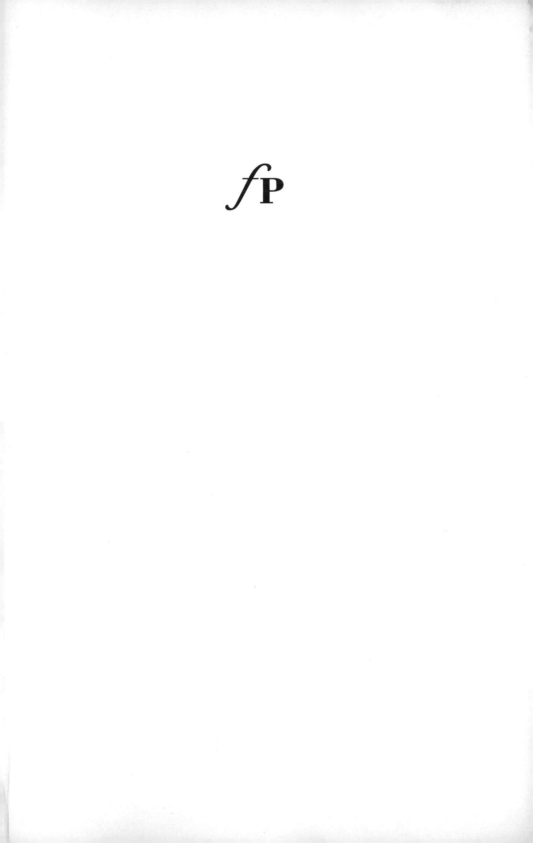

To

Mark, Abby & J

CONTENTS

Part III

PART I

The Need for the 7 Minute Solution

THE 7 MINUTE SOLUTION offers strategies to help you prioritize, organize, and simplify your life for greater meaning and productivity.

Using the 7 Minute tools, ideas, checklists, processes, and repeatable systems you will be able to use your time more effectively to energize yourself, to inspire yourself, to connect with the self you want to be, and to accomplish more in the next ninety days than you ever have before.

The 7 Minute Solution is a simple practice. You will learn to take small, manageable steps every day that allow you to make macro changes at micro levels. You can create a great magnitude of changes in your life through this daily process.

The 7 Minute Solution has two basic principles:

- Change happens in an Instant®. It happens the moment you DECIDE to change.
- You must choose to take tiny, positive, strategic steps forward EVERY DAY.

Today you are heading in one direction. And then something happens. You realize you are faced with a choice. You can choose to remain the same or you can choose to take one tiny new step forward.

The 7 Minute Solution is about deciding to change and choosing to take one more step toward a more meaningful life every day.

Welcome to the 7 Minute Community.

THIS IS AN EXAMPLE of one of the most popular 7 Minute tools, called the Daily Progress Report. This single time-management tool has changed my life. This is just one of a multitude of revolutionary ideas you will find in this book.

Subscribe to the Member Tools section of www.The7 MinuteLife.com for access to *free* downloads of this and all of our 7 Minute tools, forms, and checklists.

INTRODUCTION

THOUSANDS OF YEARS AGO, the wise King Solomon wrote, "For as he thinketh in his heart, so is he." In the Middle Ages, scientists and philosophers believed that the soul resided in the human heart. The idea made sense: when we are sad, our heart aches; when we are physically or emotionally energized, our heart pounds.

During a recent sermon, my pastor, Dan Reeves, illustrated the connections among our thoughts, our hearts, and our lives. As he took the stage that Sunday morning, the familiar sound of a human heartbeat filled the darkened auditorium.

Boom-boom . . . boom-boom.

A video of a beating human heart appeared on the overhead screen.

Boom-boom . . . boom-boom.

"The human heart is designed to pump the perfect amount of blood needed to meet the exact demands of your body at the exact time," Reeves said. "When resting, your heart pumps slowly. When exercising, your heart rate increases to the perfect level to meet your needs. You are not consciously thinking, 'I'd better make my heart beat.' Rather, your heart changes its output based on the demands you put upon it at any given time. Like your heart, your life is ready to deliver exactly what you ask of it."

With the rhythmic heartbeat in the background, he asked a question I hope you'll answer now: "What will you ask of your life?"

What a powerful point, "Life is ready to deliver exactly what you ask of it, what will you ask of it?" In this book, I will encourage you to look deeply at your life. Do you know what you really want most out of life? How would your life be different if you made the best use of your mind? Your nutrition? Your sleep? Your learning? Your time?

If you want a more meaningful life, are you asking for your life to deliver its very best?

Reeves continued his sermon by picking up a large rock that sat next to the pulpit. The dirty mass measured about twenty-four inches wide, fifteen inches across, and four inches high. It had to weigh almost thirty pounds. As he held the rock, he described the difficulty he'd had carrying it into the building. Unable to hold it and open the door at the same time, he'd had to put down the rock, open the door and brace it with his foot, bend over, pick up the rock, place his back against the door, and maneuver his way inside. From there, he had carried the rock about a hundred yards, wrestling with yet another door. Finally, sweating with exertion, he had placed the boulder on the stage, taking care not to damage the wooden floor.

The rock seemed to grow heavier in his hands as he recounted the story, and his arms were visibly straining to hold on to the rock.

"We aren't designed to carry heavy rocks all day," he said as he carefully put it down. "I can no longer feel my fingers. My arms are aching. There are simply some things in life we were not meant to carry. What do you need to change in your life? What do you need to put down?"

Then he added, "My body and my strength allowed me to carry the burden of the rock. Unfortunately, like so many people, I was straining after the wrong goal. Life is ready to deliver exactly what you ask of it—maybe it is time to ask what to seek."

Boom-boom . . . boom-boom.

As I sat there listening to the sound of the human heart beating, I wondered, *What are the rocks in my life? What rocks have I been holding onto that are keeping me from creating a life with meaning? Most important, am I asking enough of life?*

CAN YOUR LIFE REALLY BE DIFFERENT?

What do you need to throw off or set aside to live more fully and less fatigued? The good news is that, like putting down a heavy rock, change can happen in an instant. One moment you are facing one direction in life; in the next your world changes forever.

For me, that change took exactly seven minutes. I was forty-one, and as a full-time working wife and mother, I felt the constant crushing pressure of deadlines and obligations. My life sped past me in a blur from one day to the next, one month to the next, and one year to the next. I wanted more. I wanted my days to be more than waking up and going to work. I wanted my life to matter. I wanted to make a positive difference to my family and to the world. I wanted to be different, but I didn't know what my next steps should be.

My guess is that you are looking for many of the same things I continue to seek. Maybe you can relate to my story. I am a full-time working, teenage-chaperoning, pet-grooming, laundry-doing, treadmill-marching, tweeting, Facebooking, fiftyish-year-old wife, mother, and daughter. And I am creating a life of *more*—more meaning, fulfillment, significance, purpose, hope, and joy.

The 7 Minute Solution is the outcome of my desire to grow, live, and give with purpose. It is not the end of the journey; it is the story of what is happening in my life and in the lives of other friends and sojourners who are on the same path.

EXPECT CHANGE

Throughout this book, you'll be encouraged to consider what rocks— what burdens—you have chosen to carry. Are they worth the effort? Does the strain of holding on to them keep you from enjoying and experiencing growth in other areas of life? Are those burdens inhibiting your faith, family relationships, health, personal growth, creativity, or generosity? Is the weight of what's *not* working keeping you from making a positive, lasting impact on your relationships at home, in the workplace, or in your community? If so, it's time to make a change.

> You can be different tomorrow than you are today,
> seven minutes at a time.

THE 7 MINUTE SOLUTION

Definition: The 7 Minute Solution offers strategies to help you prioritize, organize, and simplify your life for greater meaning and productivity.

Living the 7 Minute Solution is not about living in seven-minute increments; it is about gleaning a deeper understanding of the seven vital signs of living with meaning: conscious awareness, motivation, growing and learning, engaging, persevering, living in flow, and living with faith.

The 7 Minute Solution is a choice. The 7 Minute Solution is about choosing to consciously focus your attention for 7 minutes every day on what is most meaningful in your life. You can be different tomorrow than you are today based on the choices you make on a daily basis. The process of moving from where you are today to where you want to be is about engaging your desire to learn and grow, while acknowledging that *today* is your only opportunity to live and breathe. The 7 Minute Solution is about taking tiny steps forward every day, while fully experiencing every moment in the present.

Life is intended to be lived, not watched; inspired, not easy; meaningful, not mundane. The ideas of the 7 Minute Solution have inspired change in the lives of thousands of people I have been privileged to meet and share ideas with during the past two decades. You'll learn from fathers who have reconnected with their children and from couples who have rediscovered joy in their marriages. You'll be inspired by the perseverance of women and men who have faced unimaginable odds—and won. You'll read accounts of triumph experienced over life-threatening circumstances—and in everyday moments.

You will meet people whose lives were very much like yours may be now. Then, in a matter of moments, their lives changed forever. Their journeys will inspire you to see new possibilities for yourself—and to stay the course when you encounter challenges.

CHECKING FOR SIGNS OF LIFE

Imagine being the first person on an accident scene and finding an injured person. The ABCs of first aid are to see if the person is a*wake,* check for b*reathing,* and then *continue care.* You shake the person gently and call out to him. If he doesn't respond, you watch his chest to see if it rises and falls, you put your hand near his nose and mouth to see if you can feel his breath. You feel his carotid artery to check for a pulse. *You check for signs of life.*

The 7 Minute Solution is designed to help you check your own vital signs. You may be up and walking around, but that doesn't mean you're truly living. Like an accident victim in shock, you may be walking through life in a state of unawareness. Chaos, distraction, interruption, procrastination, stress, and the increasing speed and demands of life squeeze the joy out of life—they can suffocate you before you know it. It's time to wake up and focus on what really matters to you. It's time to check your vital signs.

Your heart is designed to pump life-giving blood through your body, but it can't function properly without oxygen. In the same way, it's impossible to live the life you were created for if these seven vital signs are not part of your everyday existence. Action without purpose is like a heart without access to adequate oxygen—even if it is able to pump, what it delivers is not as rich or as beneficial as it should be. Now is the time to breathe in life. The 7 Minute Solution will help you evaluate your vital signs; it will shake you and call out to you to wake up! But more than that, it will equip you with the tools and systems necessary for creating a life with meaning "7 Minutes" at a time.

Begin to discover the 7 Minute Vital Signs as you ask yourself the following questions.

Are You Consciously Aware?

Life is filled with so much noise that your brain has trouble filtering out what is really important. The first vital sign to check is simple: are you aware of what you really want from your life? Life will give you exactly what you demand, but first you must clarify your ideas in writing and create an action plan.

Are You Motivated?

As you ask more of your life, you will discover gaps between where you are today and the person you want to be in the future. Motivation is the force that pushes you to stretch for your goals. By creating ninety-day goals, you will break your ultimate objectives into more quickly achievable minigoals and experience the thrill of success more often. You'll also develop a powerful momentum, because, by creating ninety-day goals, you will break up your ultimate obstacles into manageable pieces and allow yourself to experience success on a regular basis. One win leads to the next.

Are You Growing and Learning?

Your brain has incredible potential, but it functions on a use-it-or-lose-it basis. Growing and learning equip you to develop new and better ways to live. Growth is a vital sign, because it is what ignites your enthusiasm for letting go of old habits and routines.

Are You Engaged?

Mired in routine, it's easy to become a fatigued, bored zombie oblivious to the brilliant opportunities that surround you. Purposefully focusing on your highest-value activities ensures that you are engaged with the people and priorities that matter most—and also primes you to be better poised to take advantage of any new opportunities.

Are You Persevering?

Making significant changes requires perseverance. Why? Bad habits are hard to break; they're comfortable routines to return to, even if you know they're not good for you. But it's when you push through the barrier of your comfort zone that you experience amazing growth.

Are You Living in a State of Flow?

The term "flow" here means using your highest skills—your personal gifts and talents—to accomplish your most meaningful challenges. It is about channeling your abilities in a way that leads everything to click and let you know you are experiencing life at its optimal level.

Are You Living with Faith?

The vital sign of faith ties together every element of life. Because of faith, you seek a better life—a life filled with purpose and meaning—and you trust that it exists. Faith compels you to look beyond yourself, to reach out to others, to give of your time, energy, and love. A life without faith is filled with hopelessness, but with faith anything is possible.

YOUR WAKE-UP CALL

Change begins by becoming aware of where you are today. So before you begin the 7 Minute Solution, take a moment to ask yourself these Big Life Questions:

What was your life like yesterday? _____

_____

_____

_____

_____

_____

How did you feel when you woke up this morning? _____

_____

_____

_____

_____

_____

What do you want most out of life? _____

_____

_____

_____

_____

_____

What drives you? _____

_____

_____

_____

_____

Picture your life ninety days from today. How would you like to feel? What would you like to accomplish? _____

_____

_____

_____

_____

What tasks are you spending time and energy on that don't contribute to what you want most out of life? What would happen if you stopped giving those tasks your full attention? _____

_____

_____

_____

_____

_____

What would bring you true happiness and more meaning?_____

_____

_____

_____

_____

_____

Each of us desires to create a life with meaning. We seek significance. We want to reconnect with our faith and purpose. We want to know that we have been placed on this earth for a reason. But too often we go through the motions of life without *really* living. Your answers to the Big Life Questions will help you revive your life and reconnect with its deepest meaning. By answering them, you've already begun a process of discovering where you are, deciding where you want to be, and mapping out a plan to get there. Let these questions awaken your soul. Refuse to allow life to pass you by any longer.

Let's get started on the journey of awakening to the goodness, the greatness inside you. Before we explore the 7 Minute Vital Signs, let's first introduce a little more about what the 7 Minute Solution is and where the idea of "7 Minutes" comes from.

WHAT IS THE 7 MINUTE SOLUTION?

Time is free, but it's priceless.
You can't own it, but you can use it.
You can't keep it, but you can spend it.
Once you've lost it you can never get it back.
— HARVEY MACKAY

THE 7 MINUTE SOLUTION IS the life system that will equip you to escape the chaos and enjoy a life of freedom and meaning. You'll learn how to plan your day and be intentional with your time. You'll learn how to train your brain to focus on what is most meaningful in your life. The strategies you'll learn will empower you to make choices that will shape you into the person you desire to be. The end result: you will experience a more meaningful life.

THE 7 MINUTE SOLUTION WORKS

The 7 Minute Solution is very personal to me. Almost twenty years ago, I realized I wanted more out of life. I wanted to renew and restore my faith in God. I wanted to know Him, and I wanted my life to be a reflection of that relationship. I wanted my soul to come alive again. I wanted to feel my heart beat with excitement for each new day. I wanted to be filled with the physical energy that comes from living in alignment with my personal values. I wanted to be challenged to learn and grow intellectually.

I've since uncovered truths about myself and what *more* means to me. My journey of discovering the principles in the 7 Minute Solution made me realize that, for me, meaning doesn't come simply through self-discovery or personal development. As I learned what was most meaningful to me, I became more deeply aware of the needs of those around me—and my desire to help them grow and discover more in their own lives.

Since 1993, I have taught time management principles to thousands of men and women, from corporate executives in the financial services industry to pharmaceutical sales managers to the senior managing directors of hospitals to leaders of nonprofit organizations to university students. The 7 Minute Solution is based on a solid framework of practical tools that have been developed through years of usage by men and women of all ages. As you would expect, many of the first concepts were grounded in helping people improve their time management skills. But the point of the 7 Minute Solution isn't simply to become more efficient or productive. The real purpose is to help you create a life that is filled with meaning, purpose, and productivity. Freed from chaos, people are suddenly able to pursue their dreams and experience joy and renewed excitement for life.

Time is a constant for how we experience life. Time affects your relationship with your work, your family, and yourself. In order to experience life at a different level, you must make choices to have more free time in every day. Time management is not about doing more; it is about doing more of what matters to you in life.

WHY 7 MINUTES?

How long is your attention span?

In my first time management book, *The Seven Minute Difference: Small Steps to Big Changes,* I reported on several studies that indicate that because of our exposure to television, the average American adult has an attention span of only seven minutes. Several generations now have grown up watching television—a lot of it. A 2009 Nielsen Company survey reported that the average American watched 153 hours of television per month—that is, more than five hours per day. It should come as no surprise that this volume of television and the repeated pattern of seven minutes of programming interrupted by commercials would affect our ability to concentrate. Over and over again, this pattern of as little as seven minutes of attention followed by commercial interruptions has predisposed us to have difficulty focusing our attention for long periods of time.

But television is only one piece of the attention span puzzle. Right now, literally millions of things are vying for your attention, from the projects you need to meet with your team to finish to the stacks of paper on your desk to your stomach growling because you are hungry—and your brain has a limited ability to process that information. To cope, your brain switches constantly from one distraction to the next. The results are obvious: unfinished projects, an undefined sense of longing, untended relationships, and unmet goals.

To experience a more meaningful life, you must consciously choose what you will pay attention to each moment. What you focus on determines your level of fulfillment, productivity, and success.

The unfortunate reality is that most of us have been so busy surviving that we have not taken the time to clarify our values, priorities, and goals. With those critical elements left undefined, we remain stuck, scattered, and dissatisfied. *The 7 Minute Solution* will teach you how to clarify how you really want to live. You'll learn how to filter your choices through your values, priorities, and personal goals, so you can focus on making the most of every moment.

What does it take to increase your attention span and intensify your focus on projects and activities that will improve your life? I believe you can make great strides toward creating a meaningful life in just seven minutes. That's because tiny actions taken every day can change the course of your life. I call these the 7 Minute Microactions. And as you'll learn, they are simple and life changing.

7 MINUTE MICROACTIONS

All of life is really a series of tiny actions, tiny choices, and tiny decisions I call microactions. Microactions are important because they get us moving. They are a starting point, and they are the difference between being stuck (doing nothing) and taking action and moving forward. Microactions compound. If you accomplish one microaction, such as returning a phone call to help you complete a project, it may not seem like much, but over time a series of deliberate microactions compound into a tipping point. Microactions don't overwhelm you; they are achievable. And because they are so tiny, they are very doable.

Making small changes in your thoughts and behavior can result in monumental differences in your life. The 7 Minute Microactions are so simple that they are often overlooked and underutilized. But they can be the difference between mediocrity and excellence. In my own life, the microaction of writing down a short description of purpose resulted in a major change in my personal and professional life. But microactions can take any number of forms, including:

- Outlining your daily plan of action
- Thanking a coworker for a job well done
- Building time in the day to catch up between meetings
- Being on time or early for every meeting
- Writing two thank-you notes per week
- Reading ten pages of a book
- Getting up fifteen minutes earlier
- Eating more fruit
- Drinking more water

When incorporated into a daily routine, these microactions take on an even greater potential for bringing about immense new levels of productivity and growth in our work and home life. Microactions are the tiny steps toward positive growth that you take every day. Microactions are manageable and easy to accomplish. And, their power compounds over time. It is exactly because they are so easy to accomplish that, after only a few days of focusing on them, you will see results.

Consider one great example of a microaction by a friend of mine, John Arnold. He eliminated clutter and excess in his life in just forty days by adopting a single microaction. Specifically, every day for forty days, he filled a standard grocery sack with items he no longer wanted and either threw them away or found them a new home. The end result was that he purged clutter from every room, closet, drawer, and cabinet in his house, his office, and his garage and both of his cars.

The microaction created not only a physical tipping point that resulted in a new level of order but also a mental tipping point that gave him a new mind-set about material things. As John describes it, "I learned that everything I own owns a little bit of me. My relationship to material objects completely changed. I now have a new baseline for what I will allow as clutter in my life. If you had told me I was going to organize my entire home and office in forty days, I would have never believed you. But doing it one bag at a time was easy."

Microactions have changed my life, and they have the power to help you change your life, too. These split-second decisions determine what you will pay attention to, how you will focus your life, and what you will choose to do with your time. And throughout *The 7 Minute Solution,* I'll introduce you to more of these tiny, powerful life changers.

Because we have such a short attention span, we need tools to grab our attention and bring it back into the present moment. You are probably already using many tools to help yourself stay on task. You may currently be using:

- Paper calendars
- Electronic calendaring tools such as Microsoft Outlook
- Smart phones such as the iPhone, BlackBerry, and Droid
- Written to-do lists
- Post-it notes

- Voice notes
- E-mail reminders
- Rubber bands placed around your wrists so you won't forget something

All of these items act as "peripheral brains." Peripheral brains are all of the external tools that help your brain capture and store information so you can remember what you need to accomplish. It is not that we are incapable of accomplishing tasks, it is that our brains seem to race so quickly that life is experienced as a series of waves of chaos, which is overwhelming, rather than an ordered series of events. In the past, you have attempted to rely on your peripheral tools to try to bring order to the chaos of life. As humans, we seek order and simplicity.

Unfortunately, without a life system to make sense of all of this information, such tools actually inhibit your productivity rather than improve it.

You know that your current tools and systems aren't working when:

- Your e-mail box is overflowing.
- You lose the Post-it note with the phone number of your most important client.
- Your to-do list is lost, and the first thing on your new to-do list is to find your old to-do list.
- You look at your appointments on your calendar, and your heart aches because you would rather be doing something entirely different with your time.

If your current peripheral brains are failing you, you don't need more time management tools and systems. You need a life system; you need a solution. *The 7 Minute Solution* will teach you to intentionally choose how you will spend your time. And the 7 Minute Microactions and 7 Minute Tools will help you regain control of your thoughts and your attention so you can focus on what really matters to you. My goal isn't to simply help you be more productive; who wants to become more efficient at living an unsatisfied life, filled with busyness and stress? No one! That's why *The 7 Minute Solution* teaches you how to use your time, energy, and brainpower to become the person you really want to become—so you can experience the life you desire.

Your brain and its tremendous ability to dream, imagine, innovate, and grow are key factors in creating real, meaningful, sustainable change. So before we go any further, I want to give you a basic explanation of how your brain works, because understanding that you can change gives you a reason to try—a reason to wake up.

HARNESSING THE HERD IN YOUR HEAD

You become what you think about.

—EARL NIGHTINGALE, *THE STRANGEST SECRET*

The human brain is simply amazing. It is changeable and has an enormous potential to learn; the scientific term for this ability is "neuroplasticity," which means that the brain is "plastic" or changeable. Neuroplasticity is the capacity of your brain to create new neural connections, to rewire itself (known as cortical remapping) as a result of your experiences, thoughts, actions, and repetitive behaviors.

Let me give an everyday example of neuroplasticity. Driving a car is a perfect example of how the brain is plastic or changeable. Our daughter is fifteen and will soon be learning how to drive a car. As she begins that process, every action will be labored and deliberate. She will have to consciously think about the simplest steps: how to turn the key in the ignition, how to put the car in reverse, how to look in the rearview mirror. As she pulls into traffic for the first time, stress chemicals pour into her bloodstream and she feels anxiety about every decision she makes. But, within hours of driving, because the brain learns new and novel concepts very quickly, she won't have to wonder how to turn on the ignition—new mental connections will have formed. Within days of learning to drive, the excitement is still there but the stress chemicals begin to go away, replaced with new chemicals of accomplishment and confidence.

Now, fast-forward twenty years and look at how neuroplasticity has affected your driving. Every single time you have driven a car you have strengthened the neural connections in your brain to the point that driving is now so routine it can be almost dangerous. You hop in your car in the morning, turn on the radio, and, before you know it, you are pulling into your office parking lot. Now, you drive without much, if any, conscious cognitive processing. For most of the time you are on automatic pilot. Through experience and repetition your brain has become so familiar with driving that it takes virtually no effort.

Wouldn't it be exciting to think you could experience some of the same automatic positive improvements in your life when it comes to time management, productivity, and organizational skills? Neuroplasticity makes this possible in virtually every area of your life. It is one of the key concepts of The 7 Minute Solution.

We have the ability to rewire our brains by consciously choosing what we will do. To become a better golfer, play golf. To be in better shape, exercise. To become a kinder person, be kind more often. Your brain will respond in direct proportion to what you focus on. Because your brain is plastic or changeable you are also able to form new connections to compensate for lost ones. For example, after some strokes that cause loss of the ability to walk and talk, some patients are able to regain some or all of their lost abilities through intense therapy. Even though parts of the brain are damaged, the remaining cells can begin to rewire themselves to compensate for the injury.

The average number of thoughts that pass through your subconscious mind per day is estimated to be as high as 70,000. Each and every thought you have, every action you take shapes the strength and connections of your neural connections. Consisting of approximately 100 billion cells called neurons, your brain is the most powerful information processor ever designed. Every second, it processes millions of bits of information. Within 1/1,000 of a second after being stimulated, chemical and electrical impulses race along synaptic pathways throughout the neural circuitry of your brain. The efficiency and strength of your neuronal connections or pathways give you the ability to think, plan, create, and execute new ideas.

One psychologist, Dan Holmes, PhD, uses a simple analogy to illustrate how neuronal pathways are created: "I'm an old farm boy. We had a dairy, and the cattle in the field walked the same paths all the time. There were what we called 'cow paths' in the fields where the cattle had beaten down the grass. The grass was dead; the path was just dirt. But it hadn't always been that way; those paths formed because the cows' consistent behavior created the pattern. That same thing happens in our brains; we have patterns of how we process things that are partly based on repetitive behavior."

Right now, your brain is relying on habits and routines—cow paths—that you've established to make life simpler. Some of those habits, such as brushing your teeth every morning, serve you well. Others, such as procrastination and indecision, do not. But you can train your brain and develop new neuronal pathways—new habits— by repeating behaviors that support your goals and dreams. Back to the cattle analogy, if you drive the cattle along a new route, you will notice a difference in the field within just a few days. Within ninety days, there will be a clearly defined path where the cattle have repeatedly traveled.

The more frequently and consistently you repeat new behaviors, the stronger and more defined the new pathways become. *Your brain actually changes its shape and structure based on what you think about and do most of the time.* And old pathways—bad habits—are eliminated when they are not used.

WHAT PATHWAYS WILL YOU HAVE CREATED NINETY DAYS FROM NOW?

The 7 Minute Solution is built on a ninety-day foundation. The ninety-day period has been chosen for two reasons. First, life is cyclical and follows steady rhythms. Nature itself starts over every ninety days.

Winter, spring, summer, fall, followed by winter again, each season is different, bringing new opportunities, With this foundation, you will know that every ninety days you will have a fresh start and be able to bring on new challenges.

The second reason is very practical—you need a manageable amount of time to see real results in your life. A week is too short and a year may seem too far away. No one wants to wait a full year to see results.

Change requires commitment: If you want to be different ninety days from now you must use the ideas in this book. This book contains plenty of checklists and tools that you can use to improve your time management skills. But checklists, tools, and ideas won't change your life. Think about how many checklists you've left unchecked. It is only through implementing new strategies that you will change your life—and implementing those ideas takes practice. *Repetition is the key to modifying behavior.* To get the most out of the 7 Minute Solution, I encourage you to commit to using these tools and strategies for ninety days in a row.

Can you imagine what your life could be like ninety days from now? Look forward ninety days from today. Time passes in a blink. Will you be different ninety days from today? You know you want to be. And I know that you *can* be. You simply need to decide to be different; then use the 7 Minute Microactions, Tools, practical applications, and systems to make that change a reality.

SOME PLANNING TAKES
MORE THAN SEVEN MINUTES

I encourage you to begin this process of change by scheduling time to work through the initial exercises in this book. How long has it been since you took an extended period of time to reflect upon exactly what you wanted your life to mean to you? Have you defined and ranked your personal values recently? Have you prioritized what is most important to you? Do you have a written purpose statement guiding and clarifying the decisions you make on a daily basis? Do you have written ninety-day goals with specific action steps for how you will accomplish them? Do you know specifically what is keeping you from becoming the person you want to become? Are there ways to streamline and plan each day *before* that day begins? Many sections of this book will be followed by 7 Minute Practical Solutions. Don't skip them. Take seven minutes or whatever time is necessary to start planning for and living a more meaningful life.

Too often people are so busy with their work that they don't take time to plan what they want to accomplish. Did you catch that word "busy"? Being busy keeps people from living with intention. The truth is, planning is hard, and it takes time that you may feel you don't have. But executing without a plan is harder, and in the end, failing to plan costs you more time. In fact, failing to plan could effectively cost you your life if you waste your days doing stuff that doesn't matter.

Don't waste your life. I believe it is valuable to spend at least four days each year—one day every ninety days—intensely preparing, designing, dreaming, outlining, and creating a written plan of action for what you want your life to become and what you want to accomplish. You can center that plan on what is most important to you and wrap it around living a life of purpose and meaning. And when you have a very specific plan, you can effectively choose how you will invest your most limited currency: your time.

APPLYING THE 7 MINUTE SOLUTION TO YOUR LIFE

The 7 Minute Solution is about consciously focusing your attention for seven minutes every day on what is most meaningful in your life.

In an online survey we conducted in February 2011, the vast majority of people found meaning in five general areas of life:

- Family
- Love
- Friendships

- Faith
- Making a difference

We want to believe our life matters. We want to believe that by utilizing our gifts and talents we can make a difference in the world. We want to serve those around us in a way that celebrates our purpose. We seek meaningful connections with our faith, friends, family members, and coworkers. We want to belong. And we realize that to be a part of something bigger, life can't be just about us. For our lives to really matter, we must serve others.

So the question now is: are you ready to live with intention and purpose? I hope so! If so, it's time to check your vital signs. And just as you would for an accident victim, we'll start with the basics: are you aware?

THE PROBLEM: UNAWARENESS

*B*OOM-BOOM . . . *boom-boom.*

Your heart is beating, but are you truly connected to your life? When you wake each morning, do you feel the buzz of potential and excitement? Or do you move from day to day, lost in a swirl of chaos, confusion, interruptions, and distractions?

At age forty-one, I carried excess weight on an out-of-shape body. My busy days were packed but not productive. I was tired—really, really tired. Although I liked my work, after twenty years in the same job, I felt empty and worn out. A stirring deep inside my heart gnawed at me. I wanted more, but I didn't know exactly what *more* meant, and I didn't know what to do about it.

THE AWAKENING

When I saw my friend Debbie Ring walking toward me at church that Sunday morning, I knew even before she spoke that something had happened. She put her hand on my arm as if to comfort me and said, "I've got cancer." She paused to let the words sink in. "It's stage four colon cancer. I have six months to live." The jolt of her words ran through my body like an electric current.

"I've got cancer." Three words. Three terrible words. They hit me with such force that my initial inclination to run from their sting was overcome only by my instinct to protect my friend. I grabbed hold of her and together, we cried.

At home that night, I tried to remember what my life had been like the day before.

Nothing. It was like nothing. I knew then that I had been existing but not really living. I was breathing but not feeling.

How did I feel now? Sadness for my friend swept over me. I felt guilty for allowing life to pass me by. An overwhelming need to wake up shook me. I felt a growing responsibility to *live*. Debbie's three dreadful words had drawn a line in the sand in front of me. I knew I had a choice to make: I could choose to continue to move through life completely unaware, or I could choose to wake up.

In August 2001, I took the first step toward awareness. I recognized that something needed to change, but I didn't know where to go or whom to turn to.

Less than two weeks later, another awakening rocked my world—and probably yours as well. The events of September 11, 2001, continue to affect our country. But for a young man who worked in my office, the awakening of that day's events stirred intense clarity to his life. At twenty-two, Adam Staples was in the process of becoming a financial adviser. His training included a three-week course in New York City, and on the morning of September 11, Adam went to the office in the South Tower of the World Trade Center. Like everyone else that morning, he felt concerned and confused when he heard the commotion about the plane hitting the North Tower of the World Trade Center at 8:46 A.M. But security guards assured everyone that things were okay in the South Tower and there was no need to evacuate.

At 9:02 A.M., Adam leaned against the window on the sixty-first floor and looked out at the New York skyline. Suddenly a violent explosion rocked the building. An incredible noise vibrated through the air, and debris fell from the ceiling. Adam didn't stop to question what had happened. His survival instinct kicked in; he knew he had to escape.

Adam had run track at Arkansas State University, and he ran down sixteen flights before crowds began to fill the stairwells at the forty-fourth floor. Caught in a mass of people, his progress slowed. The seriousness of the moment hung in the air as Adam and the others moved as quickly as possible with the same goal in mind: get out, now.

At the sixteenth floor, Adam noticed large cracks in the walls. A few people were able to get a connection on their cell phones, and, slowly, news of the two planes hitting the World Trade Center towers passed from person to person.

While Adam hurried down those stairs, I watched the news of the terrorist attacks from the safety of my office. His parents had called to find out if we knew whether their son was dead or alive, and we couldn't offer any reassurance. My coworkers and I huddled together, silently crying and praying that our friend had found his way safely out of the building. At 9:58 A.M., I watched the South Tower lean violently to the right and disappear into a horrifying gray cloud of smoke. My head fell into my palms, and I wept.

It took Adam forty-five minutes to make it out of the South Tower. He had walked approximately six blocks when he saw the building he had been in only minutes earlier lean to the side. He stood silently in the middle of the street with hundreds of other people and listened to the horrible sound of the building collapsing floor by floor. *Thud . . . thud . . . thud . . . thud . . . thud.*

Adam was safe, and he knew his life would never be the same.

In the terrifying moments on the morning of September 11, 2001, countless lives were forever changed. People around the world grieved the loss of friends, family members, and their sense of safety. But Adam didn't watch the terrible events unfold on television or on the Internet; he lived them. In the fifty-six minutes from impact to collapse of the South Tower of the World Trade Center, he experienced a rush of hypersensitive focus and adrenaline. His life moved instantly from a blissful state of unawareness to an awareness that he might be living his last moments on Earth.

"With every step I took walking down the stairs of the World Trade Center, I wasn't thinking about myself, I thought of my mom and dad. I *felt* my parents' love and prayers," Adam says. "Since then, my greater awakening has been that this life is not about me. Whatever job I have, my most meaningful role now is as a loving husband and as a father sitting on the floor with my children. Most people are unaware of what is most important in their life." Today, Adam's life continues to resonate from his greater awakening. Yes, Adam is very successful in business, and he lives with gratitude. But he believes he has been placed here to serve: Serve his family, serve his community, and serve God, "It's not about me." Adam's life is a reflection of his appreciation for the brevity and preciousness of time.

At the end of August 2001, my friend Debbie Ring heard those three terrible words: "You have cancer." Less than two weeks later, the young man who worked in the office adjoining mine barely escaped death when United Airlines Flight 175 crashed into the South Tower of the World Trade Center only sixteen floors above him. These two incidents were my wake-up call.

The voice in my head screamed, "Allyson, today may be all you have. You need to wake up! You need to live. Don't you know there's so much more to life? Can't you see it?" And for the first time in my adult life I did see it. I saw clearly that there was more to life. I wanted to live a life of meaning and purpose. I wanted to reengage in life at a completely new and different level. I wanted to awaken my heart, my mind, my body, and my soul. I wanted to feel alive again. I wanted to breathe in life. What more would it take? My friend Debbie was dying, my friend Adam was alive—and both of them were living more fully than ever before. It was time to let go of fear and regret. It was time to embrace life in a new way, to live with faith, hope, and love.

There are no more excuses; now is the time. Every day you have a choice to make. Debbie's diagnosis drew a line in the sand for me. This moment is the line in the sand for you. Will you continue to let life pass you by? Will you get up tomorrow morning, kiss your children good-bye, spend eight or nine hours doing a good job, hop back into your car, and spend a few unremarkable hours at home—living completely unaware of all the goodness life offers?

Let me tell you from experience: there is a better choice. Adam found a safe path out of the South Tower and awoke to an understanding of what is most important to him. You have the potential to live more than eighty years on this earth. How you choose to spend your time is one of the most important factors in whether or not you will experience a meaningful life. I have chosen not to allow life to pass me by. I am awake and aware that the choices I make every day determine the quality of life I experience. I am choosing, moment by moment, to spend my time living a life that matters. How will you choose to spend your time?

Time.

The doctors told Debbie Ring that she had six months to live. But with courage, modern medicine, faith, and prayer, she lived six more years. Throughout those years, Debbie cherished her time. She lived with purpose and hope. On January 18, 2007, with her daughter lying next to her, and her two boys kneeling at her bedside, her husband, Dan, gently kissed his wife good-bye and said, "Run to Jesus, baby, just run."

I know that when Debbie passed from this world to the next, she had no regrets. Her family knew she loved them, and her faith gave them hope and courage. That's what mattered most.

WHERE IS YOUR ATTENTION?

Concentrate all your thoughts upon the work at hand.
The sun's rays do not burn until brought to a focus.

— ALEXANDER GRAHAM BELL

IT IS TIME TO WAKE UP, to move from unawareness to awareness. Awareness begins when you know what is most important to you. The life-changing events Adam and Debbie faced helped them quickly reprioritize their lives. But it doesn't have to take a crisis for you to find that clarity. Life is an evolving process. You don't usually just move from being unaware to awareness. To wake up you must learn how to concentrate and focus your attention.

Attention is your brain's ability to consciously choose what you see at any given time. The speed at which your brain processes information is remarkable. You have approximately 100 billion neurons in your brain. Each cell constantly communicates with the cells around it. One hundred *billion*. To put that number into perspective, that's approximately the number of stars in the universe—but the stars can't speak to one another. Those 100 billion neurons process millions of pieces of information every minute of the day by taking in what you hear, see, smell, touch, taste, and experience emotionally. Attention allows your brain to take those random bits of information and piece together what you experience as reality. Attention allows you to see what you want to see and hear what you want to hear. Attention allows your brain to cut through the clutter and focus only on what you deem important.

DEFINING ATTENTION

William James, in his 1890 textbook *The Principles of Psychology*, explained attention this way:

> [Attention] is the taking possession by the mind, in clear and vivid form, of one out of what seem several simultaneously possible objects or trains of thought. Focalization, concentration of consciousness are of its essence. It implies withdrawal from some things in order to deal effectively with others, and is a condition which has a real opposite in the confused, dazed, scatterbrained state which in French is called *distraction*.

Let's break down this definition of attention, beginning with the concept of the mind taking possession. When was the last time an event in your life took possession of you? When were you last swept away with emotion?

One such event in my own life was my wedding day. I remember every detail of the events on August 22, 1992. I can still see each of the friends and family members who surrounded me. I remember the scent and beauty of the flowers, the lilt of the music, the taste and texture of the wedding cake. If I close my eyes, I can still feel the emotion of that day, the strength of my husband's love as we held hands, looked into each other's eyes, and said, "I do."

I feel a similar connection to the birth of my two children. I remember every detail: how tiny they were in my arms, their soft breath against my skin, the intense and immediate love I felt the first time I saw them. In such divine moments, it is as though everything else faded away and my complete attention and focus were incredibly clear and vivid.

Harnessing attention awakens your discovery or rediscovery of meaning. Attention empowers you to make tiny daily decisions that move you into a richer, more fulfilling life. When was the last time something took possession of you? Emotion greatly affects the power and depth of your attention.

James concluded his definition of attention with this phrase: "and is a condition which has a real opposite in the confused, dazed, scatterbrained state which in French is called *distraction*."

Distraction. The word "distraction" comes from an ancient form of torture. Imagine this: An enemy ties your left arm to one horse and your right arm to a second horse. He then ties your left leg to a third horse, and your right leg to yet another horse. Then he slaps the horses' flanks, and they gallop in different directions—distracting you. It would kill you.

Try this: Stand with your arms and fists outstretched above your head, your legs shoulder width apart. Imagine what it would feel like to be pulled in so many directions. Are you living like this? Distracted, pulled in many different directions? Pulled by your job, pulled by wanting to live up to the dreams of your family? When you are stretched like this, you can't take even a single step forward toward any of your goals.

Respondents to a survey conducted by Seven Minutes, Inc., in 2009, listed distractions and constant interruptions as the two biggest challenges they struggle with daily. Distractions will always be part of your life. But if you're not consciously aware, distractions can become your focus. Flitting from one task to the next, from Facebook to YouTube to Twitter and back again, to the phone, to the text message you forgot to send, and then, oh yeah, you needed to finish that report, but first you switch on the news for a few minutes . . . it's easy to get distracted; you must *choose* to learn to live an attentive life. Living an attentive life means you are able to filter out the noise and focus in on what is most important.

MAXIMIZING YOUR 7 MINUTE ATTENTION SPAN

How good is your attention? Isn't it shocking how much information we must plow through every day? In an attempt to help you improve your attention span, here is a little information on how you can maximize your current attention span.

There are three types of attention:

1. Focused attention
2. Sustained attention
3. Divided attention

Focused attention is short term in its effect. You experience focused attention every time something startles you—a waiter drops a plate in a restaurant, your cell phone rings in a meeting, or there is a knock at your door. This type of attention usually lasts less than eight seconds, and once the event is over you seem to refocus on what you were originally working on.

Sustained attention is the type of attention the 7 Minute Solution will help you improve. Sustained attention requires complete concentration, sustained over time. It enables you to focus your complete attention on a single task at a time without interruption. Sustained attention is what might be called *thinking*. It happens when you eliminate distractions from your mind and fully concentrate on the task at hand.

Completing a project by using sustained attention carries an emotional reward. When you successfully eliminate distraction and finish even a simple task, you are physically and emotionally rewarded with chemicals called endorphins that give you a sense of well-being.

The third type of attention is known as *divided attention*. In today's workplace it is often referred to as multitasking, but in fact multitasking doesn't exist; what is actually happening is task switching or divided attention.

As we will explore more fully throughout this book, your brain has a limited capacity to consciously process tasks. As humans, we are limited to focusing our attention on one thing at a time. For example, if I asked you to take your right hand and place it on top of your head, it would be difficult for you to continue fully concentrating on reading this sentence. What would actually occur is that your brain would stop reading for a split millisecond, think about what muscles it takes to move your right arm, and your hand on top of your head. In the next millisecond your brain would refocus your eyes on this page and continue to read.

What is the problem with task switching? Divided attention takes more effort.

As you quickly switch back and forth from task to task, you have to slightly repeat each task just to get back to where you were. Divided attention is much less productive than focused attention. Instead of pumping your body full of endorphins, divided attention pumps you full of adrenaline and stress hormones. When you are fully engrossed in a project and you are interrupted, it can take you up to twenty minutes to get back in the right frame of mind.

Consider your average day. How many interruptions do you experience in an average workday? Every phone call, every text message, every e-mail binging in through the server, not to mention all the observations your brain distracts you with. And just as you mentally settle in to work on a task, your mind wanders and you ask yourself, "I wonder what is happening on Facebook? I'll just click over to my bookmarked Internet site and take a quick look." And your attention is gone.

Although much research says adults can hold their sustained focus for an average of seven minutes at a time, I am confident that by understanding the importance of focusing your attention, you will be able to improve your ability to think.

I have often wondered why I can stay completely engrossed in a movie for more than two hours but there are times when I can't seem to focus my attention long enough to complete a project that I have started numerous times.

Joe Hardy, PhD, is the senior director of research and development at Lumos Labs, a company that develops computer programs designed to improve attention, memory, and cognitive processing speed. When I asked Joe about the brevity of the average attention span, he pointed out that attention is *the dynamic allocation of your attentional resources.* It is how you select and process specific information for dynamic and changing periods of time.

"I am not sure there is a correct answer to how long a person can pay attention," he says. "Maybe the way to ask the question is 'How does performance change over time as you are working on a particular task?' The bottom line is that our 'attentional resources' oscillate over time; your ability to focus your attention goes up and it goes down. It's not just that you have a limited attention span, but also that your ability to focus your attention oscillates based on your stress level, what you have eaten, how much sleep you have had, and even if you find yourself 'bored' with a particular task. The good news is, science is discovering multiple ways to cognitively train your brain to help you increase your attention span, your memory, and your focus."

Does your life feel like swirling chaos?

Life is filled with chaos and distractions. As in the picture above, that chaos swirls around you. Imagine standing in the center of that swirl. One of the reasons we are unaware of the goodness of our lives is that there is too much coming at us. We're distracted and constantly interrupted. This barrage of information comes to us through our senses of sight, hearing, smell, touch, and taste, filtering first through our subconscious mind and then into our conscious mind. *When you have not decided what is most important, everything seems important.* You don't know where to focus your attention, and you end up feeling overwhelmed, lost, and distracted.

Attention is the skill that enables you to prioritize, organize, and simplify your life at work and at home. Improving your attention span is a skill you can learn. Deciding what is most important to you and learning to focus your attention on what you value allow you to create order out of chaos. But understanding how attention works isn't enough, you must begin to choose to take tiny positive steps forward every day.

Check Your Vital Signs

What do you know to be true in life? What are the priorities that you value most?

The average American watches five hours of television a day. How can we say we don't have enough time if we have time to watch that much television? Maybe you don't watch that much television, but if your attention isn't focused, you could be wasting just as much time. During my own process of discovering what was most important in my life, I decided to create a list of things I know to be true for me to improve my attention span. Here is my list:

1. I need a proper amount of sleep to live my most effective life.
2. I must fuel my body with nutritious food to function at a peak level.
3. I must stay active to have the mental and physical energy I need.
4. I must challenge my mind with quality information.
5. I can't do all things in one day.
6. Physical and mental clutter slows me down and makes me unhappy.
7. Life is brief.
8. I prefer simplicity and order over chaos and distraction.

These eight things are my pulse. But when I live in a too-busy state, they are easy to forget. Like a string around my finger, these eight truths remind me to stay on the correct path. If life is a path, these truths act as a compass for me; as usual with life, it is the simplest truths that are the pulse of life. I must regularly check my pulse to make sure I am not just going through the motions of life. In order to move from unawareness to conscious awareness you have to be on the right path.

When you are ready to move from the crushing chaos that so many people experience on a day-to-day basis, the first step is to prioritize, organize, and simplify your life.

This first application revolves around discovering what is most important to you.

7 MINUTE SOLUTION PRACTICAL APPLICATION NO. 1: DISCOVER WHAT IS MOST IMPORTANT TO YOU

Prioritize, Organize, Simplify

In this graphic, the eight randomly placed circles next to the word "prioritize" represent the millions of inputs of information coming at you every second of the day. You must choose how to prioritize that information. What will you decide to pay attention to? What you focus on makes you who you are and determines the type of life you experience.

It's time to begin the process of identifying and prioritizing what is most important to you. Different people value many different parts of life. Knowing what you value will help you create the life you desire. Your foundational values will often be an extension of your personality and how you want to experience life.

Below you will see a list of seventy-five values. These are foundational values, including love, friendships, freedom, learning, influencing others, laughter, and many others. Even as you read this list of words, your brain has an instant jolt of emotion. When you see the word, "love," your brain experiences a flash of love. When you read the word, "friendships," your neural circuitry subconsciously and instantly flashes through millions of happy memories and you feel the emotions of friendship—connection, caring, sympathy. Each of these written words carries emotional power and energy. These values are the fuel of life that sustains us.

I recommend you complete this process in four steps.

STEP 1. Scan quickly through the three columns. Let the words open your eyes to the importance of knowing your values.

Rank ✓	Rank ✓	Rank ✓
○ Love	○ Faith	○ Family
○ Friendships	○ Change	○ Serving others
○ Achievement	○ Philanthropy	○ Leading
○ Excitement	○ Authenticity	○ Solitude
○ Arts	○ Balance	○ Time
○ Community	○ Laughter	○ Honesty
○ Happiness	○ Influencing others	○ Knowledge
○ Security	○ Compassion	○ Recognition
○ Meaningful work	○ Money	○ Contributing
○ Helping	○ Nature	○ Inspire
○ Choice	○ Sharing	○ Pleasure
○ Freedom	○ Competence	○ Health
○ Intimacy	○ Joy	○ Self-respect
○ Success	○ Efficiency	○ Teaching
○ Adventure	○ Growing	○ Stability
○ Independence	○ Adventure	○ Expertise
○ Power	○ Peace	○ Travel
○ Learning	○ Integrity	○ Connecting
○ Fun	○ Creativity	○ Recreation / Play
○ Passion	○ Belonging	○ Making a difference
○ Comfort	○ Advancement	○ Competition
○ Trust	○ Relationships	○ Financial security
○ Order	○ Intellect	○ Decisiveness
○ Reach full potential	○ Excellence	○ Taking risk
○ Wisdom	○ Tradition	○ Leaving a legacy

STEP 2. Read each word a second time. Determine what each value means to you; then, using your first impression, make a checkmark by *all* of the values that have the most meaning for you personally. Take your time with this process. Don't try to rank them on this first review; feel free to check as many of them as you deem important. This first scan might include fifteen to twenty-five values. As you read the list, consider how the words make you feel.

STEP 3. Review the list a third time and narrow down your values by circling the words that seem most important. Of course, all these values are important, and you may want to add some that are not listed.

STEP 4. As you review your list for the fourth and final time, your first objective will be to narrow your list to your top ten values. What stirs inside your heart? Of the words you've circled, finally rank your top ten personal values.

If you are wondering why this application is a four-step process, it is intentional and very important. Remember that through neuroplasticity your brain is plastic or changeable. But change requires repetition. The more times you repeat a specific

You can find the full-size version of the Prioritize Worksheet on page 342.

activity, the stronger the neural connections become. With Step 1, as you read this list, you begin to create a few connections of happiness and expectation. You are reading meaningful and valuable words and just scanning through them somehow makes you feel better. In Step 2, as you scan the list, you actually have to put some mental effort into reading each word and they make you feel better about yourself as you read them. In Step 3, as you circle your chosen values, you are making a mental commitment that "Yes, these things really are important to me." And in Step 4, you begin to sense the excitement of how much you could accomplish with your life if you had more time to focus on the priorities that really do matter most to you. These are the things you value in life. They are your driving force.

Here is what I wrote:

1. Faith   6. Creativity/sharing ideas
2. Family/friends   7. Inspiring others
3. Health   8. Making a difference
4. Growing/learning   9. Doing meaningful work
5. Peace/freedom   10. Having financial security

Those are the values I listed as most important in my life. They are my priorities. As I look out ninety days from today, I imagine how I will feel about my life if I create a daily schedule that allows me to live in perfect alignment with those ten areas. Would my life be better than it is today? Of course the answer is yes. When I hold this list in my hands, my heart pounds and my eyes tear up just a little. It's as though the moment, so full of potential and possibility, "takes possession" of me. For a few minutes, I am swept away, imagining what it would be like to live a life focused on my priorities of faith, family/ friends, health, growing/learning, peace/freedom, creativity/sharing ideas, inspiring others, making a difference, doing meaningful work, and having financial security. There is a sense of deep congruence, and I feel powerful emotions revolving around these values.

Every ninety days, I schedule a time to be alone to go through this process. As I read the list and let the values sink into my mind and my soul, my life takes on a clearer meaning. As I look at the list of my personal values, I am able to instantly see the possibility of great meaning. When I give myself permission to step back from the noise of life and focus my attention on what I have just said is essential to me, it feels important. As I read my list out loud, I feel a sense of hope surging over me. My mind says, "Yes! Yes! Listen! This is why you are here. Wake up, Allyson! Wake up and *live*!"

Almost immediately a doubting voice pipes up: "Oh, Allyson, pick up your BlackBerry. Take a look at your calendar. Does your current daily, weekly, and monthly schedule line up with what you have just said is most important to you?"

But I'm able to quiet that doubt because I know I have the final say over my calendar; I can make choices that better align my time and my personal values. And I can never go back to saying I just didn't know what was important. I am no longer unaware.

Let me share a story of the power of knowing your personal values in business.

LIVING THE VALUE OF WOW

Dave Savage describes himself as a "total entrepreneur from birth." At forty-seven, he is an accomplished businessman. Dave's overarching mission is to surpass expectations in every aspect of his life and his business, using his personal values as guideposts along the way. As he clearly puts it, "When you surpass expectations in a business, good things happen."

In 1986, Dave had a vision of a new way to help loan officers become more successful by empowering them with the tools to help homeowners make informed, intelligent mortgage decisions.

After his WOW moment, Dave became passionate in the belief that he had developed a unique solution to a problem that affected the lives of millions of Americans.

With his single, transformative idea, Dave and his partner put a year of sweat equity and $18,000 on a personal credit card into building Wow Tools (now Mortgage Coach). The company was named after a core company value, that of delivering a WOW moment to every customer. Today the company is the leading provider of information and productivity software to more than 6,000 loan officers who have collectively helped hundreds of thousands of homeowners make better decisions about their futures.

This widespread success is just the beginning of Dave's vision of Mortgage Coach. Today, Dave is laser focused on fundamentally changing the way homes are sold and, in the process, creating long-lasting stability in the housing market.

"Informed purchases based on personal life goals help create a more stable market," says Dave. "I really believe that if everyone had used our tools, we would have avoided some of the housing-market meltdown."

In addition to Mortgage Coach, Dave Savage has started many other companies. In 2000, he started SmartReply, a permission-marketing innovator that helps companies connect and deepen customer relationships. The company was profitable, but Dave knew it could be much more. He stepped back and analyzed the industry. Even in 2002, it was obvious to Dave that mobile marketing was the future. And so he set about overhauling SmartReply into a mobile-marketing pioneer. This new strategic focus paid off and the company's growth exploded. This year, he sold the company to SoundBite, a publicly traded company that is a leader in customer-communications solutions.

In every venture Dave undertakes, he applies three core principles: (1) He delivers WOW moments. (2) He provides obvious, tangible value to both client and end consumer. (3) Last, but perhaps most important, he focuses on making complex systems drop-dead simple. Combine these three principles and you get a value system centered on delivering quality business and life-enhancing products that are a joy to use.

Values definitely matter. Step back and become crystal clear about your unique, authentic, pure, driving values. Values are the turning point between unawareness and awareness.

Now it's your turn. If you haven't already done so, complete this exercise. Take seven minutes right now to write down your top ten values in order of priority.

Once you have written down your top ten list, you will recognize that these foundational values are at the core of your being; they are your soul. Let your values drive you forward; they are your inexhaustible fuel.

My top ten values are:

1. _____

2. _____

3. _____

4. _____

5. _____

6. _____

7. _____

8. _____

9. _____

10. _____

START WITH WHAT IS MOST IMPORTANT

Moving from an unaware life to a life of awareness begins with clarifying the values that are most important to you. Many of the practical exercises and tools in *The 7 Minute Solution* are simple to grasp, yet their power often goes unrecognized. Erin Casey, who has been actively involved in helping me prepare this book, shared several great insights regarding how this first step affected her life. Erin has been studying and writing about personal development for almost two decades, but as she completed the 7 Minute Solution Priorities Worksheet, her initial reaction was guilt. Like many working mothers, she feels a constant pull between family and work. By thinking through the priorities worksheet and writing down her top ten list, she became more aware that her intentions for how she wanted to live her life and the realities of how she actually spent her time were not always in alignment. This is not an uncommon experience. Realizing the gap is actually one of the first steps to becoming vitally aware.

As Erin completed the exercise, it became clear that her top ten priorities are freedom, love, peace, authenticity, faith, family, adventure, making a difference, fun, and nature. For those who know Erin, none of those elements is a surprise. For those who simply look at how she spends the majority of her time, some of them would be unrecognizable as Erin's core priorities.

Becoming clear about her priorities empowered her to be more purposeful about what she paid attention to. She decided to choose carefully how she would spend the hours in her day. She chose to make her priorities, priorities. For her, that means taking a break in the afternoon to spend quality time with her two sons—even when she's on a deadline. It also means taking a walk at lunchtime so she can clear her mind, exercise her body, and reconnect with nature. Identifying her values and priorities created a framework for designing a better quality of life.

Meaning and purpose are different for each person. But knowing what is most meaningful to you is the beginning of the 7 Minute Solution. Truthfully, you probably already know what is important to you. But distractions and deadlines cause you to forget those values or let them slip to the bottom of your to-do list. That's why taking time every ninety days to focus on your values is so important. Your values are your nonnegotiables in life. *You need a solution or a system to remind you of your priorities.* Prioritizing your values is a cornerstone of creating a life with meaning. Once you have written your list of what is most important to you, slowly read the words over and over to yourself. Think about them. Reflect on your values. As King Solomon said, "As a man thinketh in his heart, so is he." Or, in the words of Earl Nightingale in *The Strangest Secret*, "We become what we think about." Attention and focus involve consciously choosing what you will think about, because we do become what we think about all day long.

The rest of *The 7 Minute Solution* will help you harness your attention and sharpen your focus. You'll learn strategies that will help you experience the meaning in life you desire. You'll check for vital signs and learn how to untangle yourself from bad habits and beliefs that keep you from living your very best life.

It's time to wake up and live!

PART II

The 7 Vital Signs

VITAL SIGN 1:

Are You Consciously Aware?

*Any definite chief aim that is deliberately fixed in the
mind and held there, with determination to realize it,
finally saturates the entire subconscious mind until
it automatically influences the physical action of
the body toward the attainment of that purpose.*
—NAPOLEON HILL, *THE LAW OF SUCCESS*

REE FALLING AT 120 miles per hour from 14,500 feet in the air—that's how my friend, Karon Fields, wanted to spend her fiftieth birthday.

I have always wanted to go skydiving. What would it feel like to glide through the open sky at 120 miles per hour? What would I be thinking? How would it feel to get onto a plane knowing that I would jump out only a few minutes later? Would I feel alive again? Would it make me consciously aware of everything happening around me?

Karon knew what she wanted. She wanted risk back in her life. She wanted to feel the rush of adrenaline and heart-pounding excitement. On the morning of her fiftieth birthday, Karon felt completely alive; she was excited about making her lifelong dream of skydiving a reality. When she arrived at the flight facility in Bolivar, Tennessee, she signed eight pages of waivers, sat through fifteen minutes of ground school, and got onto the plane.

"Skydiving seemed like a great idea while I was standing on the ground," Karon told me. But as the plane climbed into the sky on that beautiful Saturday morning, her heart wavered between excitement and terror. She didn't have long to worry, because within minutes the plane reached 14,500 feet. The door opened, and a rush of cold air and incredible noise blasted into the cabin. Her instructor stood up and connected their tandem harnesses. She knew it was time to take the first step toward the door. Her heart pounded wildly. Time seemed to move in slow motion; her brain could see only what was directly in front of her. Adrenaline coursed through her veins. The moment was exhilarating, exciting, and terrifying.

Karon stood only twelve feet from the door; every step toward it required extreme effort. She was attached to her flight instructor, but with Karon in front of him, he couldn't lead her; she had to be willing to take every step forward. With only a few steps remaining, her instructor yelled, "Cross your arms over your chest!" And she did. Time seemed to stand still. Through the plane's open door Karon could see the curvature of the earth below. The cold wind wrapped around her and took her breath away.

Finally only one step remained between her and the door. And she took it.

As she stood with her arms crossed tightly over her chest, the instructor yelled his final word of instruction: "Put your toes out the door!" And Karon did. At 14,500 feet in the air, she stood in the doorway of an airplane attached to a man she did not know but trusted with her life—with nothing but sky beneath her toes. The instructor grabbed hold of the doorjamb and yelled, "Rock one, rock two, rock three!" On three, they were out the door.

DECIDING TO LIVE WITH
YOUR TOES OUT THE DOOR

Life can give you what you ask of it, but not until you start taking steps toward what you want. Karon asked life for a breathtaking moment. Don't we all want that? Don't you want to wake up overwhelmed with uncontainable excitement about what the day holds for you? Don't we all want to live with our toes out the door?

Living with your toes out the door means you must first be willing to get onto the right plane—to get your life in order. In the last chapter you identified what you value most. When you know your priorities, it becomes much easier to choose the right plane.

Once you are on the right plane and headed in the right direction, it will be easier to reach the right altitude and to recognize the tools and resources you need to accomplish your goals. One of those resources is people who are willing to support and encourage you. Much like Karon's skydiving instructor, you need people in your life who have the experience and wisdom to guide you on your journey. You need mentors and friends who will stand up when you stand up and will encourage you to move forward continually even when you are afraid. Although most clichés point to the difficulty of the "first step," Karon's story demonstrates that it can actually be the final step that challenges us the most. It's then that we need friends and mentors to challenge us to put our toes out the door. I want to live with my toes out the door. I want to feel alive and be completely aware of what is most important to me. I want to be surrounded by people I trust, connected to people I love, and close to those who bring out the very best in me. That type of vibrant and full life requires that we decide to live each day consciously aware of our values, our surroundings, and our opportunities.

BECOMING CONSCIOUSLY AWARE

Did your heart pound as you read about Karon's experience? Were you aware of the fear and excitement she felt as she stood with her toes hanging over the edge of the door? Try for a second to imagine that you are on the plane. Feel what she felt. Hear the wind rushing into the cabin when the door opens. In your mind, walk with her as she takes slow, deliberate steps toward the door. When the instructor tells her to cross her arms over her chest, envision what that looks and feels like.

If you're ready to live with your toes out the door, now is the time to consciously decide exactly what you will pay attention to. Consciousness has many definitions, one of which is total awareness of what surrounds you—awareness of the life you are currently living and of who you are.

WHAT WILL YOU CHOOSE TO BE CONSCIOUSLY AWARE OF?

I can only imagine the heightened sense of focus Karon Fields felt as she stood at the door of the plane. In my imagination I can only wonder what she was focused on.

What did she see? Was she looking at the grassy fields 14,500 feet below? Was she looking at the door of the plane? Was she aware of the floor she was standing on? Was the floor painted black, or was it painted white? Did she notice? What did she hear? Could she hear the sound of the wind? Could she hear the roar of the plane's engine? Could she really hear the voice of the man telling her to put her toes out the door?

What did she feel at that moment? Was her skin cold? Or was she hot? Was she excited or scared? Did she even know she was breathing? Why do I wonder? Because this was a pivotal event in her life. It was something she had wanted to do for years. She had planned for it, she had saved up for it, and she did it.

I wonder how much of the experience she actually remembers. What was she paying attention to while she was free falling at 120 miles per hour? What can you really pay attention to in such a moment? Did she deeply enjoy the moment? Was the experience everything she had hoped for?

Not exactly. As Karon says, "There was so much adrenaline flooding through every cell in my body that after I landed I could barely speak. I couldn't sleep for two full days."

What happened? Her attention shifted. Attention is fleeting. Karon's attention was deeply distracted by the extreme excitement of her adventure. It is time to ask, what is the difference between attention and choosing to be consciously aware?

The Relationship Between Improving
Your Attention and Conscious Awareness

In the last section I defined attention and introduced you to three types of attention. Being consciously aware is the application of attention. We are always attentive to something. Now we explore how you can learn to choose consciously what you will pay attention to. Attention is a cognitive process that requires significant mental energy. The ability to choose what you will be consciously aware of is at the very depth of creating the life you want to experience.

In the introduction of her book *Rapt: Attention and the Focused Life*, Winifred Gallagher made five statements that define attention and helped me understand the magnitude of every tiny decision regarding what I consciously choose to focus my attention on.

1. "Indeed, your ability to focus on *this* and suppress *that* is the key to controlling your experience and, ultimately, your well-being."
2. "If you could look backward at your years thus far, you'd see that your life has been fashioned from what you've paid attention to and what you haven't. You'd observe that of the myriad sights and sounds, thoughts and feelings that you could have focused on, you have selected a relative few, which became what you've confidently called 'reality.' You'd also be struck by the fact that if you had paid attention to other things, your reality and your life would be very different."
3. "What you focus on from this moment will create the life and person yet to be."
4. "If you could just stay focused on the right things, your life would stop feeling like a reaction to stuff that happens to you and become something that you create: not a series of accidents, but a work of art."
5. "Your life becomes the sum total of what you focus on."

In life, you see what you consciously choose to see, hear what you consciously choose to hear, feel what you consciously choose to feel, and experience only what you choose to consciously experience. Life is filled with so much noise that your brain has learned to filter out what is unimportant so that you can focus your attention, your awareness, on what matters most to you in life.

You are bombarded with millions of thoughts, ideas, sights, sounds, smells, and physical inputs every second of your life. Each of these sensations is further impacted by the emotions you experience along with them. Your brain has a sophisticated filter. This filter constantly makes choices about what it will allow to enter your conscious awareness. It makes those choices based on what you think about regularly, what you value as most important, and what you have chosen to pay attention to in the past.

When we haven't clearly identified what is most important, *everything* seems important. The constant noise demands our attention and crowds out our time. Rather than living with focused intention, distraction and disorder become the norm. Although you are bombarded with millions of pieces of information every second, you can choose to become consciously aware of how you filter them.

Values plus attention and choice equal conscious awareness. Put another way, conscious awareness is chosen attention. When you carefully begin to choose what you will pay attention to you can begin to walk down the path of a more conscious and meaningful life.

Attention is therefore a highly sophisticated selection process. The first 7 Minute Solution Practical Application was a worksheet with seventy-five values listed on it. This is a highly targeted list. The intention of the exercise is to have you make a conscious choice, even if just for a few minutes, to focus on the really important values in life. As a time management and productivity consultant, I am aware that many people are so overwhelmed by what is happening to them that they don't even know what they should be paying attention to. All they feel is chaos and confusion, and the only thing they believe they should pay attention to is whatever is the loudest and most pressing event that is in front of them at that moment.

Contrast that life to what you would experience if you chose instead to take a conscious interruption from the chaos and noise. It would be almost as if there were a circle of activity that you could step out of for a few minute, to proactively think about what you want to allocate your attentional resources to. You allocate your budget. But have you really decided exactly how you want to allocate your time and how much time you will spend paying attention to the things that are most important to you?

What would it be like to step back for a time and *think*? How different would your life be if you could consciously plan what to pay attention to?

What if you made decisions based on the knowledge that you have a finite amount of attentional capacity? With every choice you make, you are consciously choosing not to pay attention to something else. *Attention is a zero-sum game.* There are only twenty-four hours in the day. The way you choose to spend your next minute means that you have decided not to spend that minute doing something else. As Winifred Gallagher says, "your ability to focus on *this* and suppress *that* . . ."

I want to make sure my *this*es and *that*s are right.

How many times have I chosen to watch a TV program rather than read? How many times have I found myself staring at my computer rather than exercising? Are your *this*es and *that*s bringing more meaning and fulfillment to your life? Are you using the limited amount of time you have at work to focus your attention and select your highest and best tasks during the day?

Have you made strategic decisions about how you and your team should be allocating your attention? What is the point of attention? Right now, look around the room. What do you see? There are hundreds of physical items to see. How many things are in the room you're sitting in? How many colors are there? What do you actually hear, the hum of the heater or air conditioner? Are there people talking? What do you feel? What is the temperature? Can you feel the chair you're sitting in? Do you feel your back against the fabric? Are there shoes on your feet? Do you even feel your feet until you bring attention to them? Can you feel the shirt on your back? Through our selective ability to focus our attention on individual targets, we are able to filter out millions of stimuli. The point of this information is that consciously choosing what you pay attention to will create the life you experience. Attention is a deliberate process, and it is hard to focus your attention and deliberately concentrate.

When you learn to control your brain's filter, you will be able to make conscious choices about what you want to pay attention to and how you can best use your time. These conscious choices are based on your values, priorities, purpose, and life goals. It should make sense that you will choose to pay attention to what is most important to you. The problem for many people is that they haven't determined what is most important. They're living passively, taking life as it comes. Without priorities, making choices is like setting your radio on scan and just listening to whatever song comes on the radio. If the scanner stops on a rap station, you listen to rap, even if what you really enjoy is jazz music.

We must regularly ask ourselves, "Is this what I want to consciously spend my time and attention on right now?"

Much as with a radio in your car, once you determine and clarify what you will pay attention to, you can tune in to and turn up the volume on those things. You can also turn down the volume on the things that are not as important. For example, if you determine that good health is important, you can turn up the volume on your health. You might then contact your physician for diet and exercise recommendations; create a plan for what you want to accomplish; and make more healthful choices on a daily basis. If you determine that your family is most important, you can turn up the volume on your activities with your family. Those might include eating together, planning special moments, and asking your family what they would like to do together and then doing those things.

Likewise, you can turn down the volume on things that are no longer important to you. You can tune out things that might be harmful. That could mean turning down the volume on negative thoughts, negative words, disorganization, and physical clutter. When you understand the power of attention and focus, you will see that what you pay attention to not only influences your life, *it becomes your life*. The human brain can focus its full conscious attention on only one thing at a time; out of the billions of pieces of stimulation and noise, you must deliberately choose what you will pay attention to. As Winifred Gallagher stated in *Rapt,* "Your life becomes the sum total of what you focus on." I take that a step further. I believe your level of fulfillment in life, your productivity, your successes and failures—your entire life experience—is determined by what you choose to focus on.

Giving yourself time to reevaluate your life every ninety days is important for a couple of reasons. First, as you grow and change, you may find that your priorities grow and change as well. It is important to touch base with yourself at regular intervals to determine what you want to turn up the volume on and spend more time and attention on. It is equally important to decide what you want to turn down the volume on to make time for other things.

Your brain is extremely powerful, but there is a limit to what it can do in any given moment. It's impossible to focus on everything at once. Research shows that you can consciously process roughly forty bits of information per second. But every second of the day, your brain is assaulted with much more information than your conscious brain can handle. Thankfully, your subconscious brain is able to process between 11 million and 40 million bits of information per second. To cope with vast amounts of information, your brain filters out what it deems irrelevant and uses subconscious shortcuts and routines called "cognitive models" that allow you to respond to many situations without consciously thinking about what you need to do. In fact, some studies suggest that 95 to 99 percent of our daily behavior is dictated by our subconscious routines, patterns, and habits—the cow paths that we have made through our daily lives. This implies that a maximum of 5 percent of the choices we make are conscious choices for how we want to live our lives.

For example, you may get up at the same time, wear the same type of clothing to work, eat the same lunch, work on the same projects, drive the same route home every evening, have the same conversations with the same people, and deal with the same frustrations every day.

What if you no longer want to live on autopilot? Remember the way neuroplasticity works? To change your life, you must tell your brain what to allow to filter into your conscious awareness. You must then choose what you will devote your energy and attention to. To create a conscious existence, you must choose well. Every choice you make impacts your life. You must consciously choose between watching a violent television program and reading a book of faith, between worrying about something you can't change and spending thirty minutes exercising, between starting and completely finishing a task at work and reading endless e-mails. You must choose between living in chaos and working from a written daily plan of action.

Like a muscle, the brain responds to stimulation. If you continue to live with the same routines and habits, your life will likely provide the same outcomes. But, if you decide to make new choices today and you begin to repeat those choices day after day, imagine the compounding impact those tiny decisions will have five years from now.

Life is a series of tiny choices. Creating a life with meaning is about discovering the purpose you were uniquely and divinely created to complete in your limited time on this earth. When you understand your purpose—and your brain's capabilities—you can create a meaningful and fulfilling life.

The question is, what will you choose?

ADJUSTING YOUR BRAIN'S FILTER

The brain is incredibly fascinating, and it plays favorites. Let me give you an example of the bias in your brain regarding what you choose to see and what you choose to ignore. At the age of thirty-five, I became pregnant with my first child. Until that time, I had never really noticed whether other women were pregnant. But once I was pregnant, I saw other pregnant women constantly! It shocked me to see so many pregnant women. And babies! Tiny infants were secured in car seats and in shopping carts at the grocery store. I saw babies everywhere!

Of course, there have always been pregnant women and babies. But because they'd never before been relevant to my life in such a personal way, I hadn't noticed them. When my circumstances changed, though, I became significantly more aware of people who were sharing the same experience I was living.

Here's another example. While my family was on a weekend vacation in Chicago, our daughter hurt her knee and had to shop the Magnificent Mile in a wheelchair. My husband and I spent the weekend pushing our daughter's wheelchair down the crowded sidewalks of Michigan Avenue and into and out of stores. Looking for wheelchair-accessible doors, asking where the nearest elevators were, and searching for wheelchair-accessible fitting rooms was a new and frustrating experience for all of us. We suddenly became aware of how inconvenient life must be for people who are wheelchair-bound full-time. I also became instantly aware of how many other people I saw in wheelchairs that weekend. They were everywhere. How could I have not been aware of others in wheelchairs? How could I have not noticed?

It wasn't that I was purposefully insensitive. But with our daughter in a wheelchair, our sensitivity was instantly increased tenfold.

We see what we are interested in. We see what we're working on. Our brain filters out the extraneous and at the same time is acutely aware and constantly seeking out the information, resources, and people we need in our lives. This can work to our advantage, but if we haven't told our brain what to pay attention to (or be on the lookout for), it may filter out potentially useful information. Our brain is constantly scanning and searching for what we tell it to see. Our job, then, is to teach our brain what to search for, what to call to our attention. What we want to pay attention to is people, opportunities, and resources that equip us to live by our priorities, fulfill our purpose, and achieve our goals. If we regularly review and clarify what is most important in our lives, we will inevitably become more aware of what we want and need to see.

How many times has this happened to you? You are in a crowded room waiting for a meeting to begin. Chatter and noise fill the room, and you are focused on a conversation with your boss when a person ten feet away mentions your name. Suddenly your attention changes completely. You can no longer concentrate on what your boss is telling you. Instead, your forty-bit capacity is completely focused on what that other person is saying about you.

The filter in your brain constantly scans all of the input around you until it finds something novel, surprising, or familiar. Have you wondered what part of your brain allows you to hear your name out of a crowded room? This is a process managed by your reticular activating system. It is looking for patterns that it can relate to and understand: babies or people in wheelchairs. This system controls what your subconscious mind allows to filter into your consciousness—and deletes the rest of the information.

Your reticular activating system is why you see what you want to see, whether you're looking for Oreos in the cookie aisle or your child's face in the group of fifty children in the school choir. You have been programming your reticular activating system for years; you just haven't been calling it by that name. The word reticular gives an image of creating a net, "the reticular veins of a leaf." This net acts as the conscious filter in your brain catching what you have deliberately set the bait to attract.

Think about it: when you first fell in love with your mate, everything—the songs on the radio, strangers you passed on the street, a random but heartwarming scent in the air—reminded you of that person. Your reticular activating system scanned for and picked up on everything that connected you in some way with your new love. The same thing happens when you're working on a large project. Your reticular activating system notices anything and everything that could help you complete your unfinished tasks. It keeps a running tally of the people you need to call, the budgets you need to finish, and the systems you need to develop. Your brain constantly thinks about the project; you can't get it off your mind. That's why you can see a random stranger at the grocery store and suddenly remember the name of a person you were supposed to call. You feel a physical jolt of adrenaline surge through your body as your brain triggers the reminder.

Your reticular activating system continually scans through the sights, smells, sounds, and data that surround you and makes subconscious decisions about what to catch and filter up to your conscious awareness. The exciting news is that you can program your reticular activating system to notice and make you aware of advantageous information, people, and resources that will help you experience the meaning and fulfillment you desire. You set the net for what your reticular activating system will catch by regularly reminding yourself what you value and by creating written goals.

You are already surrounded by all the goodness life has to offer; you only need to become consciously aware of it. You program your reticular activating system by priming your mind to consciously pay attention to what you are seeking.

The problem is that we are so busy, we have become accustomed to allowing our subconscious minds to decide what we should pay attention to. We become comfortable or lazy, and we forget to seek the things that help us be who we want to be. However, once you are aware of your desire to create a life filled with meaning, you can take the next step toward achieving that goal by programming your brain to seek out the things that will add true value to your life.

The flip side of the brain's powerful scanning system is that each of us has a subconscious tape that we allow to play through our minds. This tape may have negative messages on it that we have heard as far back as childhood, and it is part of the automatic pilot that often directs the choices we make. The tape plays and you hear, "You are not smart enough. Why should you even try to achieve that?" You don't deserve good things to happen to you. You need to be nicer." The tape may play these negative thoughts even after you have become conscious of them and no longer believe them. Sometimes it seems easier just to believe these old messages and live in the routines and ruts of a drab life rather than take action to change the tape.

You *can* change the tape by taking time to reshape your core beliefs. And it is worth the effort.

7 MINUTE SOLUTION:
PROGRAM YOUR RETICULAR ACTIVATING SYSTEM

Think. Write. Do.

We program our reticular activating system with what we *think, write, and do.* Language plays a significant role in the way we experience consciousness. Researchers understand that there is an enormous difference between subconscious thought and conscious thought. Subconscious thought is sensory. Conscious thought is recognized and structured as words and language.

Therefore, one of the premises of the 7 Minute Solution is that we must consciously focus our attention on what we *think,* on what we *write,* and on what we *do.* The process of "think, write, do" will allow you to turn up the volume on what you want to pay attention to.

Think

You know by now that your thoughts shape your choices, and your choices shape your life. But it's time to realize that *your thoughts also shape your brain.* Every thought you have is linked to a chemical and electrical impulse through the neuronal connections in your brain. Your 100 billion neurons make up the physical structure of your brain. And although your brain cannot change in size due to the restriction of your skull, every day your brain changes its physical structure as it continually rewires itself based on your thoughts and actions. Norman Doidge, MD, says, "I define neuroplasticity [the concept that our brains are plastic, or changeable] as that property of the brain that allows it to change its structure and its function and that is in response to:

- "The actions that we commit ourselves to
- "Sensing and perceiving the world
- "And, even quite fantastically to thinking and imagining"

The physical structure of your brain changes with every thought. Through repetition of thoughts you see true change. Neuroplasticity makes thinking critically important to becoming the person you want to be.

We experience life through our thoughts. By shaping our thoughts into words—even if those words remain unspoken—they become real to us. You really do become what you think about moment by moment, day by day, year by year. The pathways in your brain are created by the thoughts you have. Through neuroplasticity, the more you concentrate your attention on a specific thought, the stronger and deeper those connections become. The stronger the connections, the more efficiently your brain becomes at processing them; that is how new habits and attitudes are developed. If you want to experience more meaning in life, you need to spend more time thinking about what is meaningful to you.

If you actively sought meaning, couldn't you find more of it in your life?

In my own life, my friend Debbie Ring's cancer diagnosis jolted me into a conscious awareness. The impact was immediate. I realized instantly that I wanted my life to be radically different from the way it was. Unfortunately, I wasn't sure *how* I wanted it to be different. In my heart I simply knew I wanted more. My faith is very important to me, and I knew at the age of forty-one that I had been distracted from things that were most important to me. My life had become busy, but it was not productive. I was successful but not happy.

As I looked Debbie Ring in the eyes and listened to her tell me she had cancer, I felt an emotional tug—both for the pain of her situation and for the emptiness I felt in my own life. Internally, I began to experience emotions I had never felt before, but I didn't know how to articulate them. I didn't know what they really meant.

For the next eighteen months, I thought. I prayed for her and her family. I prayed for myself, I prayed for my family, and I prayed for wisdom. It was not an overnight awakening for me, but I knew I was growing toward some resolutions, even if they weren't immediate solutions. And though I didn't realize it at the time, all that thought and prayer primed my reticular activating system. The more I thought, the larger my mental "reticular net" became, and as my mental net grew, it more easily captured answers for my questions.

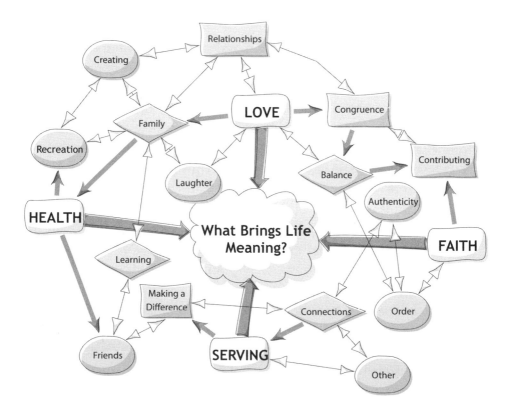

The thinking process began my search for understanding. During those eighteen months, I took unconscious thoughts and feelings and turned them into words—into conscious thoughts. I asked myself questions such as "What do you want your life to be like? What would bring your life meaning?"

When faced with important questions, I often use the simple tool of mind mapping. So many of the things I want out of life are experiential. Language limits our ability to articulate the depth of what we feel and how we describe what is most meaningful in life. How can I describe giving birth to a child—or holding the hand of a friend who has just lost a child? How can you describe solving a problem or creating a new invention to help people in life? By thinking about and writing individual words, rather than trying to tell the whole story all at once, I can define my feelings.

Write

If thought is the beginning of understanding, and if "As a man thinketh in his heart, so is he," thought is clearly important. Unfortunately, the human mind thinks at an incredibly fast speed. Some psychologists estimate that humans have 30,000 to 70,000 subconscious thoughts per day. Many times, our thoughts are fleeting. They move into and out of our conscious awareness so quickly that they're gone before they have time to make an impact on our actions and outcomes.

Thought is important, but creating some way to capture and clarify your thoughts is possibly a hundredfold more important. Your thoughts need a framework, a structure, and a place to be written down. You must translate and capture your thoughts by writing them down.

Thinking and writing are two ways to program your reticular activating system. Earl Nightingale said, over and over again, "You become what you think about most of the time." Your life is how you spend it. How fantastic is it to think that the life you experience can be altered and expanded? Regardless of the circumstances you face, you can choose to consciously decide what you will focus your attention on. If you spend your time focusing on serving, love, hope, goodness, sharing, and giving, that is what your life will become.

I speak from personal experience when I tell you that it is possible to change your life. Change the way you think, and you will change your results. And it doesn't have to take years. You can begin changing your life in a matter of minutes.

HOW MY LIFE CHANGED IN SEVEN MINUTES

I shared with you earlier how at forty-one, I had an awakening brought on by the combination of news from a friend that she was dying of cancer and the shock of nearly losing a coworker in the tragedy of 9/11. I awakened to the fact that my strategies for life were failing me. At that point, I began living out of the problem. I knew what I wanted to get away from. I knew that I didn't want to be overworked, overweight, or overwhelmed.

For years our team had a made it a best practice to participate in an annual full-day off-site planning retreat. I had worked as a financial adviser for the same firm since 1984, and by 2003 I was more excited than usual about the meeting. The meetings were not part of our company's formal training curriculum; rather, each year the three members on our team spent one day without the regular interruptions to focus our full attention not only on what we wanted to accomplish but also on who we wanted to become and how we could more fully serve each client.

Susan Naylor and I had known each other since she was a freshman in college. In 2002, I asked her if she would come to Jonesboro, Arkansas, to work for me. At twenty-six, she had the wisdom to say, "Allyson, I am not interested in coming to work *for* you—but I would love to come work *with* you." Then, only a few months later, we consciously took the time to create an agenda for the off-site retreat. We asked ourselves:

What is our core business?

How should we focus our attention?

What additional skills and knowledge do we need to acquire?

What is the highest and best use of each member of our team based on our personal strengths?

What are our personal driving values and priorities?

What is our purpose? What brings life meaning for each team member?

What worked best?

What didn't work?

What will we change?

What will we do more of/less of?

Once we understood the foundation of our business, we planned to spend the afternoon reviewing the business analytics and performance of our prior year to create a written concrete business plan for the following year.

What was our goal last year? Did we attain that goal?

If yes, what did we do right? If not, what happened?

What are our goals for the new year?

What are the concrete action steps we will implement to achieve these goals?

Who is responsible? What is the timeline?

Even as I created the agenda, I knew this meeting could be different. We were fairly clear about how to run a business like a business. But we were not as clear about our values, our purpose, the highest and best use of our time, and what brings life meaning.

Intuitively, I knew that when I was working in a job that was in line with my deepest personal aspirations, increasing revenues and better client relationships would be an obvious outcome.

What I didn't expect was that that single meeting would become a turning point in my life.

As the facilitator of the meeting, I asked our team to do a simple exercise. Before I tell you about that exercise, I have to confess something. Don't get me wrong, I love retreats. I am a busy executive, and I relish any opportunity to pause and regroup, but I didn't attend this retreat with the expectation that my life would be forever changed.

A kitchen timer was set for fifteen minutes and the only instructions were to look inside our hearts and complete the sentence "My purpose in life is . . ."

With that, the kitchen timer began counting down. At first everything but purpose swirled through my mind: the laundry waiting at home, groceries I needed to buy later, errands to run. Antsy and exasperated, I resisted the exercise, thinking "How is it possible to be completely unaware of my purpose in life? Is it even possible to define my purpose in what's left of the fifteen minutes on the timer?"

I surrendered to the possibility and decided to give it a try. With my subconscious mind racing, I focused my attention on the things I loved about life. Mentally, I listed my gifts and talents. I thought about the world around me and about what gave my life meaning and fulfillment at its deepest level.

A glance at the timer told me I had exactly seven minutes left. I scribbled words like a college freshman rushing to finish an exam. When the kitchen timer dinged, our pencils went down and I stared at these words:

> My purpose in life is growing. In life, I want to grow and change. I want to be different tomorrow than I am today. I want to grow as a wife—to be more in love with my husband, to hold hands more often, to enjoy long talks late into the night, and to share our hopes and dreams. I want to grow as a mother—to watch my children mature into their own destinies. I want to grow as a spiritual person—to become kinder, wiser, more hopeful, and more understanding. I want to work at my job with honesty and integrity. I want each day to be filled with fun and

excitement and challenge. And I want to help others bring about meaningful changes in their own lives, by sharing my discoveries and ideas.

My purpose in life is fulfilled by growing and through helping others grow.

I looked up from my paper feeling slightly stunned. I was no longer lost, trying to get away from an unsatisfying life. Now I had a clear direction. In those seven minutes, I stopped living out of the problem and started living into the solution.

That purpose statement helped me understand why I had been placed on this earth. I knew why I was here and how I wanted to use my time. I was able to look out at life and know what mattered. At that moment, I felt a deep and spiritual connection. It was one of the defining moments in my life.

It had taken forty-three years to shape my life, eighteen months to think about what I wanted my life to become, and a mere seven minutes to write it down. First I had to think about purpose; then I had to translate those thoughts into language; and finally, at that retreat, I was able to write down my life's purpose in only seven minutes.

When I finally awoke to my purpose, a whole new world of possibilities emerged. From those seven minutes, I have begun to redefine my life. I have started down a different path and have had the opportunity to share these ideas with tens of thousands of other people.

My life changed forever when I took seven minutes to write down my purpose. What I've come to understand is that until you understand your purpose and can clearly express it in words and writing, it's almost impossible to live it.

Without a clear sense of purpose, all of the organizational tools in the world won't bring you meaning. They will help you live more efficiently; they may even reduce some dissatisfaction; but to actively add value to your life, you must know your purpose clearly and measurably move into it more fully on a daily basis.

A HARNESS AND A SWORD

My friend Laurie Beth Jones is a popular motivational speaker and best-selling author. But it wasn't until she had her own awakening and discovered her purpose that her life felt truly meaningful. As she explains, "An awakening—becoming consciously aware of your purpose and all that you want from life—is a process.

"We awaken on multiple levels—we awaken to our giftedness, we awaken to our calling, we awaken to the beauty of the world around us, we awaken to the beauty of others, we awaken to our purpose, and we awaken to God."

For years, Jones tried to figure out exactly what she was designed to do. "Discovering my mission, my purpose in life was a long and arduous process," she remembers. Finally, after much thought, prayer, and soul-searching, she says, "I discovered my mission is to recognize, promote, and inspire divine connection in myself and others."

Understanding and focusing on her mission have helped her build a noteworthy career. "This clear mission became both a harness and a sword. A harness for my energy, and acted as a sword to cut away from the things I shouldn't or can't do with my life. I found that it is amazingly freeing when you get crystal clear about what you are here on Earth to do," she says.

Jones wrote her mission statement in 1994 and says that when she focuses on living her mission, everything improves. If she goes off course, her mission reminds her where her attention should be. By being faithful to her purpose, she has made a tremendous impact on the world. Her books have sold more than a million copies in sixteen languages. Her communication profiling system, Path Elements Profile™ (PEP), is taught around the world. More notably, she receives e-mails and letters from people every day who tell her how her work has changed their lives. From prisoners and prison workers, to pastors in India, to rescue workers and border patrol agents, she is encouraged by the words of those whose lives she has touched. "These letters and e-mails make me realize we must be faithful to do what we're called to do."

Mother Teresa said, "God called me to be obedient, not necessarily successful." Laurie Beth Jones adds, "It's the obedience that is measured, not necessarily results." It's time to get clear about what you were called to do so you can begin living out *your* purpose.

Do

There are three steps to the process of "think, write, do." First you have to think about what is most meaningful to you. Then you have to translate your thoughts into writing. Finally, you have to do it. Nike made a fortune with the advertising slogan "Just do it." The 7 Minute Solution slogan is "Did I do it?" Every day, consider the choices and the actions you took that day and ask, "Did I do what I said I would do today?" It is a simple yes or no question. The 7 Minute Solution is about *knowing* what you believe to be most meaningful to you and then *doing* what is most meaningful to you.

7 MINUTE SOLUTION PRACTICAL APPLICATION NO. 2: CREATE A PURPOSE STATEMENT

Now it is time for you to take action and create your purpose statement. As Laurie Beth Jones said, "Your purpose statement will act as a harness and a sword." It will harness your attention and allow you to focus on what is truly important. It will become the guiding force for how you will focus your time and attention. Stating your purpose in words—in writing—tells your reticular activating system what to notice. The act of etching your purpose on paper reprograms your brain's filter, allowing you to actively choose what you will become consciously aware of.

Earlier in this chapter, I talked about my friend Karon and her willingness to live her life with her toes out the door. Jumping out of a plane was her ultimate goal for that birthday adventure, but it wasn't the first step. First she had to be willing to go to the right place. She went to Bolivar, Tennessee, to the skydiving facility; you may need to go to a quiet place to discover your purpose.

Next she had to be willing to get onto the plane. If you really want to change your life, you have to be willing to make decisions—sometimes difficult ones. You must open your mind to the idea that what you have been doing in the past might not take you where you want to go in the future. If what you're doing now isn't working, if you don't already have the life you desire, you must do things differently than you have done them in the past. Otherwise you'll keep getting unsatisfactory results.

Once on the plane, Karon listened to her instructor, knowing he was far wiser and more skilled at the task than she. I encourage you to walk the path of life with mentors, friends, and people who can hold you accountable. Regularly ask yourself, "Whom should I be connected to today? Who holds the same values as I do? Who is on a similar path, and who is a few steps ahead of me and can help me make the right choices?" Then pay attention! Your reticular activating system will identify the right people.

When you're in the right place and you are connected to the right people, you will find yourself ready when it's time to stand up. You won't be alone. Your mentors, instructors, and confidants will be right behind you—but you must be willing to take the steps toward a greater life. And as you get closer to making those big decisions in life, there may come a point when you simply have to cross your arms across your chest and listen as your heart shouts, "Put your toes out the door!" Again, don't be surprised if you discover that the final step or two is actually more of a challenge than the first few steps. Though quite a few adages focus on overcoming inertia to take the first step, many people discover that the last steps, like those last ten pounds you want to lose, are actually what take the most concerted effort.

So move forward without fear; the first steps may not be as difficult as you have imagined. *Now* is the moment to put your toes out the door. Defining your life's purpose is both exhilarating and a little terrifying. It can take time to look inside your heart and discover what is truly important to you. But once you know your purpose, you will have the confidence to lean forward into life—and jump.

Identify Your Purpose

I was forty-three years old before I ever took seven minutes to write down my life's purpose. But once I had defined my purpose, it became so important to me that I had a "growing" logo created.

I posted the logo in different places in my home and office; I even had T-shirts made with the logo on them. I want to see it all the time, because it helps program my reticular activating system. Now I am constantly aware of ways in which I can grow and learn. I seek out opportunities to share new ideas and to make the world a better place by helping other people grow.

Having this logo in plain view reminds me of my purpose. It also brings me joy and meaning. Growing is fun for me. It's what inspires me. Learning something new, reading a new book, or meeting a new person lifts me up and energizes me.

I want you to experience that same energy, that feeling of inspiration and joy. That's why I want you to discover your purpose. You can begin the process by writing down a few words that describe what you love about life. As you think about what you love most in life, you will ignite the proper neuronal connections for discovering your purpose. Think about what makes your heart pound and your palms sweat. What gets you up in the morning?

This was my list:

God
Mark (my husband)
Abby and J (our children)
Growing/learning/reading

Writing/creating/sharing
Fulfilling work
Peace/freedom

This is a general list of the most obvious things I love about life. My list is fairly abstract, your list may be much more concrete including that you love to coach Little League baseball or you love leading and mentoring the members of your team at work.

It's time for you to create your own list. The first time you attempt to articulate what you love in life, it may be much more difficult than you think. We are so distracted by the clutter on our desks, the staff meetings, and the laundry we need to do that our brains are not in touch with what we love most. We are not used to being so blunt with ourselves, and sometimes we even feel guilty that how we spend our time and what we really love are not in congruence.

It took me eighteen months to clarify what I loved most in life. Don't be concerned if this exercise evolves over time, as you grow and change—what you love most in life may change as well.

Allow your brain to express your emotions in words. The act of writing down the things you love most in life will cause you to notice them more often and become aware of them. How cool is that?

How long does it take to write down what you love most in life? You might be surprised at how hard this exercise can be. You may be so pushed and pulled by stress and distraction that you may find it difficult to stop the noise in your head long enough to articulate seven things you love most about life. But when was the last time you took even a few minutes to write down what you love about life?

Is it any wonder we don't enjoy life more? How can we enjoy life if we are not sure what we are supposed to be enjoying? How ridiculous is it that our lives are so incredibly busy and inefficient and so full of noise and stimulation that we shut out the important parts, such as acknowledging what we love and are passionate about?

You may be reading this and thinking "That makes sense. I'll come back and write down my answers later." Don't wait! Take a few minutes right now to think about and *write down* what you love about life, what you appreciate, what you want more of. It's not enough to simply think about it. To make the most of this experience—to best use the time you're investing in reading this book—you must write down your answers. By writing down what you love in life, you are creating new neuronal pathways in your brain. These new pathways will become stronger as you go through the exercises in this book. How strong do you want the connections to become? You have control over that: "As a man thinketh in his heart, so is he." Think. Write. Do.

Take the time now to write down what you love. What is most important to you? You can write on the page in your book, or you can go to www.The7MinuteLife.com, click on "Member Tools," and print a copy of the Discovering Your Purpose Worksheet. The words may come from the priorities list you created at the end of the previous chapter.

What do you love most in life?

1. _____

2. _____

3. _____

4. _____

5. _____

6. _____

7. _____

Think about the words you've written down. Let the words sink in. How do they make you feel? What images come to mind?

Your purpose will often revolve around what you love most in life. Let your mind wander; search your heart for what you believe to be your purpose in life.

I would like to share three beliefs I have about purpose:

1. Purpose is what we do for others; it's about serving.
2. Purpose is how you use your gifts and talents to change the world.
3. Love is the foundation of purpose.

What Inspires You to Serve Other People?

How can you use your gifts and talents to change the world? Your purpose is not about you. It isn't about how you can make your life better; it's about what you can do for other people to make their lives better. The great news is that by improving others' lives, your life will be filled with the reward of joy.

A few years ago, after I shared these principles with a team of financial services executives, one of the men in the group stood up with his written purpose statement in his hand. He was visibly shaken. At six foot four, the executive looked like a football player. Emotion choked his voice when he said, "I want you to know I am thirty-three years old, and I've just figured out that my purpose in this life is . . ."

In a slow, quiet, confident voice he continued, ". . . to make sure my twin autistic boys know their daddy will always love them."

Simple. Outwardly focused. Grounded in love. That was it.

His realization filled the room with emotion. He and I cried, and many of the other participants fought back tears. For thirty-three years, this man had lived a good life. And in just seven minutes he had connected with a purpose he had likely felt but had never slowed down long enough to articulate clearly. His purpose of being a loving father touched everyone in that room. And it still gives me goose bumps to know that from that moment forward, every choice he made was based on the enlightenment of this new awareness of his purpose to love his children.

Now It Is Your Turn to Discover Your Purpose

Spend as much time as you are comfortable with on this exercise. It could take seven minutes, it could take an hour. It may even take months for you to discover your purpose. Regardless of how long it takes, I am positive that the process of discovery will be a blessing. By focusing your attention on what you love, you will become consciously aware of your life and what is most meaningful to you.

You can find the full-size version of the Discovering Your Purpose Worksheet on page 343.

This exercise gives you the opportunity to write about why you've been placed on this earth with the gifts and talents you've been given. Give your life the gift of attention by creating your written purpose statement now.

7 MINUTE LIFE™ STORY: THE IMPACT OF CONNECTING TO YOUR PURPOSE

Will writing out your purpose make an impact on your life? It did for me, and it has for the thousands of people I have worked with during the past few years. I want to close this chapter by sharing an e-mail I received on Sunday, September 20, 2009:

Dear Allyson,

Since Tuesday I haven't stopped thinking about your workshop. While I am always stressed and always high-energy, I have an enormous amount of stress right now. After spending a day with you, I now know that I don't have to live this way. I can take how I am "wired" and transfer that to positive behavior. My stress has changed my life from being a relaxed man of happiness, to a man I would not have recognized eighteen months ago. I am financially overextended and I am constantly worried. I know I'm not alone.

Throughout our day in Dallas, everything you said impacted my life: making changes, focusing on purpose, recognizing life's challenges as the opportunity for growth. I'm reading your book, *The Seven Minute Difference*. I am committed to making the sacrifice and change for my wonderful girls, and part of that is changing myself to be a better man.

I would like to share with you what I wrote during the "7 Minutes" you gave us to create our purpose statement. This is what I wrote almost verbatim:

My purpose is to be a present and supportive husband, a doting father who is available and kind at all times. The purpose of my life is to not make the same mistakes and to not let my life be defined by those mistakes. My life's purpose is to be a supportive and loving son: a present and open brother: and a generous, gracious and growing friend. My purpose is to not be driven by deadlines and goals for work. It is to be driven by experience, impact a journey of internal peace and understanding. My purpose is to be a faithful servant and to be forgiven for my sins. My purpose is to be a man of optimism and joy! My purpose is to not let my frustrations and difficulties affect my relationships with those around me. My purpose is to love. Love Jill. Love Sydney. Love Eloise. Love my friends. Love my experience. Love life.

You have given me the tools to be the man my family deserves. The man my coworkers need. And, the man I'm dreaming of becoming.

I'll go skydiving with you anytime. Thank you.

Mark Schwab

Mark and I have kept in touch, and he has told me several times that the 7 Minute Life™ workshop was a turning point in his life.

Today Mark lives a peaceful, more focused life. Clarifying his purpose helped him align his daily decisions and activities with how he really wants to live. "By thinking, writing, and doing what I say I will do on a daily basis, I have made a conscious decision to focus on the things that give my life meaning professionally, personally, emotionally, and spiritually. It has helped me live a life of clarity, peace, and fun. I have a sense of satisfaction when I finish my daily job, but I also realize now that work is not the only thing in my life," he says.

Mark's "AHA!" moment came in an instant during the workshop that day. "I became consciously aware that there is another way to live life. Up until then I don't think I realized there were other options. I felt boxed in which is a terrible way to live—trapped, confined, stressed, anxious," he says. "I realized it's possible to live a life of fulfillment, joy, and peace—and still be a viable professional who can do a really good job; you just have to structure your life differently. The 7 Minute Difference was that difference for me."

How much of Mark's story is your story? Can you relate to his feeling of frustration and despair? Can you imagine how it would feel to be freed from the bonds of financial and relationship stress? Mark woke up. He took the time to identify his purpose, and then he chose to change his life one decision at a time. He was motivated by love. What motivates you?

VITAL SIGN 2:

Are You Motivated?

> *Do or do not . . . there is no try.*
>
> —YODA (*STAR WARS*)

FOR EARL BELL, pole vaulting came almost as naturally as walking. He made his first jump at five years old. He loved the feeling of flying through the air, especially when the result was beating his competitors or his own record.

With his natural talent, a top-rated coach, and three brothers who pushed him to be his best, Earl excelled at pole vaulting. But after his freshman year in college, he had his eye on buying his first car. He planned to take time off from training during the summer so he could work and earn enough to buy a car. Earl's brother Bill recognized Earl's special talent. In fact, he saw a champion. Bill encouraged Earl to quit his job and focus on his training. He gave Earl a car and supported him so he could devote his time and energy to pole vaulting. In return, Earl trained harder than ever.

Like most things in life, pole vaulting can be broken down into sequences that must be mastered. The basics include timing, balance, and coordination. Some of the other critical parts are run speed, pole plant position, body alignment, and of course physical strength, stamina, personal motivation, and mental toughness.

How hard is it to compete as a world-class athlete? Earl worked with his coach, Guy Kochel, seven days a week—up to five or six hours a day. Over and over again, day after day—repetition and finally mastery.

Fast-forward only a few months to the spring of 1974. Earl Bell wrapped up his sophomore year by competing in the NCAA Outdoor Pole Vault Championship. During his freshman year, Earl's personal best jump topped out at 16 feet, 8 inches. Now at nineteen, with a year of intense motivation, training, dedication, and focus, Earl qualified for the championship finals. On his first attempt he cleared 17 feet, 8 inches by one-half inch. Earl had increased his personal best by an entire foot over the course of one year.

The thrill of achievement was short lived as his opponent cleared it as well. Now the bar was raised to 18 feet, 1 inch—five inches higher than Earl had ever jumped. Five inches, by itself, doesn't sound like much. It's shorter than your average stair step. But when you are pole vaulting, five inches equates to months of all-out, hyperfocused, back-breaking training. Consequently, Earl stood upon the runway, pole loosely in his hands, eyes transfixed on the bar, saying to himself, "It's just too high, I can't make it. I have never jumped that high."

Then, with the enthusiasm of a teenager, *he changed his mind*: "Oh, well, I'll just run and do my best." And with that thought, Earl Bell won the NCAA Outdoor Pole Vault Championship. It was the jump of his life!

Earl went on to break the world pole vault record in 1976 and earn his first bronze medal in the sport at the 1984 Summer Olympics.

Today Earl Bell trains others who are aspiring for mastery in their sport. Athletes come from around the world to work with coaches and trainers and one another at Bell Athletics in Jonesboro, Arkansas. As a result, the bar keeps moving higher; competition and training push these athletes to improve. What is it though that differentiates the Earl Bells of the world from athletes with an unrealized dream? Consider his story.

What happened to Earl Bell in that pregnant pause before jump-ing that allowed him to clear the bar and to soar to new heights in an instant? There is no single factor, but inner and outer motivations came together.

Earl's brother's financial sacrifice and encouragement were undeniable triggers motivating him and opening a path to training with its hours of coaching. Earl had also pushed himself forward with his love of jumping, the thrill of winning, and the allure of doing better. And in that final moment, the one and only thing standing between him and an almost unprecedented increase in performance was a choice to change his mindset. He got no new training; his body did not miraculously change, nor did his skill level. The only thing that changed was his mindset. He changed it by choice.

Understanding what motivates you is a key to living a more meaningful life. You need external motivators triggering your desire to move and internal motivators big enough to embrace and pursue the transformation. Both are necessary.

INSTIGATE, VALIDATE, INTIMIDATE, MOTIVATE

Motivation is an inside job, but sometimes you need someone or something to instigate change—and instigators are not always pleasant. The word "instigate" means "provoke or incite." In Latin, "stig" is related to the word "stick," as in to stick or prick your skin. Ouch!

In my life, the dissatisfaction of being completely out of shape, slightly overweight, and extremely exhausted continually stuck me. The constant "sticking" of unpleasant reminders served as a vital-sign check. Eventually, I knew I had to make some decisions. One of the most exhilarating parts of this process was coming to the full understanding that I possessed the freedom and ability to decide. I had become aware not only of the world around me but of all the options available to me. I realized that I'd been frozen in the familiarity of blame, insecurity, hurt, and dissatisfaction. Now I felt compelled to face unknown paths and make new and different decisions. It dawned on me that:

I could simply DECIDE to change.

I started telling myself, "I have DECIDED!"

"I have DECIDED . . . to lose weight."

"I have DECIDED . . . to get in shape."

"I have DECIDED . . . to get rid of the clutter in my home."

"I have DECIDED . . . to get the proper amount of rest."

"I have DECIDED . . . to eat foods that give me energy."

"I have DECIDED . . . to read."

"I have DECIDED . . . to laugh."

"I have DECIDED . . . to love."

Those decisions revived me! Having them written out clearly and being able to look at them constantly motivated me to seek out a solution. My written purpose statement was part of that solution. It illuminated a different life path, one with options. And once I decided what I would do differently, I began taking the first intentional steps down that new path.

VALIDATION AND INTIMIDATION

Just as we may need external prompting to make different choices, mentors and friends can help us along the path of change and awaken motivation within us. My friend and colleague Colin Stewart did that for me.

In 2003, shortly after I had discovered my purpose, Colin sat in my office, looked me in the eyes, and said, "Allyson, I've known you for years. You are one of the most talented people I know; it's time to up the ante in your life. You can do better than you are doing now. You can do a *lot* better."

Colin may not remember that conversation, but it was another vital-sign check—and a turning point for me. First my friend validated me; then he thoughtfully intimidated me. I needed to hear both. It was time to up the ante.

Earl Bell shared a story that illustrates the impact of validation and intimidation. Zack, a young man who attended a Bell Athletic pole vaulting camp, was an incredibly talented high school athlete. He had the speed, he had the build, and he loved to pole-vault. But for some reason he never jumped higher than ten feet. No one could figure it out. One day an athlete Zack admired approached him and said, "Zack, you can do this. You are talented. You have the perfect speed, you have the perfect build, and you have all the right techniques. You can do this. Today is your day. Dude, *jump higher!*"

That day, Zack jumped higher. *A lot* higher. He jumped eleven feet.

How would you like to improve your life 10 percent in one day?

Validation and intimidation. Like Zack, I needed someone to look me in the eye and tell me I could do it. And then I needed someone to tell me "Allyson, *jump higher!*" I wanted to jump higher, and I just needed to find the motivation to do so.

Now it's your turn. Find someone who believes in you enough to validate you. It could be a friend, a coworker, a boss, or a mentor. Then look at yourself in the mirror and say, "Today's the day; it's time to jump higher."

MOTIVATION

Emotional moments can inspire the desire to make a change. External circumstances can instigate change. Other people can push you to improve. But desire is only the beginning. To move beyond desire to decision and then to real change, we must be motivated. Motivation sustains us long after the emotional moment subsides.

What Is Motivation?

Motivation is derived from the verb "motivate," which means "move." Motivation moves a person; it causes people to take action. Motivation causes motion; it is an inner drive for action, a desire not just to decide but to do.

Where does motivation originate? Why do some people seem so motivated? And how can we develop more motivation?

In my quest to understand motivation, I interviewed the professional counselor and marriage and family therapist Dr. Dan Holmes. I hoped he would explain motivation and reveal the secret of how you and I can have more of it in our lives. Instead, he caught me completely off guard when he offered this insight: "Almost all people are seeking change. They want to be different tomorrow than they are today. But before I can help people discover what will motivate them to change, I first have to help them understand what stronger motivation they have *not* to change!"

Too often we don't change, even when we are truly inspired. We may be motivated to change, but stronger motivations hold us back.

"Unfortunately, far too many people feel stuck. People find themselves repeating recurring behaviors that I refer to as loops. They keep doing the same things, expecting different outcomes," Holmes says. "It's like owning a car that won't run. No matter how many different colors you paint the car, it's still the same car. A lot of people make superficial changes; they don't want to discipline themselves enough to make major changes that will help them get out of these loops."

You may be motivated by fear of the unknown, and that fear may keep you from changing your behavior. Or you may be motivated by a desire to grow—to move forward and search for a solution. But, the pain of where you are now, or the yearning for something new must exceed the perceived cost of moving forward before motivation moves us. Whether it's pulling you back or pushing you forward, motivation is the inner drive that compels you to live the way you do. It's time to uncover the motivation to move toward a more meaningful life.

Our life experiences and choices shape our motivations. Holmes refers to this as the paradigms through which we see the world. Paradigms are our way of thinking about our lives, of experiencing the world around us. They are based on our experiences and perceptions. Our beliefs and perceptions are real to us, regardless of their validity, and they have a dramatic impact on what motivates us and how willing we are to embrace change.

Various psychologists throughout history have tried to bring order and understanding to what motivates humans. Abraham Maslow's Hierarchy of Needs is one of the best-known explanations of motivation.

Humans have an innate desire to grow. We are motivated to become more, we want to find meaning and purpose in life; but far too often there are large gaps between where we stand today and where we want to be in the future. And those gaps are often littered with physical and psychological obstacles that must be faced and overcome.

Maslow's Hierarchy of Needs

SELF-ACTUALIZATION
personal growth and fulfillment

ESTEEM NEEDS
achievement, status, responsibility, reputation

BELONGINGNESS AND LOVE NEEDS
family, affection, relationships, work groups, etc.

SAFETY NEEDS
protection, security, order, law, limits, stability, etc.

BIOLOGICAL AND PHYSIOLOGICAL NEEDS
basic life needs—air, food, drink, shelter, warmth, sex, sleep, etc.

Maslow's theory explains that we are motivated to reach our higher needs only after our lower needs are met.

1. **Biological and physiological needs.** Air, food, drink, shelter, warmth, sex, sleep, and so on
2. **Safety needs.** Protection from the elements, security, order, law, limits, stability, and so on
3. **Belongingness and love needs.** Work groups, family, affection, relationships, and so on

4. **Esteem needs.** Self-esteem, achievement, mastery, independence, status, dominance, prestige, managerial responsibility, and so on
5. **Self-actualization needs.** Realization of one's potential, self-fulfillment, seeking personal growth and peak experiences

Consider the poverty of a child in Ghana, West Africa. Each morning a nine-year-old girl wakes up in a ten-by-ten-foot dirt dwelling. She is hungry and knows that the only food she will receive that day will be at night and only if her mother can find work to barter for food. Her first job will be to walk more than a mile with her twin sister to bring back several gallons of water. At eight pounds per gallon, this is exhausting work for both of them.

They sleep on cardboard mats. They have no shoes. They watched as their older sister died from a simple cold. Without adequate food, water, and shelter, the girl will not be motivated to understand how an education could change her life. She will not grow beyond her daily needs of thirst, continual hunger, and fatigue.

According to www.charitywater.org, "In Africa alone, people spend 40 billion hours every year just walking for water." Can you imagine?

Your answer should be yes.

You can't move forward until you personally get rid of some of the same obstacles that face you every day. Poverty is an example of a "loop" or "cow path" that humans become trapped in. But poverty is not the only example.

Rethink this same scenario, but place yourself in the picture. For how many years have you felt that your job or your current circumstances were trapping you like the ten-by-ten-foot room? How many times have you felt hungry—not for food but for a deeper substance? How many times have you felt thirsty?

You won't be able to motivate your team to achieve new sales goals (achievement—level 4 of the hierarchy) if you have not fully made them aware of their value on the team (belonging—level 3 of the hierarchy).

It may be more difficult for your engineering and design team to focus on creating beauty and balance in a new product (self-actualization—level 5 of the hierarchy) when the economy has them worried that they may lose their job next quarter (safety—level 2 of the hierarchy).

Wanting change isn't enough. As Dan Holmes said, "You must first understand what stronger motivation you have *not* to change."

What is the pay-off of not changing? What is holding you back? What old tape is playing? Why are you not willing to change?

It All Begins with a First Step

It all begins with the first step—and before you know it, two hours and forty-three minutes have passed. At least that's what happened for JoAnn Dahlkoetter.

Dahlkoetter was living in Portland, Oregon, working on an internship for her PhD in sports psychology, when she discovered that she enjoyed running. She started training with a running group, and before long, she started competing in races. The more she trained and competed, the faster she ran.

As a PhD student in sports psychology, JoAnn was not only learning about her field, she was experiencing it firsthand. As she trained, she honed her ideas about what it takes to compete as an athlete at this level. JoAnn developed a concept she used in her own training as the three Ps of the performing edge:

- Positive images
- Power words
- Present focus

For weeks JoAnn visualized *positive images* of every aspect of the race. Day after day she visualized the course, clearly picturing every portion of the race. Each night before she went to bed, she closed her eyes and visualized herself doing well, getting through the obstacles with ease. Those positive images filled her with excitement, energy, and confidence.

The *power words* she spoke each night before she went to bed bolstered her confidence. She repeated powerful phrases such as "Every day I'm getting stronger," "I believe in myself," "I am confident," "I am becoming a faster, stronger athlete every day."

And *present focus,* the ability to live in the moment, kept her focused on each step so she didn't worry about how many steps awaited her.

"It Was the Race of My Life"

JoAnn's training led her to the San Francisco Marathon. Butterflies filled her stomach, but she trusted her training. "I kept repeating to myself, 'I've trained for this race. I am rested, and I am ready to go.' I repeated all my power words and power phrases right until the starting time," she says.

As the race began, she practiced present focus. "When you're running a marathon, people tend to think about all the miles they have already run, and many people are worried about all the miles they still have ahead of them; but not me. I was living in the present moment. I kept telling myself, 'It's only this mile that matters. JoAnn, the only mile you can do anything about is the one you're running right now.' So I just focused on *this* mile."

At about mile eighteen, a stomach cramp threatened to take JoAnn out of the race. But instead of stopping, she made the choice to slow down, breathe deeply, and trust her training. Gradually the cramp subsided, and she was able to pick up the pace. Then fatigue set in. "At a certain point it becomes a mental game. I really doubted if I could make it. I was just so extremely tired, but I kept saying 'It's going to be okay. It's got to be okay.' I came up to another marathoner, and I knew he had to be tired, too. I asked him to tell me a story—to tell me something, *anything,* to distract me from the fatigue and pain I was feeling." She focused her mind on the man's story—and forgot about her pain and exhaustion.

When the finish line finally came into view, JoAnn says, "Moments earlier physical fatigue overwhelmed me; now adrenaline pumped through my body. Pain turned into passion. I was close; it was only a hundred yards away. The finish line just steps ahead of me; not one more mile but just a few more steps. I used powerful images, positive words, and present focus.

"I ran even faster as I drew closer to the finish line and saw the tape in front of me. With my arms outstretched beside me and behind me, my head high, my eyes focused on the finish line. One step more, and my body broke through the tape."

Despite her pain and fatigue, JoAnn pushed herself forward and she won the San Francisco Marathon with a time of 2:43:20. She used positive images and self-talk to stay focused on her goal. The motivation to continue resulted in what she calls the race of her life.

The Philosophy of Motivation

Today, Dr. JoAnn Dahlkoetter is a sports psychology expert and coach and the bestselling author of *Your Performing Edge: The Complete Mind-Body Guide for Excellence in Sports, Health, and Life.* For the past ten years, she has served on the medical staff at Stanford University Medical Center. And with more than twenty years of clinical experience, she is an internationally recognized performance consultant and coach to Olympic athletes, as well as being a world-class athlete in her own right. She teaches others how to use motivation and training techniques to improve their results.

"Motivation is basically an inner desire. Regardless of if you are an Olympic athlete, a corporate executive, a salesperson, or a teacher, you have to be hungry for success, hungry for results, hungry to be the best person you can be. That is motivation," she says. "It starts with a dream; motivation comes from within. It has to be an inner desire, an inner fire, a willingness to achieve something you are passionate about."

Remember Earl Bell? He had numerous external motivators that were absolutely essential. However, when his defining moment came the realization of his gifts was defined by his internal motivation. External motivation will produce nothing more than a resounding thud against the glass ceilings of your limiting mind-sets without the liberating force of internal motivation.

Dr. JoAnn, as she is known professionally, has profiled numerous highly motivated people. After studying high-achieving athletes and top business performers, she discovered that those men and women don't possess superhuman powers, but they do share similar traits. In fact, she identified seven characteristics of motivation. The good news is that those traits can be developed by anyone who truly wants to excel in life.

The Seven Characteristics of Motivation

1. Enthusiasm and desire.

   To be truly motivated, you must have a love of what you do; it must pull you. Top people in every field have a hunger, or fire, that fuels their passion to achieve. So to accomplish anything in life, you need to begin with a vision or dream. The more clearly you can picture that dream in your mind, the more likely it is to become a reality. JoAnn visualized a magnet on the finish line, pulling her forward and drawing her in.

2. The courage to succeed.

   Once you have desire and enthusiasm and you are motivated to achieve a specific goal, you must fortify your dream with courage. Courage empowers and emboldens you to make your dream a reality. It takes courage to sacrifice. Anyone can dream, but it takes courage to persist when you are tired and feel like quitting. Everyone faces obstacles. Only those with courage are able to overcome those obstacles and pull through.

3. Self-direction.

   Champions decide early on that they are training and competing for themselves, not against other people. They are motivated to move forward not for their parents or coaches, not for the medals or money—but for themselves. A drive from deep within pushes and directs their thoughts and actions.

   Goals and motivation are closely intertwined, but the goals that drive champions forward are born out of that inner fire, out of passion. Self-directed goals motivate and inspire on an entirely different level from goals set forth by another person or external motivators such as money.

4. **Commitment to excellence.**
   High achievers are committed to becoming their best. Peak performers set priorities: they make a commitment of excellence to make their dreams come true. When Dr. JoAnn works with Olympic athletes she asked them to rate themselves on a scale of 1 to 10 on where they are now in their training and where they want to be. She then asks them to commit to making an effort every day to becoming the best at what they want to do.

   Excelling in any area of life requires a commitment to strive for excellence; that commitment demands focused time and attention. What would it mean to be the best at being you?

5. **Discipline and organization.**
   Discipline and organization are often the most difficult life skills to develop. Many people can be truly motivated to accomplish great things, but motivation must be backed up with discipline, consistency, and organizational skills. Discipline means working hard on a daily basis and sometimes on a minute-by-minute basis. Discipline can be learned and improved. And if you love what you do, it's easy—or at least easier—to be consistent and disciplined in your efforts.

   As part of their discipline, peak performers stay motivated by generating the optimal amount of excitement and energy at exactly the right times.

   Throughout this book, I've referred to the human heart's ability to pump exactly the right amount of blood throughout the body to deliver the perfect amount of energy at any given time. Discipline does the same thing. Discipline and organization allow you to dig down deep, to hold on, to persevere. Discipline is not an emotion, it's a decision. Organization is not an innate skill, it's a choice.

6. The balance between focus and relaxation.

    Staying motivated is a dance between the balance of intense focus, which generates energy, and relaxation, which rejuvenates and restores. Champions are able to maintain their concentration for long periods of time. They can zoom in on what is critical to their performance, and they can zoom out on what is not critical.

    Being in control of your attention and focus is essential to staying motivated. Like a radio scanner and its ability to tune into viable stations and skip the static, you must learn to focus your attention and turn up the volume on what is most important to you.

    Equally important is relaxation. To be creative, able to meet physical challenges, or even simply "be present" for your family and friends, your body needs the rejuvenation and restoration that comes only through relaxing. For some, relaxation is an act of discipline. Recalling that the word "recreation" is actually "re-creation" may help you prioritize your need to relax.

7. The ability to handle adversity.

    Setbacks and difficult situations are inevitable; everyone experiences challenges. But adversity builds character. Elite athletes know that when the odds are against them, they have greater opportunities to grow, to explore the outer limits of their potential. Adversity is often the spark that ignites our inner fire. Rather than avoiding pressure, allow it to open the door to deep personal growth, because personal growth renews and restores motivation.

    I want to live a life fueled by that inner fire, from a place of faith and continual growth, don't you? The good news is that we can! It's possible to increase your motivation. The seven characteristics of motivation are traits that can be learned or developed.

    Where does your motivation come from? We've looked at motivation from a cognitive and emotional perspective; now let's take a look at the science of motivation.

The Science of Motivation

For most of us, motivation is activated by a trigger. That trigger may be an emotional experience, a sense of competition, or a feeling of desire instigated by someone or something external. There are two common triggers of motivation:

1. Escaping from pain
2. Moving forward to pleasure

You may be motivated to start a new health regimen after having lunch with a friend whose appearance dazzled you (escape the pain of self disappointment). Or, it may be something as simple as the inspiration you feel to clean your kitchen counters after visiting a friend's well-organized home (move toward the pleasure of a clutter-free environment).

With either of these triggers, there is a gap between where you are and where you want to be. It's not as though you didn't already know about the gaps; in fact, "what-if" or "I wish" thoughts of change may have been circling in your mind for months or even years. But the trigger of seeing others living in a way you admire compels you to take action in your own life.

The problem with gaps—the discrepancies between where we are and where we want to be—is that they make us feel as though our lives are not in alignment with our true selves. The gaps in our lives cause stress, but they also make us aware of what is missing in our lives; they ignite the desire to change and grow. When you sat in your friend's home, your brain experienced a gap between your current existence and what it would feel like to live in a home that was in alignment with your desire to live in a well-organized, clutter-free home. When you had lunch with your friend and saw her vibrancy and fit physical appearance, your brain recognized a gap between your current weight and what you could look like if you shed the fifteen pounds you have been talking about losing for the last two years.

Here's how motivation works at its simplest level.

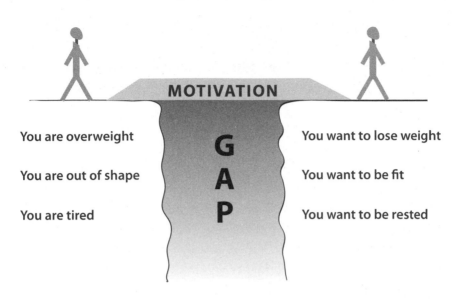

You are overweight	**G**	You want to lose weight
You are out of shape	**A**	You want to be fit
You are tired	**P**	You want to be rested

You need motivation to move from where you are today to where you want to be. Motivation is needed to fill in the **GAP**s.

UNDERSTANDING THE PARTS OF THE BRAIN

I love the science of neuroplasticity and motivation. I want to help you clearly understand the whys and hows behind the choices you have been making—and how you can make better choices in the future.

The Prefrontal Cortex

The prefrontal cortex is the thinking part of the brain. This is where life happens! In this space just behind your forehead, ideas are created, thoughts are pondered, imagination grows (or dies), judgments are made. This part of the brain is highly specialized in humans; this is where you define meaning, plan for the future, and imagine. Your values, priorities, purpose, goals, drive, motivation, learning, love, and hope all live here.

One of my favorite authors and psychologists, Mihaly Csikszent-mihalyi, PhD, says in his book *Finding Flow: The Psychology of Engagement with Everyday Life,* "What we call thinking is also a process whereby psychic [mental] energy gets ordered. . . . Thoughts order attention by producing sequences of images that are related to each other in some meaningful way." This ordering of your attention happens in the prefrontal cortex of your brain. He continues, "To pursue mental operations [thinking] to any depth, a person has to learn to concentrate attention. Without focus, consciousness is in a state of chaos. The normal condition of the mind is one of informational disorder: random thoughts chase one another instead of lining up in logical casual sequences. Unless one learns to concentrate, and is able to invest the effort, thoughts will scatter without reaching any conclusion."

Take the time to read that again. Think of what it would mean to your life to have ordered thoughts, to be able to concentrate your attention and to stop living in mental chaos.

Often referred to as the area of "executive function," the prefrontal cortex is responsible for thinking, planning, focus, attention, impulse control, willpower, making big life choices, choosing appropriate behaviors, and establishing and working toward goals.

Place your forefinger just above your left eyebrow and hold it there for a moment. Think about the connection of your physical self and your mental self. Ask yourself, "What are my deepest desires? What do I really want out of my life? What specifically will bring meaning to my life?"

Every thought you think and every word that passes your lips shapes the life you experience. Verbalizing your thoughts and desires and writing them down creates new neuronal pathways—pathways that will help you consistently make choices that improve your life. That's why a written purpose statement is so important. It etches your purpose in your mind and pushes you not simply to think about it but to live it out!

This single idea motivates me to want to think about, write, and do things that matter. Knowing exactly what is most important to you and holding your written purpose statement in your hands can change your life.

Why Change Is So Difficult

Why is change so difficult? The best word to describe why it is so difficult to change is due to the biological and chemical process of homeostasis. Homeostasis can be described as what causes the human body to crave internal stability. Your body seeks equilibrium. For example, humans have a normal body temperature of 98.6° F. regardless of the temperature outside or inside. Your autonomic systems regulate your body temperature at a constant level. Another example is your blood sugar, which is kept level as your body combines blood glucose with insulin and glucagon. Even if you haven't eaten a single bite of food for a day, your blood sugar levels will remain fairly stable. From your blood pressure to your need for sleep to your desire to exercise to how much you eat on a regular basis, your body has created a regular and familiar path of what to do.

When you decide to change, your body will fight you because of this homeostasis. Your body will say, "I don't want exercise, I don't want to eat less food, I don't want to go to bed earlier, I don't want to focus my attention."

Because of its desire for consistency, your body and mind crave the familiar. If you attempt to make several radical changes at once, your body will push even harder for "normalcy." That's why rapid radical changes seldom stick. Every January 1, millions of people make radical resolutions—and fail almost immediately because the changes are too far from normal. We want change to be fast and easy, but the reality is that small, consistent changes in your behavior and thoughts will produce much greater results. That's why *The 7 Minute Solution* encourages you to take tiny steps—what we call "microactions"— toward change every day. As you take small steps, you will strengthen the neuronal pathways and make the connections you need to continue in the path of growth. Repetition defines a distinct path, and isn't it easier to follow a clearly marked path than one that is hidden by grass and debris? Strategic repetition is the key to sustaining positive change.

Dopamine

Dopamine is a neurotransmitter that is produced in the middle part of your brain. A neurotransmitter is a chemical that allows neurons to communicate with one another.

Everything you have ever wanted in your life you have been motivated to strive for because it felt important to you.

Every choice of how you spend every minute of every day is built upon what you feel is most important. In fact, you are reading the words in this paragraph because you're experiencing a sense of anticipation that you will learn something new.

A full understanding of this single concept could change your life. Dopamine influences everything you do; it affects every aspect of your life. Dopamine is the drug of anticipation. Everything you want causes a dopamine release, and you want it because it releases dopamine. Every decision you make is based on the anticipated release of dopamine.

ABC's hit television show *Extreme Makeover: Home Edition* is a perfect example of how dopamine affects the brain. We are called together when Ty Pennington picks up his megaphone and introduces us to the family receiving the new home. Your brain is flushed with dopamine, and the anticipation begins to build as you meet the parents and the children and follow them through their current home room by room. You are delighted by the excitement as they are swept off in a limousine for a much-needed one-week vacation while their home is torn down and rebuilt by hundreds of community volunteers and generous sponsors.

When the big bulldozers arrive, you silently cheer as the clock begins the seven-day countdown. The anticipation of providing a completely new, safe, beautiful home to a family in need places your heart right there. It is only a sixty-minute show, and as the clock continues to click down to the final moments, I feel like a kid standing in the cheering crowd waiting to see the tremendous gift of love built during this life-changing, Herculean, seven-day effort. Close to a thousand people crowd around the family as the anticipation builds for that final cry of "Move that bus! The dopamine level in your brain at that moment rises by 100 percent, and you are flooded with hope and inspiration. You feel as though you just helped build that house. You feel as though you are part of that family. And you feel motivated and inspired; you feel great!

Dopamine is very powerful, but the supply of it is limited, and once it is used it is gone and must be recycled. It can be produced synthetically, but it cannot pass through the blood-brain barrier, so what you have is all you will ever have. Your dopamine levels affect your movement, memory, learning, sleep, and mood. Dopamine levels are depleted by stress, anxiety, lack of sleep, certain antidepressants, drug use, poor nutrition, alcohol, too much caffeine, and even sugar. You can increase your natural supply of dopamine through daily exercise and simple nutritional decisions, including eating ripe bananas, whole grains, almonds, avocados, artichokes, dairy products, lima beans, pumpkin seeds, sesame seeds, and most foods rich in antioxidants, which include many vegetables and fruits, especially blueberries, cranberries, and strawberries.

The problem with dopamine is that it is a neurotransmitter of anticipation. After watching shows such as *Extreme Makeover: Home Edition* or *The Biggest Loser,* you feel as though you can conquer the world, but after the closing commercial you find yourself back on the couch. Dopamine is only a launching point. And although dopamine is extremely powerful, it is also fickle. You can't rely on it to help you create significant, lasting changes. Creating lasting change requires us to make goal-driven choices on a daily basis. There is an enormous difference between midbrain, reward-seeking, short-term behavior and prefrontal-cortex, well-planned, well-thought-out decisions that are driven by desire and executed on a daily basis regardless of feeling. Rather than being driven by emotions or primal urges, your goal is to create values-based habits that ultimately create new neuronal pathways of change.

FILLING THE GAPS AND CREATING NEW PATHS

Each person is motivated by different outcomes. But I hope that you are gaining a deeper knowledge of how you can train your brain and create new neuronal pathways in response to what motivates you. First you must *think,* then you must *write,* then you must *do*—and do it over and over and over again.

Imagine that your neuronal connections are a field of very tall grass. Picture yourself standing at one edge of the field and knowing that you want to go to the opposite corner of the field. As you take the first step into the field, the chest-high grass pulls at you; it makes every step difficult. You can see over the grass, but it is hard to walk through it. With much difficulty and considerable effort, you slowly make it to the other side.

The next day, you want to accomplish the same task. Stepping off from the same entry point, you can clearly see where you walked yesterday; the grass is slightly bent, and now you know where to step. Your steps are still labored, the grass is still very tall, and it is still difficult to walk, but because you've walked the path before, you know you will make it to the other side.

The very next day, you repeat the journey. It's no longer as overwhelming. Each day you repeat the task, your steps are easier. If you walk the same path for ninety days, what will happen to the field of tall grass? A distinct path will develop, and the steps that were once such a battle will become routine.

Motivation is much the same way. Would you rather follow a difficult path or an easy path? Of course you'd rather go down the easy path; we choose familiar paths over change. But once you understand that new familiar paths can be created through repetition, it can be inspiring to realize that you have the freedom and ability to choose a life different from the one you've lived in the past. It's time to look forward. It's time to take one more step. It's time to live life one mile at a time. It's time to live in the present, with a vision to create new pathways for your life.

Life is a series of new grassy fields, and each time you are presented with a new challenge, you will be faced with a series of new decisions. Will you rely on old habits and old routines that have not worked well and have not taken you down the paths you want to experience?

Like the bending of grass, the neuronal connections in your brain are deepened and strengthened each time you repeat an action. Don't be afraid of new challenges; rather, consciously work to make yourself aware that as you try to incorporate new and better work habits into your life, homeostasis and familiarity may be pulling you toward a different path.

Think back to the priorities you have already written down. Remember mine: faith, family/friends, health, growing/learning, peace/freedom, creativity/sharing ideas, inspiring others, making a difference, doing meaningful work, having financial security.

Go back to your purpose statement. As bestselling author Laurie Beth Jones says, "Your purpose statement is both a harness and a sword." How can you start spending your time today that will be congruent with whom you want to be at the end of the day?

Before you begin the process of setting ninety-day goals, place yourself in the following picture.

There are people who wake up early a couple of times a week to go jogging, and that is great. There are also a few who have taken the time to create a more structured routine, and they call themselves runners.

There are the devoted few who run marathons; they spend months training and preparing for each race. But in life there are those even rarer who win the marathons. Combining passion and drive with goal setting and rigorous training, these men and women set huge personal challenges and meet them. Step by step, day by day, moment by moment, your goals must inspire you and call you to be your very best. If you want more out of life, define what that more is by creating written ninety-day goals.

You will shortly begin the process of creating ninety-day written goals. Your personal goals will be built on the foundation of your priorities.

As you set them, remember that champions choose their goals based on their internal drive—not external pressure. Your goals must be in alignment with your values and purpose. If they're not, they will lead you down the wrong path and widen the gap. It is only when your goals are in harmony with your priorities that you will be motivated enough to take the conscious, daily steps necessary to reach them.

How you focus your attention, the thoughts you allow to run through your mind, the words you speak to yourself, the actions you take, and the feelings you experience shape you. Your life can be powerfully positive, it can be neutral, or it can be painfully negative. The blessing is that you decide how to fill the gaps. You decide which paths to create. You choose who you will become.

So the question is "Who will you be ninety days from today?" What books will you have read? Who will you have met? What will you eat? How much will you exercise? How much will you sleep? What will you focus on? What will you pay attention to? What will the reality of your life become? Will you find meaning? Ninety days is coming; you will blink, and ninety days will have passed. Who will you be ninety days from today?

Before you create your ninety-day goals, I want to share a story of how one man challenged himself to win.

Thriving in Hard Times

John Weller is an inspiration. He is a certified mortgage planner and has been in the mortgage industry for eighteen years. Using the last analogy, John was definitely like a well-trained marathon runner. After the U.S. banking crisis hit in 2008, many mortgage professionals left the industry, and those who stayed were overloaded with new regulations, paperwork, and restrictions. John had always been serious about his business and was driven to help people make better and better-informed decisions about mortgage loans and purchasing homes, but the degree of difficulty to accomplish his goals had dramatically increased overnight. By 2009, for more than a decade John had been ranked among the top two hundred mortgage originators in the country as reported by *Mortgage Originator Magazine* and the *Scotsman Guide,* both of which serve mortgage companies and professionals. John viewed himself as successful, enjoyed his work and his clients and coworkers, but he really believed that inefficiencies and distractions were holding him back from something greater and that in the new banking environment, just working harder wasn't going to cut it. He believed that the crisis in his industry could be an opportunity to take a gigantic leap forward if he implemented a few foundational changes.

At the end of 2009, John read my book *The Seven Minute Difference* and spent a few days working through the exercises, including identifying, prioritizing, and organizing his values, mission, and life purpose as well as his areas in need of improvement. "I found this process empowering and inspirational and relatively easy using the simple fill-in-the-blanks exercises found in the first few pages of the planner," he says. "I was surprised how easy it was to just jot down notes and fill in answers to the prompts as I went through the book over the Christmas holiday in '09. I liked the idea that each exercise was only supposed to take seven minutes." As his answers flowed out of his head and onto the worksheets, John began to realize that his values and priorities weren't always exactly in line with the typical tasks, calls, and meetings that filled his days. So he laid out some ambitious goals and priorities, including some new benchmarks that had not been part of his previous goal setting or planning.

John's normal day as a loan originator typically included an hour or two of e-mail, two to three hours in the car commuting to and from work and meetings, and three to four hours helping borrowers and realtors solve problems and put together mortgage loans to purchase and refinance homes.

"At least half of my time was spent responding to various urgencies and problems on loan files, borrowers' qualification problems, realtors upset with appraisals, etc., sort of like a fireman putting out a myriad of little fires that randomly pop up in various locations. I'm not complaining; my job really suits me because I enjoy problem solving and puzzles and I know that ultimately there is a human family and their home on the line every time I get a shot to handle one of those fires. I have a mild case of dyslexia, and I use the technique of working backwards from the 'ideal end result' back to 'What can I do today?' to dictate what the next action should be. Anyway, the challenge has always been that the more loans I manage to bring in, the more problems there are to solve and often the problems on the current loans compete with my being able to bring in clients and their loans. The ultimate challenge being that the demands of new clients and their problems tended to rule what constituted my day as opposed to me proactively choosing my actions and objectives each day."

While working through the exercises in *The Seven Minute Difference,* John was particularly struck by the simplicity and power of the "one-yard-line" concept that sometimes just a last little bit of "finishing" power added to a task or call can yield tremendously higher results than running out of gas just short of the finish line. "I loved the concept that if a call or meeting was going to take seven minutes or seventy, it was that last one minute that could make the biggest difference as to whether or not I crossed the finish line or I might be stopped right at the one-yard line." John also began to utilize *The 7 Minute Life™ Daily Planner.* This tool aggregates many of the time-management and productivity worksheets found in this book. He also really liked the idea of using his planner as a scorecard to record all his activities rather than just as a to-do list that ultimately grew into a quagmire of incompletions. Specifically, he discovered his priorities and purpose in life, not just work, and decided to set 2010 as the "Year of Deeper Relationships," which he had realized was one of his key values in life.

He decided to focus on deepening his relationships with his best clients, his referral partners, his coworkers, and especially his family.

In reevaluating his life purpose, he said, "I was reminded that the people in my life are what is most important to me, not *just* getting things done." Each time he met with someone in person or on the phone, he truly wanted to engage with them at a deeper heart level. He wanted to listen, he wanted to connect, and he wanted to contribute something valuable to their lives.

"I took a little extra time and put in a little extra heart when it mattered as my way of powering across that one-yard line. I firmly believe that because of developing the habit of writing down a name and celebrating with a smile and a deep breath each time I was able to really connect with someone, I felt more fulfilled in my work and was able to better focus on my highest priorities throughout the day. I think the act of physically writing the names of those I connected with in my planner as I made each call or completed each meeting was far more effective for me personally than trying to type it into a computer record somewhere. Also, some of my best connections by phone happened while in the car thanks to my one-hour commute each way, and I frequently pulled over to have those conversations so I could really listen and take notes. Incidentally, I think the people I was talking to 'got it' that *they* were my priority in that moment since they usually knew I pulled over to have that conversation with them. While this habit sometimes extended my commute, I really think it also brought me closer to the people I care about."

Let me put a framework on what John did and how you can do it, too. In late 2009, John began to use the 7 Minute Tools shown throughout this book to focus his strategic thinking into small repeatable actions and habits to maximize his success. In business, many of us are often too busy to stop and clarify what is really most important to us and what will really make the biggest impact on a given situation. But John took what we call a "strategic interruption" from his day-to-day routines and made a decision to narrow his focus on how he could deepen relationships and cross finish lines. When interest rates dropped in mid-2010 and huge sales opportunities arose, John was able to virtually double and triple his normal sales volume. In the midst of that boom, he was also able to recruit two very important support team members who were key to the fulfillment of those sales in an environment in which everyone else was too busy, overcommitted, and stressed out.

Very quickly, John's phone began to ring off the hook and his inbox was overflowing with lead opportunities from all the family, friends, and clients John had been connecting with all year. He and his team were ready to deliver top-quality service to double and triple as many clients as his next highest competitor. Because of his strategic planning in 2010, out of hundreds of thousands of mortgage professionals in the United States, John moved up to number fifty-one in the country with $103 million in closed loans in a single year. "While we all worked very hard to achieve that success in 2010, we did it in the spirit of fun, teamwork, and of making a positive difference in human lives through their finances."

After a decade of producing at a very high level, John's goal of deepening relationships and making small adjustments so as to "finish" nearly doubled his production in one year.

CREATING YOUR NINETY-DAY GOALS

Your *purpose* identifies what you want to do with your life and how you want to use your gifts and talents. Your *goals* help you live out your purpose. Written goals, when combined with a plan for achieving them, can clearly make a difference in your life. In his book *Goals: How to Get Everything You Want Faster than You Ever Thought Possible,* Brian Tracy encourages readers to do three things:

1. **Write down your goals.**
   It is not enough just to have a vague idea of what you want to achieve. You need to develop specific, measurable goals and write them down.

2. **Make plans to achieve your goals.**
   For every written goal, you need to determine three or four or five specific actions that will help you reach that goal.

3. **Work on those plans every day.**
   Most goals cannot be achieved by sporadic and occasional effort but require daily attention and action.

Are you seeing a theme? Focused, written goals combined with daily, purposeful action lead to meaningful, lasting change. When you have clear goals, you are one step closer to fulfilling your purpose. Goals can be personal or professional, tiny or grand. They may be achieved tomorrow or within ninety days, or they may be aimed at leaving a legacy beyond your lifetime. Take a few moments now to think about what you want, about what will help you fulfill your purpose. Begin by making a shopping list of the things you want in life. For example:

- Is your health important to you? Could increased energy help you achieve your dreams?
- Would improved relationships enhance your life?
- Do you want to enjoy exciting or educational experiences?

Now is the time to dream! Make a list of the things you would like to do, be, and have. If you have trouble thinking of things to list, go back to your purpose statement, priorities, and values. What would help you live out your purpose? Articulating your goals and writing them down alerts your reticular activating system to tune in to the people, resources, and solutions that will help you achieve them. Use the 90 Day Personal Goals Worksheet on page 344 to write down each individual goal in the present tense, as though it has already happened.

Follow each goal with five action steps that will allow you to accomplish it within the next ninety days.

After you have written down specific action items for each goal, prioritize those actions and select a timeline to accomplish each one. Then place each actionable item in a scheduled time slot on your calendar. Of course, some goals may require more action steps to accomplish than others; it is not necessary to limit yourself to five action steps.

Review Your Goals Daily

Repetition is a critical component of changing habits. Part of the theory behind the science of neuroplasticity is that change occurs when you put your brain to work every day. It's like driving cows down a new, specific path day after day. With each trek, the path becomes more clearly defined. Repetition creates stronger neuronal connections and new, more efficient neuronal pathways. Reviewing your ninety-day goal worksheets frequently also strengthens your neuronal connections and pathways. Like the act of writing down your goals, reading them repeatedly encourages your reticular activating system to kick into gear so that your brain automatically scans for solutions, innovations, ideas, and processes to accomplish each goal.

For example, one of my personal goals states: "*Goal:* I am in the best physical shape of my life."

The reality is that I may or may not be in the best physical shape of my life at the time I write the goal. But it is important for me to write every goal in the present tense, as though it has already happened. To create new pathways and to motivate me to take the first step into the "grassy field" of exercise, it helps for me to be able to see myself standing on the other corner in excellent physical condition. It also helps to visualize myself in a new pair of cute size six jeans. By writing my goals in the present tense, I'm able to rejuvenate goals that might not have inspired me in the past.

90 Day Personal Goals

Minute Life

Date:_____

Goals		Completed By
1. *I am in the best physical shape of my life.*		_____
Action: *I walk 2 miles four times per week.*		
Action: *I do calisthenics two times per week.*	What was the outcome?	
Action: *I walk the dogs 20 minutes per day.*		
Action: *I drink 60 oz of water per day.*		
Action: *I sleep eight hours per night.*		
2. *I am continually learning.*		_____
Action: *I read one book per week.*		
Action: *I have a list of what I want to read.*	What was the outcome?	
Action: *I read 10 pages a day to increase my knowledge.*		
Action: *I listen to books & lectures on my iPhone.*		
Action: *I fully participate in my Mastermind group.*		

•   •   •

Just as my goals are written in present tense, so are my action steps. So if my goal is "I am in the best physical shape of my life," my action steps might be:

1. I walk thirty minutes four times per week.
2. I do calisthenics two times per week.
3. I walk the dogs once a day for twenty minutes.
4. I eat healthful foods that fill me with energy.
5. I drink sixty ounces of water per day.

7 MINUTE SOLUTION NO. 3: CREATE A 90 DAY PERSONAL GOALS WORKSHEET

Use the following 90 Day Personal Goals Worksheet to write down what you will focus your attention on. The neurological effect I experience when actually writing down my personal goals is so powerful that they not only motivate me to action but bring a burst of excitement even as I write them down.

The pursuit of meaningful personal goals is another solution for creating a meaningful life.

Start and finish every day by reviewing your ninety-day goal worksheets. As you focus your attention on the goals you want to accomplish, your reticular activating system will put itself to work both consciously and subconsciously to reach those goals. You will find yourself waking up with new ideas for how to solve a problem. Or you will be driving down the street when a burst of inspiration forces you to pull over and write down all of your new ideas.

You can find the full-size 90 Day Personal Goals Worksheet on page 344.

Just as attention means that you must focus on *this* and suppress *that,* the goals you choose today mean you are choosing not to pursue other goals.

CREATING GOALS THAT DRIVE YOU

In an effort to better understand why people are willing to set ever more challenging goals, I interviewed Dan Pink, bestselling author of *Drive: The Surprising Truth About What Motivates Us.* In order for goals to move you they must carry intrinsic motivation, which he defines as, "The joy of the task [is] its own reward." We work best when we love what we do, when we would almost work for free, when we will do whatever it takes. One of the biggest problems we have with our jobs is that we are so busy accomplishing goals that we didn't establish for ourselves that we don't have time to accomplish goals that are personally important to us. In a different book, *A Whole New Mind: Moving from the Information Age to the Conceptual Age,* Pink makes another insightful claim when he says, "meaning is the new money."

When you establish your ninety-day work goals, realize that in a ninety-day period there are approximately sixty workdays of eight hours each for a total of 480 hours. My guess is that most of us work far more than that. But are we really working on projects that matter for eight hours a day? Or are we focusing our attention on things that pull us away from our purpose and our goals?

The next ninety workdays of your life could be radically different if you use these planning tools. Sit down alone or with your team, and decide what you really want to accomplish over the next three months. You may want to focus on only two or three major work goals per ninety days.

As you create your written 90-day work goals, step back and focus on what really moves the bar. Simplify your goals into meaningful accomplishments. Write your work goals in the present tense, as though they have already been reached. Then follow each goal with action steps that you personally have control over.

7 MINUTE SOLUTION PRACTICAL APPLICATION NO. 4: CREATE A 90-DAY WORK GOALS WORKSHEET

The 90 Day Work Goals Worksheet is strategically one of the most powerful tools in this book. Bringing order to your thoughts and to your workday is one of the goals of this book. To do this you must first decide what you want to concentrate your focus and daily activities on accomplishing. By now you are seeing how limited your time at work is. You may think you have eight hours to accomplish your tasks, but after you account for the stream of interruptions, you may really have only three or four hours in which to think and be truly productive.

As you write down your 90-day work goals, you instantly release your subconscious brain to set out a net to scan for and to capture millions of new ideas for potential new solutions to reach your goals. But you must first narrow down what you want to accomplish. Your written goals give you strategic focus. And when you deliberately think through what actions you need to take to reach each goal, the only thing left to do is to execute them.

Before you write down your 90-Day Goals you will want to make sure your written goals are in alignment with your priorities and your purpose. You may struggle with creating your written 90-Day Goals—when presented with the 90-Day Work Goals worksheet— many of our consulting clients stare blankly at the page, they just don't know where to start. They ask, What do I need to set my goals? Where do I start? How do I gather the information I will need to set my goals?

It can be as simple as looking out 90 Days from today and list specific statements in present tense, for example you might say in the next 90 Days:

- Our revenues increase by 5 percent
- We increase customer satisfaction by 1 percent
- We increase market share by 2 percent
- We complete and implement the new product design

You can find the 90 Day Work Goals Worksheet on page 345.

Each 90 Day Work Goal should be written in present tense and be followed by five concrete action steps. You may have a goal that requires twenty different steps, but as you translate the action steps into your daily activities, by the end of one week you may have completed three of the steps, and then the next week you may complete two more. The 90 Day Work Goals Worksheet is strategically one of the most powerful tools in this book, because it gives you that vital framework to prioritize, organize, and simplify your goals onto a single sheet of paper.

Once you strategically define and clarify your written 90 Day Work Goals, your job becomes very simple—*do what you say you want to do.*

Regardless of whether you work for yourself or are part of a team, it is essential to set down a vision in writing for the goals you hope to accomplish at work in the next 90 Days.

If you work on a team, the most important aspect of 90 Day Work Goals is communicating them to the entire team *clearly.* An overwhelming amount of time in the workplace is lost due to poor communication of goals.

MOTIVATION, GOAL SETTING, PURPOSE, AND MEANING

Who do you want to be ninety days from now? Every turning point involves a starting point. If you haven't defined your goals and the action steps that will help you achieve them, do so now.

Motivation, goal setting, purpose, and meaning are completely intertwined. Once we discover our true motivations in life and set goals, we find that those goals pull us forward, motivating us even more.

One of my friends and mentors is Shelley Shepherd, the president of Laurie Beth Jones. Not long ago we were discussing motivation and purpose, and she commented, "There are some really, really deep tracks in each of our lives that are embedded at a very early age. There are many things in life we are naturally attracted to or naturally gifted at accomplishing. These tracks are hard coded into our brain, and I think one of the greatest blessings in life is when our purpose in life is in alignment with these "tracks."

"I believe there are paths for our lives and we should attempt to clarify and establish personal goals that are in alignment with our purpose. When we do this, we will definitely find more meaning in life."

Shelley defines meaning as the feeling that resonates within her when her life and work are in alignment with her values and purpose. There's that word again, alignment. As you write down your goals, do a vital-sign check and ask yourself:

- Am I motivated to accomplish this goal because it pulls me toward my purpose?
- Will achieving this goal help me become the person I was designed to be?
- Does this goal benefit the world around me? Is it focused on something larger than myself?

When your goals support your purpose, they free you to live with excellence. As you work to do what you said you would, you will find yourself deeply involved in the next vital sign: growing and learning.

VITAL SIGN 3:

Are You Growing and Learning?

The mind is not a vessel to be filled
but a fire to be kindled.
—PLUTARCH

IF YOU WANT LIFE to be different tomorrow than it is today, *you* must be different. When you are ready for growth, you realize that you can't remain the same. You dedicate yourself to learning new skills and expanding your knowledge by reading books, listening to audio series, attending conferences, and spending time with friends and mentors who challenge you to grow. And as you grow, you change; your creativity expands, and your brain pours forth new ideas. You become different. As a result, you experience life with a sense of newness and excitement.

Humans are created to learn, grow, and change. Curiosity captivates us. We are energized by the novel, surprising, and challenging. Our brains perform best when we are encouraged to expand our knowledge and use our critical thinking skills.

Either we are growing or we are using our valuable and limited time stagnating. Like muscles that atrophy with disuse, the brain craves stimulation. Without it even basic thought becomes difficult. Clearly, growing and learning are vital signs of a meaningful, vibrant life.

REBUILDING A LIFE

Imagine going to sleep one evening completely healthy and waking up seven weeks later, unable to move. That's how Seth James's story begins. He had been under the weather with fever and chills—nothing serious. Fatigued by fever, he went to bed early one evening. No one was expecting what happened next.

Seth's wife called his parents, Larry and Jill, in a panic the following morning. She couldn't wake him, and fluid was coming out of his mouth. By the time medics arrived at the young couple's home, every organ in Seth's thirty-five-year-old body was shutting down. As they tried to revive him, he slipped into a coma.

Later, doctors diagnosed Seth with adult Reye's syndrome, a disease that attacks the liver and brain. But the most serious damage came from the respiratory failure. Prolonged lack of oxygen caused extensive damage to Seth's brain.

For weeks Seth's family took turns sitting with him, desperate for him to wake. Finally, at the beginning of the seventh week, Seth's wife was reading to him when he spoke for the first time: "Quiet! I can read! Be quiet, I can read!" His wife smiled and said, "Okay, okay."

Seth's family was overjoyed to have him back. They knew, however, not to expect a quick recovery. Seth's body had been devastated by the oxygen deprivation. The only thing he could move was the forefinger on his right hand. He would have to relearn even the most basic motor skills, starting with how to swallow.

For the past five years, Seth has worked to relearn how to function. To do that, he has had to reestablish and generate new connections and pathways with his remaining healthy brain cells. Like other types of cells throughout the body, neurons are designed to perform specific functions. Neurons, however, are unique in that they have the capacity to learn to perform new tasks. As his brain had lost a significant number of neurons, Seth's recovery required his remaining cells to adapt—to learn to do new jobs within his brain. Through repetition-filled rehabilitation sessions, Seth calls on each cell to create new connections and take on new responsibilities.

The regeneration of Seth's body has been nothing short of miraculous. He can speak. He has regained much of the use of his right hand and his right and left arms, and he can lift both of his legs. On good days, he is able to stand in his power chair for up to ten minutes. He recently relearned how to sit unassisted for a few moments at a time. He can pick up small objects and when handed his toothbrush he can brush his teeth. "We're working on his ability to eat. He has a special fork, and I sit with him every night, and we work with it over and over and over again," Jill says.

Seth continues to improve his motor skills on a daily basis. He recently learned how to pick up and hold a cup. "He can pick it up when he is thirsty, and he can drink it by himself. This single skill is improving his life," she says. "Imagine not being able to quench your own thirst. This new skill is a big accomplishment."

The process of rewiring Seth's brain has been slow and time-consuming. The Jameses continue to research and explore every possible medical technique that could help their son regain mobility.

Through small steps of recovery, Seth continues to astonish doctors and thrill his parents. "Our son wasn't supposed to live," Jill says. "But I have watched the miracle of how Seth's neurons have rewired themselves through the repetition of his therapy. The brain is plastic. Seth can do today what he couldn't begin to do a year ago. Neuroplasticity gave him back to us. We needed a miracle, and we received it one connection at a time."

GROWING FOR A CHANGE

We are inquisitive by nature; the challenge to figure out how to do something new drives us forward. That's because, as humans, we are designed to grow. Our brains make new neuronal connections and pathways every time we take in new information. But even though we are designed to grow and learn, it isn't always easy. Seth's parents and physical therapists have spent thousands of hours working with him to teach him basic life skills. But Seth had to want to learn, and he had to make a daily effort to do so.

In the previous chapter, you set ninety-day personal and work goals for yourself. You've been given the ability to learn how to do the tasks you will need to do, to develop the habits you will need to develop, to accomplish those goals. But you have to want to grow and change. The good news is that every time you seek out new challenges and take steps to develop new skills, you are taking a step toward becoming the person you desire to be. Continue taking those steps on a daily basis, and in ninety days you *will* be different than you are today.

The word "growing" carries with it the idea of improvement, expansion, and making something more robust. As you grow and learn, you create new concepts and shape your brain. You change, becoming a new and different person. All positive changes stem from the ability to grow and learn. Think about these important points:

- You can change your physical body by exercising and eating right.
- You can increase your earning potential by acquiring new knowledge.
- You can improve your relationships by learning how your words and actions affect others.
- You can create a deeper and more divine relationship with God by seeking truth and understanding through faith.

Beyond developing new skills and beneficial traits and habits, growing and learning are the sources of much of life's meaning and richness. When you experience a revelation—an "Aha!" moment—it is often accompanied by an overwhelming motivation or drive to do something with that new information because learning releases dopamine! Such a breakthrough moment can provide a solution to a problem that may have plagued you for years. It might inspire a simple fix, such as coming up with a new routine that will simplify your morning; suddenly life is better for everyone in your home. Or it might bring clarity to a major operations problem at work. Suddenly (or so it seems), you have an answer that solves a multimillion-dollar dilemma. Such moments seem abrupt, but in reality they are a culmination of learning, growing, and awareness. They may feel instantaneous, like meeting the love of your life for the first time, but in actuality your brain and its reticular activating system have been seeking the perfect solution, circumstance, or soul mate for quite some time.

Although you may be content not to learn, evolutionarily speaking it has always been to your benefit to learn. When a cave woman heard rustling in the bushes and dismissed it as simply an interesting sound and was eaten by the lion, her sister cave woman was motivated to learn.

Your brain learns whether you plan to learn something new or not. Every day is filled with new learning opportunities. You learn about the world around you from the news you read and hear. You expose your mind to the opinions and thoughts of everyone you speak to. The millions of marketing messages you hear and see each week create desires and wants that you didn't even know existed. The question is not whether you *will* learn; the question is what you will *choose to* learn.

What are you learning right now? Are you presenting your brain with the right learning opportunities? Are you feeding your mind with books, activities, and challenges that will pull you forward?

Do you realize that what you learn today shapes you into the person you will be tomorrow? You are a combination of everything you have learned in your life to date. You have literally learned your way into your current personality. You have learned your way into your current level of integrity. You have learned your way into your relationship with God. You have learned every aspect of what you've accomplished and who you are. Every experience causes your brain to learn.

Although learning is inevitable, it is also a daily choice. You make decisions every moment that shape how you think and behave. There are only a few things you haven't taught your body to do. For instance, you didn't teach your heart to beat, your body to regulate its temperature, or your lungs to breathe. Those are automatic physiological actions. But consider the vast scope of what you have learned in your lifetime:

- **You have learned how to see,** how to observe varying wavelengths of light and comprehend them as color, shade, depth, and beauty. You have learned how to see the majesty of sunsets. You can recognize the shape and expressions of the faces you love most. And you can enjoy the immeasurable gift of seeing a smile on your child's face.
- **You have learned how to hear,** how to interpret varying lengths of sound waves that would mean nothing to the human ear without the brain's ability to put those sounds into context. Yet sound profoundly impacts every moment of our lives, from the ability to decipher complicated patterns of sound that make up human speech to the pleasure of hearing the sound of your mother's voice in the first few months of your life to the sound of your children laughing and the sound of birds singing.

You have learned how to walk, talk, eat, laugh, read, drive, and love. You have learned to embrace life or to be afraid of life. You have learned to rejoice and to mourn. The great part of learning is that every day offers a clean slate to learn afresh and move your life in a new direction.

Your life is the sum total of these learned experiences. Your life will grow into what you choose to learn in the future. What will you choose to learn today?

YOU HOLD THE KEY

For much of my life I believed there was a secret box under lock and key that held the answers to all of life's mysteries. I believed a rare few people had been given the key to this secret box, and throughout their life they had the privilege to peer inside and find the answers I desperately sought. It wasn't that they were better, exactly, it was that they had access to knowledge.

In reality there is a secret box. You have felt it calling out to you. But it is not external to you; it lies deep within your heart. It calls to you and says, "You can be different tomorrow than you are today." Inside this box is the ability to learn.

For many years I searched for the box and its key. But when I realized that the potential to learn was within me, I realized I already held the key to meaning and fulfillment, the key to significance, the key to life itself.

The key is growing. Growing, for me, has come from opening my heart to a deeper understanding of my faith. I love to grow and learn, and as I age, I want to focus my attention on learning more about what really matters.

The truth is everything in life is a mystery—until you set your mind to solving it. Everything in life is a challenge—until you set your mind to overcoming it. Learning is a process that shapes your brain, your behavior, and your life.

FOR THE LOVE OF LEARNING

My favorite days at work are those when I acquire a new skill, especially when the learning is almost unexpected. Often there is a question that has been bubbling in my mind for days or even months or years. I've discovered that the answers to questions often come when I'm working on a project that requires me to lay out various scenarios with various pieces. The effort forces me to use various cognitive skills, as when putting together a very difficult puzzle. I lay out the different pieces of what I'm trying to put together, and suddenly I experience a eureka moment. I gain a sense of comprehension; knowledge comes into focus. The answers arrive, and they all make sense. The puzzle fits together, and every piece has a place.

As I mentioned earlier, such moments may seem sudden, but

they don't happen by chance. For hours, days, or even years, I have been learning, studying, and seeking knowledge. During that time, my reticular activating system has been working in the background, learning what new information to allow to filter into my conscious awareness as I grow.

Learning excites me; it reinvigorates my passion for my work. And when the answers arrive and the pieces all fit together, I find new energy, strength, and meaning. These are some of the best days of my life. They are when I get to peer inside the secret box and watch the mystery unfold. The answers arrive, and the knowledge comes. This is when life takes on new meaning.

I know that if you're like me, you are looking for more from your life. If you want more, you cannot remain the same; you must choose to change. Learning is the process of growing and changing. Learning is a critical part of life. So as much as I want you to understand the benefits of learning, I think it's important to discuss how our brains learn.

HOW YOU LEARN

A few months ago, I set a hot iron on our kitchen counter and told my then fourteen-year-old daughter, "Be careful. Don't touch the iron. It's still hot." Before I could get the word "hot" out of my mouth, my daughter reached out touched the iron just to make sure I was telling the truth. Of course the iron was still hot, and the shock of the pain forced her entire body to recoil; her eyes turned from a gleam of curiosity to tears. Of course she has known since she was tiny not to touch a hot iron, but curiosity overwhelms us, and sometimes we think, "No, really, this time it will be different!" But now I'm positive my daughter will no longer feel compelled to touch a hot iron. Experience is an excellent teacher.

Experiences—pain, pleasure, desire, fear, love, hurt, rewards—instigate learning. They are the visible or tangible lessons. What you can't see is what goes on inside your brain when you're learning—and that's where all the action is! Learning actually occurs at the cellular level in your brain. Each of your 100 billion neurons is charged with chemical and electrical power to think, imagine, create, and learn every day. To help you understand how the cells in your brain are structured, picture each cell as a tree in a forest. Given proper nutrition and hydration, each of your brain cells, or neurons, is capable of growing numerous branches called dendrites. The thicker and stronger the branches, the more branches of nearby trees (or neurons) it can communicate with.

Your thoughts run through your brain like squirrels run from limb to limb and from tree to tree, except that the electrical impulses in your brain travel at up to 268 miles per hour and every neuron can potentially connect with up to 15,000 nearby neurons. Neurons don't really fire well by themselves; there just wouldn't be enough power from one single neuron. They fire in neural circuits, and the key is their combinational power. Every thought you have, every move you make, every heartbeat, every breath is controlled by trillions and trillions of connections (adults are estimated to have 500 trillion synaptic connections). Just stop for one moment and imagine the night sky as if you could see trillions of electrical connections being sent among the stars. And your brain never turns off or even takes a single break over your entire life span.

The magnitude of these connections makes the potential for human learning seem limitless. The key to learning is making sure that the cellular structure within your brain is strong enough and broad enough to connect in new and efficient ways. Learning stimulates new connections, and repetition strengthens them. Learning also changes the physical structure of your brain.

Now, admittedly I am a tad more geekish than the average fiftyish-year-old woman. (For example, you probably don't spend your Friday evenings watching YouTube videos about the brain.) The first book I read was *The Brain That Changes Itself: Stories of Triumph from the Frontiers of Brain Sciences* by Norman Doidge, a research psychiatrist and psychoanalyst at Columbia and the University of Toronto.

I was swept away by the idea that the brain was plastic or change-able, and I wanted to understand how it worked. Next, I read Daniel

Amen's *Change Your Brain, Change Your Life: The Breakthrough Program for Conquering Anxiety, Depression, Obsessiveness, Anger, and Impulsiveness.* I read *Rapt: Attention and the Focused Life* by Winifred Gallagher, followed by *Flow: The Psychology of Optimal Experience* by Mihaly Csikszentmihalyi; *Spark: The Revolutionary New Science of Exercise and the Brain* by John J. Ratey and Eric Hagerman; *Find Your Focus Zone: An Effective New Plan to Defeat Distraction and Overload* by Lucy Jo Palladino; and many others.

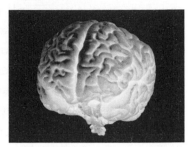

This is an illustration of the human brain.

Continual learning is one of my core values. I love reading. Words fascinate me. When I am reading a book and suddenly the words on the page open my eyes to new learning, something happens physically. Learning is challenging and exciting, and it renews me. I believe that learning is a key factor in neuroplasticity because every single thing you learn makes you different. You change as you learn.

You can use the "7 Minute" idea of reading ten pages of a book per day, or you can download books from www.audible.com to your smart phone or any MP3 device and listen to books while you exercise or clean your home.

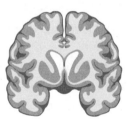

My learning about the science of neuroplasticity was at my own pace, on my own terms, but it was from that learning that I was inspired not just to tell people that they could change their brain and change their life; I wanted to create practical and repeatable tools and systems for creating change.

The cortex is only one-quarter inch thick, as shown in this illustration of a dissected human brain.

With this in mind, to understand neuroplasticity we must begin with an understanding of how the brain works.

The brain weighs approximately three pounds. Its exterior is a grayish/pinkish color and looks like earthworms packed tightly into a confined space. Slimy and gooey-looking, the part that hosts the most important part of your consciousness is described as being the consistency of cold porridge. (This is my thirteen-year-old son's favorite part of the book. Gross and interesting are a great combination. And when it comes to learning new material, the more novel an idea and the more it intrigues us, the easier it is for us to learn.)

The outer layer of the brain, the cortex, is only one-quarter of an inch thick. It is the cortex that gives us the ability to see, feel, hear, and speak. The prefrontal cortex, located above your eyes, houses the ability to think, plan, and imagine. Our ability to formulate new ideas begins in the prefrontal cortex.

This is an image of a single neuron.

I hope I've captured your attention and you're willing to learn just one more scientific fact that is critical to understanding how you can change your life.

The neurons in your brain look like tiny trees with many branches stretching from the top, a cellular body that looks like a tree trunk.

The genius of the brain is that the branches called dendrites can grow! Picture the dendrites as the muscles of the brain. As you use them in new and productive ways, the dendrites grow in number and lengthen, much as the muscles in your body grow when you exercise physically.

The most amazing part of the construction of the neuronal network is that, like trees in a forest, the dendrites—the connections in your brain—are not hardwired. A tiny gap called a synapse exists between each two neurons. An electric impulse begins a chain of chemical reactions that cause neurotransmitters to flow from one neuron to another. This exchange causes another electric impulse, which causes additional chemical reactions, and so on. The interchange of electrical and chemical activity is the basis of human thought. *The magnitude of the potential connections that can be made by the 100 billion neurons in your brain means that you have tremendous potential to think, imagine, create, and learn.*

Geeky? Yes, but when I understood that every thought that ran through my brain was a chemical and electrical impulse passing through millions of neurons, creating stronger and stronger connections, I knew that everything I learned, everything I thought, everything I did would either strengthen these connections in a positive way or cause neglected connections to die. That is why continually learning and growing are essential to creating a meaningful life. It's also why being intentional in our daily choices is so critical. The more consistently we make choices that move us toward fulfilling our purpose, the easier it becomes to make positive choices on an ongoing basis; success begets success. Intentionally repeating behavior strengthens neuronal connections, which in turn makes choosing wisely easier.

HOW LEARNING CHANGES OUR BEHAVIOR

If you touch a hot iron, your behavior changes instantly. But change doesn't always come instantly. Successful athletes are motivated to achieve, and they use a similar approach for reaching their goals. After setting themselves on a course of improving their physical endurance and achievement, they regularly test themselves, asking "Am I faster/stronger/more agile this week? Where is my weakness? How can I eliminate or neutralize it?"

How will you measure your progress toward change? You must regularly pull out a measuring stick. Look for evidence of the progress you're making; for example, are you drinking sixty ounces of water per day? Do you have a mentor? Are you choosing to read ten pages of a book per day?

Like an athlete, you'll want to continue practicing to achieve your goal. Keep in mind that you'll "play like you practice," so give these daily efforts your very best.

Learning begins by taking in information.

↓

Growth comes by repeating learned behaviors over and over again.

↓

When actions are repeated consistently, new neuronal pathways are developed and new behaviors become familiar and routine.
New habits are formed.

↓

New habits help you create a new life.

"Practice makes perfect" became a cliché because it's true. Think about every movie or TV afternoon special about athletes you've ever watched. Lots of screen time is spent on their decision to achieve and the drama of their achievement. You learn about the hours of sweat, determination and practice, practice, practice because there's usually a ten-second montage, complete with inspiring music, showing the repetition involved in mastering their skills.

Learning to embrace a mental outlook that expects repetition (with or without theme music) will help you create the results you are longing for.

Becoming More Efficient at Learning

The brain is a very efficient learning machine and is able to quickly process enormous chunks of information. It has learned to work from what scientists call "cognitive models." A cognitive model is simply the ability to recognize patterns and associate them quickly with previous experiences. You have created millions of patterns that exist in the form of neuronal pathways in your brain. You have a pattern for the path you drive to work. You have a routine for what you do when you wake up every morning. In fact, you have patterns for 95 percent of the activities you do each day.

Sometimes our models become outdated. They may no longer serve us well, but because they are familiar we continue to use them. For example, you may find yourself repeating patterns of behavior that cause you to be habitually late for meetings and constantly overwhelmed by physical clutter and disorganization. You know this behavior is not in your best interest; you may even wish that it is a behavior you could change. But because it is familiar, it is the cognitive model you continue to live with. When our cognitive models become outdated, they act like ruts that keep us from getting very far very fast.

To create new connections, we must force ourselves to think new thoughts. This requires conscious effort to take new steps in life. For example, if you are out of shape, you must consciously choose to exercise day after day; otherwise your cognitive model will keep you on the couch or working at your cluttered desk right up until bedtime.

From an intellectual standpoint, we learn by associating past experiences with our current circumstances. The human brain looks for patterns; we associate new information with what we have experienced in the past and then cross-reference and associate that information with even older information to build resources and responses that enable us to make decisions in the present.

Our brains continually review what we have learned in the past and make choices based on those experiences. We naturally ask ourselves, "What worked best the last time? What would have worked the least?" But to create change, we must instead ask, "What choice will lead to the new outcome I desire?" Learning, then, is the process of realigning what you want to accomplish with what you choose to experience.

Intercepting Automated Responses

One of the most interesting theories on how the brain learns is explained by the piano theory. If there are two pianos in a room and you strike middle C on one of them, the middle C string on the second piano will instantly start vibrating. Even though each piano has approximately two hundred strings, only the middle C string and those closest to it will vibrate. Although the tone fills the whole room, only the matching strings will vibrate and respond.

This is how you react when confronted with a new situation or an opportunity to learn. When you are presented with new information, your brain responds like a computer processor and looks for the closest fit or closest match with something you already understand. Out of all the information stored in your brain, those neurons begin to vibrate like the piano strings, and through chemical and electrical charges what you already know is brought to your conscious awareness for you to try to make sense of the new situation.

We use the piano string theory to help you understand how you create stronger connections between neuronal cells in your brain. The cow path story is something that resonated with you, and we associated that concept, which you already understood, with the new concept of creating deeper connections and paths in your brain through repeating positive habits over and over again. As you associated the old concept with the new concept, learning occured.

One of the problems with the piano string theory in business is that when a company is presented with a challenge or a new situation, it often falls back on the old ideas of what has worked in the past rather than using the old ideas as a launch pad for new learning, new creativity, and new opportunities to solve unique problems in better ways.

The brain is a powerful parallel processor; it has the capacity to process information at an amazing rate. To break or create habits, you must intercept your automated responses and consciously choose what action you will take. You must constantly ask, "Is this the best use for my attention at this moment? Will my life become richer and more meaningful through my spending time focusing my attention on this activity?" For example, checking e-mail on your smart phone at all hours of the day and night may be a habit for you. But if you're at the dinner table with your family, sitting in church, or working on a major project, checking your e-mail isn't a cognitive model that serves you; it is a distraction. A better use of your attention would be to live in the present moment and focus on the people or task in front of you.

MEMORY'S ROLE IN LEARNING

Through your ability to learn, your neuronal connections are constantly being modified. But without memory, those cellular changes would not be able to be recalled. Memory is how you recall what you learn. Like a sponge, learning is how you soak up all of the inputs of information presented to you. Memory is how you filter the information and choose what you will store in your conscious awareness. Your memory allows you to make progress. Without memory, you would be forced to relearn the same thing over and over again.

If you've seen the movie *Groundhog Day,* you may remember that Phil, the character played by Bill Murray, relived the same day over and over again until he learned the lesson of compassion and empathy. He couldn't move forward in time. Similarly, you could function without memory, but it would be extremely difficult to grow, change, or move forward in life.

"Imagine what your life would be like if you had no ability to remember or learn. Imagine starting each day without having the benefit of the successes and failures of the previous day. Or the day before. Or *any* day before. Without learning or memory, the most mundane tasks would become complex problems," wrote Andy Hudmon, PhD, in his book *Learning and Memory.* "For most people, the inability to distinguish family, friends, and strangers would be a frightening prospect."

Learning and memory are closely intertwined. There are three stages of memory: sensory memory, short-term memory, and long-term memory.

Sensory Memory

Your life is first experienced through your senses of sight, touch, hearing, taste, and smell. Every experience of life is registered by your sensory memory. "Sensory memory—sometimes referred to as *immediate memory*—acts as a gateway into the short- and long-term stages of memory," Hudmon explains. "Sensory memories are extremely short-lived (typically between one-fifth of a second and a few seconds)." That length of time stuns me. You have only one-fifth of a second to a few seconds to decide what information is important and what is not.

In this incredibly short amount of time, your brain determines what is unimportant. It filters out input that it believes to be unnecessary, and it places the information it believes to be interesting or important into your short-term memory. Sensory memory is like a vapor that evaporates before it reaches your conscious awareness.

Short-Term Memory

The information your brain deems important moves from your sensory memory into your short-term, or working, memory. Your short-term memory is like an erasable chalkboard. It is limited in both the quantity of information it can store and the length of time it can store it. How many times have you been learning something new when the phone rang and wiped out your concentration? In that split second, you lost the information you were so excited about. In fact, you could still feel the excitement of what you were thinking about, but you couldn't remember what you were so excited about.

Or think about how many times you have thought of something important as you've been walking down the hallway to your office. It could have been something you wanted to do or the name of a person with whom you wanted to schedule an appointment. But by the time you reached your office and sat down at your desk, you couldn't remember what it was—even though you knew that the thought, whatever it was, seemed important.

Short-term memory is a useful but unreliable place in which to store information. We know that timing is crucial to the learning process. Your brain gives you only a few seconds to decide if information is truly valuable. If it is valuable, you must work diligently to create the necessary neuronal connections and associations to transfer that data from your short-term memory into your long-term memory.

Your short-term memory gives you a a ten- to twenty-second window to decide what you will move into long-term memory. When an idea comes along and you experience an AHA! moment, it is as if a balloon were floating by. The more tethers you can tie to it, the more likely you are to hold on to that thought. Repetition is like adding lots of ropes to what you are learning. The more things you can associate to what you are learning the better. Facts are one kind of tether.

But, stories and narratives provide multiple tethers that improve your ability to remember them. For example, when I first met the volleyball coach and math teacher at my children's school, she told me the shocking story of her surprise wedding!

Michele and Alan Lawson had invited about one hundred friends and family over for a barbecue on a Saturday afternoon. Most of the guests thought they would announce their engagement, but everyone was what I can only describe as "open-mouth stunned" when Michele and Alan stepped forward and said they were getting married in ten minutes. She changed from her shorts into a denim sundress and he changed into clean shorts and a Tommy Hilfiger shirt. The minister walked out from his hiding place, and they were married.

The novelty alone makes this story memorable. In my entire life, I had never heard of a surprise wedding, but it is such a fabulous story of love and romance that not only do I remember it, I tell other people about it all the time. It is a viral story—and, I am sure some of you reading this book wish you had come up with the same idea!

Unfortunately, not every idea that you need and want to learn is that novel. When you read a book of this size, it is impossible to move every concept or idea from short-term memory into long-term memory. As a speaker I often teach full-day workshops, and I am aware that the average participant retains only a small fraction of what we talk about. I have heard estimates that the retention from attending a regular workshop is as low as 7 percent. In order to learn from and be able to apply each concept from your life experiences, you will need to take several specific actions.

When I read a book, I always have a pen in my hand; as I read, I go back and underline the concepts I want to remember. In theory, you're reading this book with your short-term memory, which means that many of the words you read will be held in your brain for up to twenty seconds at a time. That is only long enough to place the words later in the paragraph into context for your understanding. If you want to learn, you have to take cognitive action to shift what you are reading from your short-term memory into your long-term memory.

Learning is based on two concepts: repetition and association. When reading a book, you have a much higher potential to learn and remember a concept if you repeat it. Read the concept. Underline the concept. Reread the concept. You can also increase the odds that you will remember a concept by associating a new idea with something similar that you already understand. Another way to move concepts to long-term memory is by telling other people about what you have learned, which is another form of repetition.

YOUR SHORT-TERM MEMORY is unreliable. That is why it's so important to have a single safe place to capture the ideas you want to remember. We created the 7 Minute Life™ Daily Planner and all of the 7 Minute tools out of this need.

A key function of having a paper-based planning system

and keeping it with you all the time is that it acts as a *peripheral brain* that is far more reliable than your short-term memory. By writing down fleeting thoughts, creative ideas, and other things you don't want to forget, your brain will not be forced to continually remind you of things that pop up in your short-term memory. We know that our short-term memories are unreliable. We repeat what we don't want to forget over and over, or our subconscious mind reminds us of forgotten tasks when we are trying to focus our attention on accomplishing other tasks. Allocating your attention to repeating ideas over and over again is a bad use of time and can be corrected with a simple tool. Everyone uses peripheral brains in the form of Outlook calendars, e-mail, Post-it notes, notes on the mirror, and even writing notes on the palm of the hand. It is amazing what we will do to rid ourselves of the fear of forgetting.

Having one safe location for all of your ideas will dramatically boost your personal productivity. No more lost phone numbers, no more looking for what you were supposed to pick up at the grocery store on the way home from work, no more phone calls you were supposed to return and forgot to.

Your short-term memory is so fragile that something as simple as needing to pick up your dry cleaning can pop into your mind a dozen times during the day so you won't forget. Such mental interruptions are an incredible waste of mental energy and time. Don't rely on your short-term memory to run your life. Use a written system to capture everything you need to remember in one safe, retrievable location.

Why Doesn't My Short-Term Attention Work Anymore?

Your short-term memory may be working exactly as it was created to work. Short-term memory was designed as a short-term storage tank only. When I asked Andy Hudmon, PhD, assistant professor in biochemistry/molecular biology at the STARK Neuroscience Research Institute in Indianapolis, Indiana, about the problems we face with attention and memory, he again called television as one of the primary culprits: "The visual cortex in the brain processes visual information very quickly. As you sit in front of the television, the visual cortex portion of your brain can process the information as quickly as you see it. The speed that television has delivered information to you for your entire life is now affecting the way you want to receive all of your information. The colors, the fast edits, the moving pictures, the beautiful faces—television is all like candy for the eyes and the brain. And, because it is being delivered so quickly, not only has television programmed your neural pathways for seven minutes of content and a few minutes of commercials; it has also programmed your brain to run at a faster processing speed." Television has programmed your brain to want all information delivered at a faster speed.

The speed of television has made it more difficult for you to focus your attention for longer periods of time on tasks that require more than just being fed information, for instance, when you need to remember information, think about information, or write about information. Your brain does not want to slow down long enough to focus. Your brain can process pictures much faster than it can process words, which is making paying attention to simple conversation much harder for average individuals. Speaking to one another is simply not entertaining enough. The implications of this are jolting.

Next I asked Andy if our short attention spans have anything to do with our brains having some sort of "mental fatigue"? I wanted to know if the neuronal cells in the brain could grow tired when you think, in the same way your muscles fatigue when you exercise. Andy replied, "I don't believe there is any mechanical reason that the neurons in your brain would experience periods of "mental fatigue" at the cellular level. Like your heart muscle, your neurons never tire of firing. In fact, your brain never turns off. From the moment your brain is formed, it is always working. Even at night when you are resting, your brain is actually more active than when you are awake."

Finally I asked him why we had such incredible short-term attention issues and his answer was not what I expected, "As a scientist, I would go back to the beginning and ask, 'what was the purpose of allowing humans to have such easily distractable attention spans?' And, the answer is fairly easy to understand; for cave men and women, being able to be distracted by a slight movement or a tiny noise in the bushes might be the difference between becoming dinner for a lion and living to see another day. Distraction in this sense is an evolutionary survival skill."

He also said, "As organisms, we benefit from sampling new things. When we are distracted to look at and observe the new and novel things that pass into our life we learn and grow. and that is a good thing."

Possibly we are attempting to rely on short-term memory for functions it was never intended to be used for.

Long-Term Memory

Long-term memory is different, in that it can hold memories for hours, days, or your entire lifetime. Learning is tied to your ability to remember long periods of time. Learning is the neuronal process of moving information from short-term memory to long-term memory.

Much of learning takes place through what is known as "association." Association is one of the most efficient ways to learn. Metaphors and stories are great teaching tools because you can immediately associate the story with the intended learning outcome. They are tethers that tie what you already know to what you are learning. Associations allow you to build on what you already understand. For example, the story of Seth James being able to successfully rewire his brain helps you understand change as being possible in your own life. The premise of the 7 Minute Solution—that every day you need to step back from the noise and chaos of the overwhelming busyness of life and take seven minutes to create a written plan of action—helps you remember what to do and how to do it. You can associate the lack of clarity and stress you have been feeling with the outcome of living a life with more meaning and a deeper connection with your purpose.

You also need time to think!

John Phillips the COO of Christus St. Michael Health System in Texarkana, Texas, shared a profound thought: "As a leader, I need time to think." He continued by commenting that many corporate leaders, business people and entrepreneurs are so caught up in the busyness of work that they miss focusing on an important aspect of their job. "Leaders should realize they are paid to clarify the strategic plan. We are paid to think, not just to be busy."

Life would be easier if we could simply install a new piece of software or a new training program in our brains. But if you merely install new software on a flawed operating system, you still have a flawed operating system.

Periodically you need to step back from your business and ask:

- What are the key values that drive our business?
- What unique problems do we solve?
- What are our goals?

Plan for a series of "strategic interruptions" that allow you to think. Learning and memory cannot be separated from having time to think. Henry Ford said, "Thinking is the hardest work there is, which is probably the reason why so few engage in it." In today's busy world, we can fall into the trap of believing that time spent thinking is wasted. Nothing could be further from the truth. It's when we devote quiet, uninterrupted time to thinking that we come up with ideas that can move us forward.

Like the cognitive models we use for recurring tasks, our brains want to associate a stimulus with a memory and a response. Associations create stronger neuronal connections, which in turn create a stronger memory. Your brain is constantly looking for the closest fit to make sense of every new situation. It is waiting for the right piano string to vibrate. As with our habits, repetition increases these connections, as do emotions, smells, and physical activity. That's why speakers include emotional stories in their presentations; if they can connect their message to an emotion, you are more likely to remember the point of their speech. Scientists aren't entirely certain how long-term memory occurs, but it seems obvious that we must be intentional and motivated about learning if we want information to become fixed in our minds.

Let me share a few examples from my life.

Each morning I would wake up and get into the shower, and my mind would literally begin to race with all of the tasks and phone calls I knew I needed to accomplish that day. The mental chatter would sound something like this:

"At 9:00 A.M., you have a meeting with John."
"At 10:00 A.M., you need to call Ann to check in on her father's surgery."
"Don't forget to sign Abby up for art lessons."
"The left front car tire is low."
"You need to take your suit to the dry cleaners for the presentation on Thursday."

The mental chatter wouldn't end. From the shower, through breakfast, through getting dressed, and especially during my drive to the office, I had this silent conversation replaying itself in my short-term memory, like a tape replaying over and over again so I wouldn't forget.

Unfortunately for me, this story doesn't have a happy ending. The mental chatter in my head of what I needed to do and wanted to do was in an unreliable location. My short-term memory was not a trustworthy tool, and as soon as I walked into my office, the mental reminders that were circling were quickly erased by the telephone that was ringing, the emails that had accumulated, and the people that were knocking on my door.

I didn't have a system in place to transfer thoughts into a safer, more reliable location such as a piece of paper or an online location.

The solution is to record what you need to do in writing *as you think of it*—so you won't forget.

Concentration and Short Attention Span

Still intrigued by why we have such difficulty focusing our attention, I again asked the neuroscientist Andy Hudmon, PhD, several specific questions regarding the brain's mechanical ability to focus and concentrate. Neurons have been built to fire when called upon. You physically should be able to pay attention to individual tasks for extended periods of time. It is likely that our attention issues are behavioral and not physical; we don't have brain fatigue as much as we have boredom. If it were true your brain had a physical limitation of a seven-minute attention span, how could you watch a two-hour movie and have it hold you in rapture? How could you listen to your favorite opera and never move a muscle?"

From Hudmon's perspective, it isn't that we are physically incapable of concentrating for periods of longer than seven minutes. Rather, our culture's short attention spans result from the combination of learned behavior (multitasking) and the fact that we don't find the information being presented interesting enough or engaging enough to hold our attention.

Could it be possible that we choose not to focus? That we choose to let our mind wander—to find pleasure rather than forcing our brains to focus? The good news is that we can retrain our brains. We can recondition our brains to focus on and engage with the world around us. What would life be like if we purposefully, intentionally focused on our tasks?

A Structure for Learning

In the previous chapter, you set some goals for your life. I'd also like you to set some goals for learning. I like to learn in ninety-day increments, and I would encourage you to establish realistic goals for what you would like to focus on and learn during the next three months. Look forward ninety days from today, and ask yourself these questions:

- What new skill sets and competencies will I need to become the best person I can be at my job?
- What skill sets and competencies do I need to develop to do a better job of managing my finances?
- What new skill sets and competencies do I want to develop over the next ninety days to have a better understanding and framing of my personal faith?

Then think about how you learn. Do you learn best when you read a book, or is it easier for you to recall information after you've heard it explained by a teacher or audio program? Or do you learn best when you're doing a specific task? Some people are visual learners, others are auditory learners, and still others are kinesthetic learners who learn by doing. For many people, a combination of these three types of learning styles is most effective.

7 MINUTE SOLUTION PRACTICAL APPLICATION NO. 5: THE LEARNING WORKSHEET

Learning happens every day. Each time you become aware of something new and you make a conscious connection to older information, you build upon your depth of knowledge. The main issues with continual learning are:

1. Prioritizing *what* you want to learn
2. Deciding *how* you will learn
3. *Making time* to learn

Take a few minutes to prioritize a list of specific things you want to learn. Would you like to learn more about the amazing science of neuroplasticity? Then read *The Brain That Changes Itself* by Norman Doidge. If you would like to read one of my favorite books for salespeople, read *The Go-Giver: A Little Story About a Powerful Business Idea* by Bob Burg and John David Mann. Do you want to learn about nutrition, fitness, communication, or leadership? Simply prioritize what you want to learn, decide the most effective way for you to learn about that subject, and finally schedule the time to implement your learning plan.

Learning and growing are my passions in life.

You can download the full-size version of The Learning Worksheet at www.The7MinuteLife.com.

THE VALUE OF CONTINUAL LEARNING

In 1991 Mark Duckworth started Optus, Inc., in the basement of his parents' home. At twenty-three years old he had an office desk, a computer, and the innovative idea that he could buy and sell used telephone equipment. In less than two decades he created a business with annual revenues of more than $20 million.

Mark says, "I am always learning something new. I have a passion for this business and for learning. I love to be creative, to think of something new, to think of something innovative we could offer our customer, or a way to grow and improve our business. Our business is not about selling telephones. The sole purpose of Optus is to make our customer's professional lives easier. That is our value. That is our mission."

Then he said, "Starting this business when I was so young, 'continuous learning' has been critical to my success. For the first half of my career I was 'doing and learning.' In the last ten years I have intentionally focused on formal learning through continuing executive-level seminars, industry peer groups, personal reading and research, as well as leaning on outside advisors. We also encourage learning for our employees. We have a tuition reimbursement program, and we are bringing in more formal training to different parts of our business.

"As a business leader I have three targets to serve: our customers, our employees, and our community. At Optus, it is our pleasure to help our customers; it is a privilege; that is what we are here to do. We create relationships in which we become almost indispensable to the customer. Telephones are a commodity; what we are selling is ourselves. And we also serve our employees and our community. It is all about the experiences and relationships you create with people."

At the end of our interview, I asked Mark about what was most meaningful to him. "I have a wonderful wife, DJ, and our incredible son. I think love is the key to everything. You have got to love your family, love your friends, love what you do, love life, and love yourself.

I think it's the glue that makes everything else work. You've got to have a lot of love."

Mark Duckworth has proven the value of continual learning.

NEW GROWTH

Adapted from The Seven Minute Difference

NEW LEAVES

My purpose in life revolves around "growing." I want to grow personally and to encourage others to grow. In nature, growth is a cycle. Each spring, an oak tree leafs out; throughout the summer, the leaves gather sunlight and process it into vital nutrients that help the tree grow. As autumn arrives, the leaves change to orange, then fall from the tree, whose branches remain bare until the following spring, when the cycle begins again. Without the loss of old growth, no new growth would be possible.

So many people's lives are full of "dead leaves." They cling to old ideas, hurts, bitterness, anger, tension, and stress out of sheer habit, even though those familiar feelings hold them back in their ability to grow and be happy and fulfilled. Other habits can be even harder to break—continuing to perform old routines that are no longer productive, failing to delegate work that no longer needs personal participation, clinging to practices that have ceased to produce the benefits they once offered. Even when we sense that long-held feelings, habits, and activities are actually holding us back rather than feeding our growth, we hang on to them, seeing them as precious treasures, refusing to simply let go. It is easy to litter our lives with these "dead leaves"; but once identified, we can give ourselves permission to let them fall from the tree so we can once again experience the beauty of new growth.

Getting rid of "dead leaves" is a simple decision of will. When one of my close friends recognized that he was slipping into depression, he made a conscious decision to free up more mental space by parking his car several blocks from his office so he would have a few extra minutes to walk and become aware of what he was grateful for. Another example is a middle-aged man whose marriage ended due to circumstances out of his control; he found it best to physically leave his surroundings. He wanted a fresh start.

From changing our habits to changing our location to decluttering our physical surroundings to achieve new growth and make true advances toward our purpose, we need to be willing to shed our old leaves. Once freed of counterproductive habits, outdated ideas, and negative feelings, we can create space for new ideas to form, new habits to grow, and new depths of joy, kindness, forgiveness, love, and peace to develop.

Determine which of your old practices or beliefs might be preventing you from achieving new growth. Decide to drop those obstacles from your life, and replace them with information, experiences, and thoughts that help you create a more meaningful life.

Old Practice / Dead Leaves   replace   New Practice / New Leaves
                                     with

_____   _____

_____   _____

_____   _____

_____   _____

_____   _____

_____   _____

One final note of caution: It is natural for old habits, or dead leaves, to threaten your progress. Remember, growth—even when it is beneficial and desired—can be difficult at times. Memories of old, familiar ruts may trick you into believing that your comfort zone is comfortable. For real, lasting change to occur, you must become comfortable with being uncomfortable. You must be willing to let go of the dead leaves completely. Only then can you develop the new habits that will empower you to connect and engage daily with the meaning you desire.

VITAL SIGN 4:

Are You Engaged?

We are what we repeatedly do.
Excellence, then, is not an act, but a habit.

—ARISTOTLE

ENGAGING IN LIFE is about connection. It means that you have chosen to involve yourself in or commit yourself to something or someone. When we are engaged, life moves like the gears of a smoothly operating machine; each connection ignites purposeful action. When we are engaged, we feel connected to the values and people that mean the most to us; we feel alive in our passions and our mission. Engage your body. How do you feel? What do you see? What do you hear? As you engage your senses life doesn't just pass you by, you begin to experience life in the present moment. Engage in your work. So much of our lives are spent working. The structure of daily life revolves around the work we do. Are you engaged in your daily tasks? Are you challenged by your goals? Are you connected with the people you work with?

Picture the 7 Vital Signs of the 7 Minute Solution as yet another gear connecting you to life. Each of the vital signs of conscious awareness, motivation, learning and growing, engaging, persevering, living in flow, and living with faith continually moving and working in unison with your entire self. Only when you fully engage in life, living moment by moment, will you be able to connect with meaning.

But too often, we do not take the time and energy to really engage in a task because we are lost in the busyness of life. We race from one urgent, monotonous task to the next, doing just enough to move on to the next task without really focusing on what's at hand.

Busyness isn't the only reason we disengage or disconnect from our values or other people. Our beliefs about others and ourselves can pull us away from important relationships with family members, friends, and coworkers, even from our faith.

One reason relaxation is essential is that it gives us the emotional energy and physical stamina to engage in the relationships and activities that are important to us. Busyness and weariness can sometimes result in a tendency to "phone in," that is, make a minimal effort at what we tell ourselves is a priority.

To fully engage is to live in the moment, to actively experience what is going on in your life. In other words, if your goals are to make memories with your children and to be an encouragement to others, stop texting while you're at the Little League game and stop making a mental grocery list when a neighbor stops by to chat.

At the end of 2009, John Weller decided that deepening relationships was one of his top priorities. He wanted to connect with people in a radically different way. He wanted to listen to them and what was in their hearts. If he spent time with them, he wanted to make an impact and a difference. In sales, time is one of your most valuable currencies, and every day you have a limited number of hours. You might as well use that time to really connect with people, understand what's important to them, and then achieve a successful result.

LIMITED CAPACITY OF TIME

I would like to introduce another brain concept to you called "limited capacity." This actually has two aspects. The first is obvious: you have twenty-four hours a day, seven days a week, to accomplish everything you want to do within a single week. You can easily understand that there is a finite limit to how many tasks and activities you can squeeze into each week. You can see that every hour matters. There are only 168 hours, and after you subtract sleeping, grooming, eating, and commuting, you are left with a very limited amount of time.

Take the idea of limited capacity past the constraints of a week and look at this image of the next 90 Days on a single page. As you look at the individual squares in this illustration, your awareness of the importance of the need to engage grows stronger. In your next 90 Days you have roughly sixty working days and twelve weekends to experience life. Consider how much of every single work day is scripted for you before you even walk into the office. How many of your hours will be spent in office meetings, on prearranged conference calls and in reading and replying to e-mail that doesn't directly apply to you. The balance of the time you have left is what we would call discretionary time. These are all of the hours left over after everything that is required has been done. I believe it is in the discretionary work hours that creativity and growth can be achieved. But, how much discretionary time do you really have? Do you have one hour of discretionary time per day—this would be sixty hours in the next ninety work days?

As you look at how few discretionary hours you have in the next quarter, you begin to understand the magnitude of every minute in your day.

In order to begin to understand the power of the 7 Minute, 90 day platform, I want you to count out ninety days from today. Then, think of the next ninety days from this point of view: "What will you ask of your life? Life is ready to deliver exactly what you ask from it."

What will you ask of your life in the next ninety days? How much time will you spend focusing on your priorities in life? What will you specifically choose to learn? How much time will you set aside to spend with your family and friends so you can engage in life?

Much of time management is choosing to make better, more deliberate choices of how you will spend your time. When I look at this graphic illustration of a 90 day calendar, I am instantly aware that, if I want time to focus on what is meaningful in life, I have to make it. Only you can make those decisions for yourself.

The 7 Minute Life™ 90 Day Calender Worksheet

You can download the full-size version of 7 Minute Life™ 90 Day Calendar at www.The7MinuteLife.com.

LIMITED CAPACITY OF YOUR BRAIN

The second idea regarding limited capacity is that not only is your capacity limited to the time on your calendar, but your brain lives under the constraints of limited capacity. Your 100 billion neurons have the potential to process enormous amounts of information simultaneously at the subconscious level, but at the conscious level your brain is limited as to what it can process.

How limited is your brain's processing capability? In his book *Flow: The Psychology of Optimal Experience,* Mihaly Csikszentmihalyi reports that our brain's processing capacity taps out at 7,560 bits of information per minute, or 126 bits per second; put this into perspective by understanding that processing language requires 40 bits per second. "In a lifetime of 70 years, and assuming a waking day of 16 hours, this amounts to about 185 billion bits of information," he wrote. ". . . It seems like a large number, but in actuality most people find it tragically insufficient."

Consider how your brain's limited processing ability affects you every day. How many times have you attempted to have a coherent telephone conversation when an e-mail pops up on your computer screen and you attempt to read and respond to the e-mail while you are supposedly listening to your boss? In a similar vein, how many times have you dialed into a conference call that you were supposed to pay attention to and, instead of listening, you found yourself mindlessly doing paperwork and completely missed the information on the call?

While you have enormous capability to grow and change, if you want to process information effectively the first time it means you need to choose what you consciously pay attention to. To be fully engaged means to be fully present in the task you are working on with full intent, unbroken concentration, and full focus and attention.

Have you ever been engaged in tasks at work that sweep you away, when time stands still and you feel that your life matters? In such moments you find deep fulfillment in your work. But far too often you find yourself wandering through the workday with no clear direction, multitasking rather than focusing. When a coworker comes in to ask you a question, you don't even stop typing the e-mail you are sending. This is not engagement. It drains you of energy and fills your workday with stress.

Understand that your limited capacity can keep you from total engagement because you constantly feel the pressure of a lack of hours in the day, or it can empower you to make every engagement count. Gaining a deeper understanding of your limited capacity can give you the freedom to stop trying to do all things and force you to realize that because there are a limited number of hours in every day, you should focus on fully engaging in only those activities that are of the highest value.

Limited Capacity of Conscious Thought

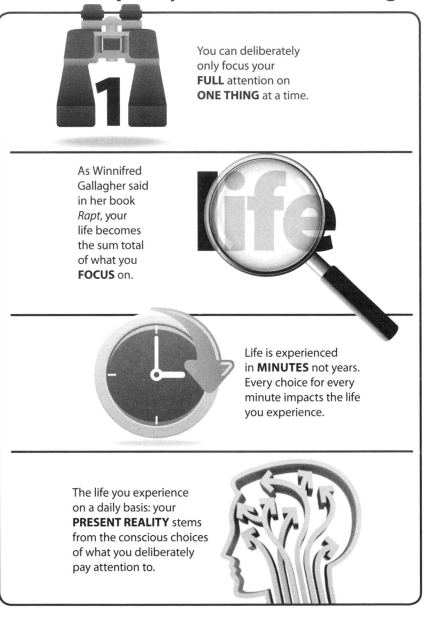

You can deliberately only focus your **FULL** attention on **ONE THING** at a time.

As Winnifred Gallagher said in her book *Rapt*, your life becomes the sum total of what you **FOCUS** on.

Life is experienced in **MINUTES** not years. Every choice for every minute impacts the life you experience.

The life you experience on a daily basis: your **PRESENT REALITY** stems from the conscious choices of what you deliberately pay attention to.

In 2010, John Weller actually reduced the number of projects he focused on and instead focused on making sure each conversation he had was held at an entirely different level. His life was more than about business; it was about adding value to each person's life and connecting as people. He did so by listening and by taking more time with each conversation so that he could fully understand what the best result could be. Because he carefully planned whom he would spend time with, he was able to be more purposeful in every engagement. That focus made his work more fun and more fulfilling. He was more fully present.

Engaged or disengaged with life? We connect with people when we meet with them face-to-face, is it a surprise it is difficult to build a relationship via e-mail? Don't let another day pass without engaging with the people you love most.

TOE TAG: NO PULSE, 10:51 A.M.

Do you remember the last time you realized you had missed an opportunity? I'm not talking about missing an opportunity to buy your favorite brand of shoes at half off, although that would be a shame. But some missed opportunities come at a much greater cost.

Have you ever lost a loved one—a grandparent, a parent, a sibling, or a child—without having the chance to say good-bye? The pain of that loss can seem unbearable. But what if, to make matters worse, you had become disconnected from that person because you'd been too busy to spend time with him or her? Or what if you were estranged because of differences of opinion—differences that really didn't matter in the face of the love and respect you still had for that person underneath the disagreement. How much more painful would that loss feel, knowing you would never have the chance to hug that person and tell them that you loved them despite your differences? That's the position Brian Shambo and his father found themselves in one day.

Brian, a junior in high school, left school to run a quick errand.

His mother had given the seventeen-year-old boy permission with the strict warning to be back at school by 10:45 A.M.

He didn't make it.

On the way back to school, a car ran a stop sign and sent the teenager's car careening through the intersection, screeching across sixty feet of asphalt until it finally hopped a curb and came to a violent stop against a retaining wall that served as the entrance to a neighborhood.

Sitting dazed in the mangled car with his knees jammed through the dashboard, having torn the tendons in his right ankle by bending the accelerator pedal into the floorboard, with massive bruising on his chest from the seat belt and four chipped teeth from hitting the steering wheel, Brian's first coherent thought was getting back to school. "I just wanted out of the car. All I could think about was my mother saying 'You need to get back to school in forty-five minutes.' "

After attempting to get out of the vehicle, Brian passed out, his body hanging out of the open window. He later awoke with a volunteer EMT shaking his arm and frantically asking him questions before he blacked out again.

But Brian didn't simply lose consciousness or go into shock. His heart stopped beating, and his lungs stopped taking in oxygen. The EMT crew battled to revive him, but after several minutes of no response, they gave up. Finally an EMT took a black marker and wrote on Brian's lifeless foot, "No pulse: 10:51."

They loaded his body into a helicopter and headed toward the hospital, still attempting to revive him.

The next thing Brian remembers was the *woosh, woosh, woosh* of the helicopter blades. Unable to move, he stared at the medic who sat next to him. "He was looking at my arm when he caught a glimpse of me looking at him. When I blinked my eyes, he looked very surprised," Brian says. The medic had been trying to start an IV in a final attempt to save him, but because Brian's veins had collapsed he couldn't get the fluids started. "So I almost assumingly said, 'Why don't you try again?' "

On the eighth try, the medic was able to hit a vein and said he couldn't believe it. He explained that they had already called Brian in to Carolinas Medical Center as dead on arrival, DOA. There was no medical or physical reason for Brian to wake up, and I believe there was a greater purpose at work.

Brian and his father had been constantly at odds. Brian describes their relationship as a "love/fear" relationship in which Brian was constantly looking for approval. Lying there in the emergency room, Brian was less concerned about his injuries than his father's reaction. He felt certain that his dad, a "Vietnam vet, by-the-book man," would blame him for the accident. He had always told Brian that if he was in an accident he caused, he wouldn't drive for a while.

His father was two cities away, and it took him about forty-five minutes to drive to the hospital. The only information he'd been told over the phone was "Your son was in a very serious accident, and we need you to come to the hospital." Can you imagine the thoughts that would be racing through your mind if you were the parent whose child waited for you at the hospital? Would you be able to focus on your driving? Would you think about the last words you'd spoken to your child?

When his father walked into the hospital room, Brian's first words were "Dad, it wasn't my fault, I promise." His father came near and saw the damage, the cast that ran the length of his son's right leg, the neck brace, the horrific bruising. Then he saw his son's foot and the note the EMT had left: "No pulse, 10:51." "It was the first time I saw him cry," Brian remembers. "Probably the only time I have seen him cry." His dad left the room to try to call home. Brian's sister later told Brian that they couldn't understand a word he was saying because he was so emotional. In that moment, Brian and his father reengaged on a new foundational and emotional level. They connected to the true meaning of their relationship: unconditional love.

On that day, Brian was in a terrible accident. He died. Then he and his father experienced two miracles: a second chance at life and the opportunity to start over, to engage in their relationship.

Why does it take a tragedy to make us aware of how disengaged we are from our lives? Brian Shambo's story of how he connected with his father gives us a glimpse of the possibilities all of us have. How many opportunities do you have every day to connect with those you love? More important, how many of those opportunities do you miss?

The impact of this event was to tear down the harsh "father-son" relationship in which Brian was constantly looking for his father's approval. It was an event in which his father was forced to lighten up or let life pass him by. It changed Brian's life in the sense that he and his father have led a much more meaningful life with each other. Of course, some of the father-son relationship had to remain in place due to Brian's age. Brian concluded, "And as time went on, we were able to rebuild on our new foundation, and not work to tear down the old structure. The event itself took care of that. It really just accelerated our ability to have a more meaningful, deeper relationship."

WHAT DOES HAPPINESS HAVE TO DO WITH ENGAGING IN LIFE?

We can choose to live a lifeless existence of routine experiences and barely-there relationships, or we can choose to reconnect with life. If you've read this far, I'm certain you want to be fully engaged in life. How can you make that your reality?

The first step is usually becoming clearer about what and who you want to engage with and what you want to engage in. In conducting research on engaging in life, I read Shawn Achor's book *The Happiness Advantage: The Seven Principles of Positive Psychology That Fuel Success and Performance at Work*. Achor spent twelve years at Harvard studying the psychology and science of happiness. Quoting from the book: "In a study appropriately titled 'Very Happy People,' researchers sought out the characteristics of the happiest 10 percent among us. Do they live in warm climates? Are they all wealthy? Are they all physically fit? Turns out, there was one—and *only* one—characteristic that distinguished the happiest 10 percent from everybody else: the strength of their social relationships."

But I wanted to know more, so I set up a telephone interview with him. I wanted to know if being happy would really make a difference in business.

During our call, I asked Shawn, "What is the happiness advantage?"

He replied, "Happiness gives people and companies a huge competitive advantage. The happiness advantage is the discovery that nearly every single business and educational outcome improves when the brain is positive; when your brain is happier and more positive, it shows higher levels of intelligence, productivity, creativity, and you're able to work longer, faster, and people perceive you to be more charismatic. Our brains work better when they are in a positive state of mind."

Shawn Achor defines happiness as "the joy you feel striving after your potential. For me, this has a parallel with fully enjoying life." He continued, "The reason I like this definition, which came from the Greeks, is that it's joy, not momentary pleasure; it's something you can feel even in the midst of suffering and the ups and downs of life. But it's also tied to you living toward potential; it is happiness along the journey, not just something you have whilst you have your first success. So in other words, it is journey-oriented instead of goal-oriented."

It is interesting that social relationships were the common denominator in happiness among people. I would also say having positive business relationships would have a very strong correlation with the individual level of success in business regardless of what business you are in. We refer to relationships as 7 Minute Life™ Connections, and we have seen how increasing the number of people you stay in touch with on a daily basis impacts your level of engagement at work and increases your happiness advantage.

7 MINUTE LIFE™ CONNECTIONS

Let me share two tools regarding how you can improve your social connections and relationships to engage with in life:

> 7 Minute Life™ Connections Personal Worksheet
> 7 Minute Life™ Connections Business Worksheet

You can download the full-size version of The 7 Minute Life™ Personal Connections worksheet at www.7MinuteLife.com.

You can download the full-size version of The 7 Minute Life™ Business Connections worksheet at www.7MinuteLife.com.

Knowing that your time is limited, it only makes sense to become as deliberate as possible with your 7 Minute Life™ Connections.

Stop and take seven minutes to make a list of up to thirty people in your personal life whom you believe you should make a conscious effort to be more connected with, from your younger brother to your high school basketball coach to your college roommates to your best friends. When was the last time you spoke to those people? When did you last have lunch together? Relationships make life meaningful and happy; make time to nurture your relationships.

Your 7 Minute Life™ Connections for business may be more difficult. Write down the names of people you should connect with at a business level. This list can include current clients, prospects, mentors, people you would like to know, and people you feel you should know. Here is another 7 Minute idea: as you think of names to go onto your personal list and business list, put every single person's cell phone number and e-mail address in your smart phone or your computer. How much time do you waste every month looking for e-mail addresses and cell phone numbers? Then write down the names of two to three people whom you will call, have lunch with, or meet for coffee. Choose carefully who you want to ask to be on your 7 Minute Life™ Connections Personal and Business List, and then spend time to engage in their lives.

As a strategic planning tool, the 7 Minute Life™ Connections Business List is proving to be one of the most important. We are so busy with daily noise and activity, it is incredibly easy to lose sight of how to strategically grow one's business. You want to regularly ask yourself, "who is our target market? Who should I speak to about the products and services we offer as prospective clients? Which of our current clients do we need to know better?" As Dave Savage put it, are we continually surpassing their expectations? Are there people in related industries who could mentor you? Should you form a small mastermind group to help you build your business connections?

A PRACTICAL STRATEGY FOR UTILIZING YOUR 7 MINUTE WORK CONNECTIONS

In the last several years we have added a new category of 7 Minute Life™ Business Connections: people with whom we are partnering.

I have set a goal of hosting a two-hour conference call or a two-hour face-to-face meeting each month with someone in the financial services industry who is a superstar. These people have risen to the highest levels of success no matter what measure you use, from their sales revenue rankings to their incredible client service models to the depth of their professionalism to the breadth of their investment strategies. We call these meetings "partnering UP," because these mentors became partners in our desire to learn and grow. And their amazing success stories pull us "UP" and enable us to see the bigger picture of what we can become.

In many of these meetings I have felt like a fly on the wall inside a secret meeting, gaining a clear edge over our competition. Often I leave the meeting wishing I could have known this information ten years earlier. Surprisingly, most of these people whom I ask to "partner UP" with are not people I know personally; they are superstars in our financial services firm, and they are the serious leaders in our company. Because I also want to become a better writer and I love to learn from other people, some of these calls are with famous authors, such as Shawn Achor and Bob Burg, both of whom I e-mailed and requested time to speak with. I'm getting much better at knowing exactly who needs to be on my 7 Minute Life™ Connections Business List, and since I often don't know the people personally it can be an effort to find their contact information. But almost always people with whom I "partner UP" love to help. In these partnering sessions, it has been our team that has moved "UP."

Think about the people you have admired in your industry. Would it be worth sending an e-mail to them to ask for a few minutes of their time? What could you learn from meeting with one person a month who is running a company that has ten times the revenues of your company? Engaging with such men and women has been one of the highlights of my career.

Take 7 Minutes right now and list seven people in your industry you admire. Do you know how to connect with them? The next micro-action is to determine how to contact them. You can check LinkedIn to see if one of your connections knows them, or as I have, you can go directly to their website to find out how to contact them. There are only three steps to meeting new connections: 1) List who you want to connect with. 2) Find out how to connect with them. 3) Schedule a time to connect with them.

Connection	E-mail	Phone
1.		( ) -
2.		( ) -
3.		( ) -
4.		( ) -

5. _____ ( ) - _____

6. _____ ( ) - _____

7. _____ ( ) - _____

You will want to be able to complete the full list of thirty 7 Minute Life™ Connections, but this is a great start.

YOUR HIGHEST-VALUE ACTIVITIES

Enhancing productivity and increasing meaning is not merely a matter of getting more done. *The secret to true productivity and meaning comes from getting the right things done by giving your highest value activities the highest priority.* It seems so obvious that it should hardly be called a secret, but how many times have you spent all day buried in being busy and yet felt like you achieve virtually nothing?

To truly understand this concept let's take a moment and look at how you currently feel you need to spend your time. If you already have a to-do list for today I invite you to get it right now. If you do not have a to-do list, then take a few moments and write on a blank sheet of paper any task you feel you should do today.

Once you have your list examine it through the lens of these three questions:

1) What is the pay off?

Analyze the pay off of every task on your list. Your highest-value tasks will have a measurable payoff directly related to your values, purpose, or goals. Which tasks actual generate more leads for your business? Close more sales? Complete a project? Push you over a significant hurdle? Eliminate a critical obstacle? Stengthen a relationship with a key client? Or, allow you to live into one of your deepest desires? Those are the tasks you want to target with aggressive attention at the front end of your day. You want to invest in those activities before any other activities. Even if all you do is a single microaction on those tasks, address them before all others.

2) Which activities should you *not* be doing?
Be ruthlessly honest with yourself about every activity you engage in. Have you said "yes" to things you shouldn't have? Are some tasks convenient ways for you to feel busy, while not really producing many results? Are there tasks you could delegate or pay someone else to do? What would the consequence be if you ignored some activities or completely eliminated them? Is that an acceptable cost to pay? Keep in mind that every moment invested in a low-value task is a moment that you lose to spend on those activities that bring you meaning, joy, and forward movement.

3) If you could only do five things on your list, what would they be?
This question will be much easier to answer if you spent time on the first two questions. It will also force you to rapidly and definitively define what is most important. Those five items will be your highest priority. Those five items are the first five activities that you should act upon the moment you walk through the door of your office.

You can drive your highest-value activities to the top of your priority list every day using a simple planning strategy that I like to call 5 before 11. Your 5 before 11 is a list of five high-value actions you strive to achieve before 11 A.M. Using a 5 before 11 list will condition you to strategically take control of your day. It will help you bypass ineffective organizational techniques and achieve greater results with less effort. Doing so will ensure that every day you are investing time in the activities that most engage you with life. A 5 before 11 plan is one of the foundational 7 Minute microactions that will empower you to prioritize, organize, and simplify your life. So, where did 5 before 11 come from?

MIMI BOCK: 5 BEFORE 11

In 2007, I was in a twenty-foot by twenty-foot hotel meeting room in Vienna, Virginia. There were eighteen attendees, I was the instructor, and our host was Mimi Bock. Mimi has spent the bulk of her adult life working in the financial services industry, most recently leading a $400 million division of a multinational company.

Mimi had hand selected the group that was in this room. They were part of a pilot program aimed at seeing if there were a way to truly help people create a framework of processes and systems that could dramatically change their lives and increase their productivity and sales. Time management and organization were of course a topic, *but on this day even my life would change forever.*

Over the previous three years I had created a single sheet of paper that I called the Daily Progress Report. It was a successful organizational tool developed to help you create a daily written plan of action to physically track your progress on a daily basis. On the top right corner of that single sheet of paper I encouraged people to create a written list of their "TOP PRIORITIES." This list was suggested to help them focus in on what they wanted to accomplish *each* day. We all joked that we had 900 top priorities and as a result often felt overwhelmed.

Mimi had been using my system for about two months. She wanted the attendees of the session to know that she was already "eating the cooking" we were dishing up. About an hour or so into our session, Mimi shared:

> My life is complicated—just like yours. I know that if I want balance in my life, I must begin by organizing my top priorities. I have a critical need to feel that every day I have gotten something done that is important to my business and my personal life. But, every day there always seems to be a handful of things *hanging over my head*—getting in the way.

Those things—those few things that show up on my top priority list over and over and over again, just hanging there. Then I wake up and a week has gone by—sometimes even a month—and they are still there. I knew I had to do something to *focus*.

She continued:

I realized that there are a few hours in the morning *where I have more quiet than craziness. A time where I have a better chance of focusing before life gets in the way.* I needed a way to take care of the things that were hanging over my head and crushing into my life. *I realized what I needed was the ability to take care of these things so I could "live."* And I knew for me, if it was going to happen, it was going to happen in the morning.

It was almost like there were a few tasks that were bigger than top priorities and they needed to capture my full attention and they needed my time. Without my time and attention, I was dragged down and my deeper priorities suffered.

I knew right then that I needed one more tool.

And, in that moment Mimi realized the answer for herself.

"I am going to commit to getting five high-value tasks accomplished before eleven o'clock every morning. I'm going to call it my five before eleven list."

It was like a spark had ignited in the room. The physical energy of the people rose dramatically. People's heads tilted up, their backs straighten, their eyes widened—they just got it! *5 before 11!*

We all got it.

The phrase meant something. We instantly understood that we were trying to do too much with too little time. Instead, by having a limited number of five tasks, there was an instant renewed sense of commitment and excitement.

It was one of those rare moments in life where something so profound happened that its meaning and power were not lost in the moment. Mimi would later say, "It was like a mantra in my head. It became a simple reminder. It was nice. It was catchy. As a result it was rolling around in my head. It was something I thought about doing every morning. 5 before 11: it just had a nice ring to it."

Comments from the eighteen people in the room started immediately. "That's just so right!" Heads were nodding. One person said, "How many times have I come into the office all fired up with a list of twenty tasks, and found myself dog tired heading to my car at the end of the day realizing I didn't do a single one?" Another attendee added, "And, when I do that, I feel *bad*—really, really bad."

As Mimi and I recently reflected on why the 5 before 11 concept was important she added many additional insights:

> Part of it is the power of the checkmark—simply getting it marked off your list and getting it done. But it's also the emotional piece of it, the part that resounds in your life when you do what you say you will do and you do it well. You feel worthy. It makes you feel like you are good at what you do. And you begin to feel organized, accomplished, and able. Then guess what happens? You *want* to do it again! The longer you continue to use 5 before 11, the shorter the list of things left undone in your life becomes. You then find you have more time to focus your attention on deeper priorities rather than important tasks.

Mimi also believes that you need to be *very thoughtful* about what makes it onto your 5 before 11 list. You can so easily lose sight of the *bigger picture*. There are so many bigger picture things that we want to get done in life that may never make it on a 5 before 11 *task* list. Differentiating between a *big picture, deeper priority* goal that can't be accomplished all at once and important activities or tasks is critical. That said, she continued:

But I've come to realize that my 5 before 11 tasks need to be attached to my *bigger picture* goals—those goals that connect with my values and purpose. These are the things that bring meaning to my life. Let me give you two examples.

For me, one of these big picture priorities was and still is:

I want to be a better mom. I want to be a more connected mom.

I want my son to feel like I am there for him. That is a *much bigger picture* value in my life, and, I don't want to wake up five or ten years from now and realize time has slipped away. Time that you can't get back.

A simple but *connected* 5 before 11 *task* that leads me toward fulfilling that goal might include:

- PICK UP POSTER BOARD

Now, you may be thinking to yourself, Big deal! Poster board? Here is when I realized how such a small task can become a *huge* deal. Without 5 before 11, I might say to myself as I get ready to leave the house, "Mimi, don't forget to pick up the poster board." I drive straight to the office like a Pavlovian dog—only one cup of coffee in me so far. I get hooked on e-mails and then my meetings start. My day is filled with issues, challenges, meetings, and e-mails. It's now 7:30 P.M. and on the drive home I am thinking about all of the things I didn't get done that I wanted to get done. I then walk through the door and my seven-year-old son is standing at the door with a huge smile on his face that dissolves into a frown. He says, "Mom, where is the poster board? You promised we'd work on it tonight." So yes, the poster board is the small *task*, but the *bigger picture* value of not having to stare blankly at your child saying, "Oh, my gosh! Honey, I forgot it," is what makes it a huge deal. The emotions that are tied up in these moments have lifelong implications particularly if they are repeated many times over. I can tell you that when I added tasks like "Buy Poster Board" to my 5 before 11 list I never forgot again and didn't have to see that look of disappointment on my son's face over something so seemingly simple.

Mimi's second example was from her work.

I want to be valued as a talented leader and owner of my business.

She said:

Each quarter I had to deliver to my boss our division's Quarterly Business Review. As a business executive I was busy—*really busy*. Each quarter it would've been easy to wait until the last minute to work on this report, and then to take two or three days before the report was due and pull several late nighters. Or I could choose to use the concept of 5 before 11 and have a series of individual *tasks* placed on my 5 before 11 list over a period of a couple of weeks. *Planning this out took time.* I was very intentional about what I needed to do. I could take my time and think, "What information do I need to gather to make this report the best it can be?" I could ask, "Who else do I need to speak to about this report?"

"One of the important sections of my QBR was the presentation of our region's profit and loss statement. Every quarter there would be gaps in the reports I would use to determine our standing and every quarter my boss would ask me about those gaps, expecting me to fill these gaps with detailed information. *These are the things that can keep you up at night.* I was beyond wanting to walk into these quarterly meetings "kind of" having an idea of why my profit margin had risen or declined. I wanted to know it cold. We all know that you don't know things cold after cramming for a test!

Using the 5 before 11 list for at least two weeks prior to my QBR presentation, I'd first add a task: Review the reports/write out all questions. Then I would add a task to have my assistant set up a meeting with my finance manager and then I'd be sure that the meeting happened. He would walk me through the quarter's profit and loss statement, answer all of my questions and I'd still have time to really get my head around it. That was knowing it cold.

When I asked Mimi for her last piece of advice regarding the power of 5 before 11 she said:

Using this tool just makes my life better. You'll feel organized, accomplished, and more able. My suggestion is that everyone try it for *one* week. Sit down for fifteen minutes the day before, preferably before you leave work, and think about those irritating little items that are holding you down or tasks you know you must get done the next day. Write them down. In the beginning the list may be many more than five. Start with four must do's and add at least one aggravating, hanging-over-your-head task. I promise you, after knocking out thirty-five high-value tasks that are connected to your deeper priorities, you'll be hooked!

I completely agree with Mimi and yet over and over again we see people struggle to know exactly what their personal highest-value activities should be. To help you clarify what your specific highest-value activities are so that you can readily select the best possible 5 before 11 activities, we have created one final tool for engaging, called "Your Highest and Best." Completing this one-page worksheet will rapidly help you turn the corner from slogging through your day feeling bored and frustrated to living into your gifts and passions so that you are engaged, creative, and productive.

7 MINUTE SOLUTION PRACTICAL APPLICATION NO. 6: HIGH-VALUE ACTIVITIES

All high-value activities point toward the bigger picture. Learning how to focus on your high-value activities is a four-step process.

1. Write down what you love to do at work, at home, in your hobbies. What do you really enjoy doing?
2. Validate your strengths. What comes easily for you? Your goal is to spend the bulk of your time on what you do best.
3. Based on what you enjoy doing and are good at, write down your highest-value activities. Answer this question: if I were living my ideal life, how would I spend my time each day?
4. Clearly define for the outcome. How would you benefit if you focused your time and energy on doing your highest-value activities? The reality is that if you intentionally planned your day, spending the bulk of it on these activities, your life could change overnight—and it would change forever.

Take a few minutes now to fill out the Highest and Best Activities Worksheet.

Once you have clearly identified your highest and best activities, you will truly begin to see their worth. Let me illustrate this idea by relating it to the experience of shopping. When you buy a gallon of milk at the store, it is doubtful that you waste much mental energy on the purchase. But when you help your child decide where to go to college, you might spend several years

You can download the full-size version of the Your Highest and Best Worksheet at www.The7MinuteLife.com.

researching universities, and the monetary investment is enormous. Education is a high-value activity.

Like many of the concepts in this book, awareness is the beginning of knowledge. If you have been doing the same job for years, you may be spending 80 percent of your time focusing on low-value activities that don't engage you and don't create meaning in your life.

Take the time to track exactly how you have been spending your limited amount of time. Once you see how you have been spending your time, compare your *actual* activities to your *highest and best* activities. Then using 5 before 11, start moving away daily from those life-depleting low-value activities to life-enriching highest-value activities. *One of the simplest truths is that as you spend more time on meaningful activities, your life will become more meaningful.*

CREATING A ROAD MAP FOR YOUR LIFE

How did you spend your time last week? If you broke down last week into fifteen-minute increments, how many of those time blocks could you say were focused on doing what you love, utilizing your strengths, and spending your time on activities that bring profitability and greater success to your life, your business, and your relationships?

How does your actual use of time compare to what you wrote on the Highest and Best Activities Worksheet? If you're like most people, the comparison is pretty depressing.

Why?

Because you are so busy trying to decide what's important that you don't know what to do to feel really fulfilled at the end of the day. When you don't know what to focus on, you try to do everything and commit to things you don't have the time, energy, or desire to do. After a while, your life becomes a series of unfinished tasks and broken promises. Years of disappointment stack one on top of the other until it feels easier and safer to disconnect.

Thankfully, life doesn't have to be that way. You can engage in and enjoy life every day. It takes a little planning, but you can decide what activities to engage in. If you plan your time with your purpose and goals in mind, you will constantly move toward more meaning and greater fulfillment. When was the last time you thought about how you should be spending the minutes in your day? Are you compelled to agree to time commitments because you feel you "should"? Your "should" in life should be based on your priorities, your purpose, and your goals. One key to the 7 Minute Solution is making sure you let the right "shoulds" into your life.

The life you experience is made up not just of years but of minutes. In order to fully engage in life, you must get a grip on your minutes. That is why time management matters. That is why microactions matter.

If you are willing to take the idea of focusing your time and energy on high-value activities, you will find yourself doing more of what you love, utilizing your personal strengths, and being internally rewarded by the accompanying feeling of fulfillment when your life is firing on all cylinders.

What I really wanted in life was not another to-do list; rather, I wanted a *forward-focused strategic plan.* As I interviewed leaders in various industries, I found that their focus had something I lacked. On a regular schedule, all these men and women stepped out of their daily business of life and focused their full attention on a much bigger picture. They taught me to take whatever time I needed to think about what my life should become.

If your thoughts are scattered, confused, constantly multitasking, pulling you in several different places at once, that is how you will experience life. Consider the power of the 7 Minute Tools that we have talked about up to this point in this book. What if you used them to create a forward-focused strategic plan for your life, with your personal values serving as the framework of your life and your purpose serving as the foundation, with your goals in the center of your plan radiating outward with specific action steps that you could immediately implement in your daily life?

The following chart is an example of how you can track
your time in fifteen-minute increments during the
workday. This simple exercise is very revealing.

Minute Life

15 Minute Increment Tracking Sheet

Time	Activity	Time	Activity
5:00		1:00	
:15		:15	
:30		:30	
:45		:45	
6:00		2:00	
:15		:15	
:30		:30	
:45		:45	
7:00		3:00	
:15		:15	
:30		:30	
:45		:45	
8:00		4:00	
:15		:15	
:30		:30	
:45		:45	
9:00		5:00	
:15		:15	
:30		:30	
:45		:45	
10:00		6:00	
:15		:15	
:30		:30	
:45		:45	
11:00		7:00	
:15		8:00	
:30		9:00	
:45			
12:00		10:00	
:15		11:00	
:30		12:00	
:45			

Somewhere deep inside my heart I knew that working from a plan
with focus, I would be much more likely to engage in life.

Why don't we have a plan?

Because we have a love-hate relationship with planning.

Even the word "plan" has a negative connotation. When the leader of your team tells you that it is time to create a two-year business plan, you secretly groan and a sinking sensation hits you in the pit of your stomach.

Old plans have forced you to commit to things you knew you couldn't accomplish. And you realize each time your boss sets a lofty goal that it will demand even more of you. At the same time, there is a part of you that loves plans. When we see what it is possible to accomplish when an entire team buys into a new strategy, a strategic plan gives us hope. It inspires us. It enables the blossoming of creativity and freedom for new paths to engage and challenge us. When we clearly see new possibilities, there are a newness and a novelty that capture our imagination and make work fun again.

IMPLEMENTING THE 7 MINUTE SOLUTION WITH THE MICROACTION OF 5 BEFORE 11

Definition: The 7 Minute Solution offers strategies to help you prioritize, organize, and simplify your life for greater meaning and productivity.

Every vital sign we have discussed so far is helping you create a framework to prioritize, organize, and simplify your life for greater meaning and productivity. On page 8 of this book I introduced the concept of applying the 7 Minute Solution to your life, and I said, "*The 7 Minute Solution* is about choosing to consciously focus your attention for 7 minutes every day on what is most meaningful in your life." By now you've gained a few ideas regarding high-value activities and how you can engage in a more meaningful life. But you may still be looking for that one practical tool that can change your life. What if you could dramatically improve your love-hate relationship with planning? What if you could execute your goals in strategic plans and be completely able to track your progress? I believe you can do this by implementing the concept of 5 before 11. Once you have your plan in place, you've defined your high-value activities, and you've created written goals with written action steps, it becomes very easy to translate your goals into daily actions.

I am asking you to take seven minutes at the end of every workday to create your list of the five high-value activities that you will commit to completing before 11 o'clock the next morning.

THAT IS ONE of the big reasons this book is called *The 7 Minute Solution.* Taking 7 Minutes every day to *think.* Taking 7 Minutes every day to decide how you will spend the minutes of your day. Taking 7 Minutes every day to choose how you will focus your attention on what is most meaningful to you. This is the 7 Minute Solution.

As a strategic consultant, I know that most people are not working from a daily written plan of action: This single idea of taking seven minutes a day to step back and actually think about what you value most in life (your priorities), look at your purpose (this is what drives you and sustains your energy), and finally review your ninety-day goals (this helps you identify your high-value activities)—then take 7 minutes to create your written 5 before 11 list.

Then, your first priority the next morning is to do what you said you would do.

Accomplish 450 High-Value Activities in the Next Ninety Days

High-value activities are purposeful activities that move you toward your written goals. They are often microactions that concretely help you live out your purpose, passion, and deepest values. Given all that you do in a day, doing five high-value activities may not sound like much. But imagine doing it for ninety days. If you implement the 5 before 11 concept, you will succeed in taking 450 steps toward your goals. How different could your life be in ninety days if you took 450 positive and strategic steps toward living the life you have always wanted but were too busy to achieve?

If you are serious about wanting to complete those 450 steps, then making time to complete your five high-value tasks before 11:00 A.M. is essential. By scheduling your high-value activities before 11:00 A.M. you give them priority over lower-value activities. Face it, each day holds a finite number of hours. Those hours are like concert tickets. Only so many people are going to get seats for the concert, and it all depends on who gets into line first. Make sure your high-value activities are at the head of the line every day. You don't want to find yourself at the concert of life, sitting in the parking lot and missing out on the best the world has to offer.

The most significant outcome of utilizing these tools has been reclaiming my time. The more organized I am and the more attentive I am to accomplishing specific tasks in the most efficient manner, the more discretionary time I have to create a life with meaning. Planning your time, purposefully engaging in your highest-value activities, and living with your values and priorities in their proper place bring great meaning. You'll feel more, enjoy more, and love more.

Of course, as with any new habit, it's not always easy. Some days the "too-busy" mantra fills my head and I'm tempted to forgo planning so I can just push through and get things done. And just when I think I'm on a roll and I have everything under control, life happens.

Get ready; life is going to happen. It might be a call from the school nurse that throws you off course for the day. Or it might be something more involved: the death of a loved one, a pink slip from a job you loved, a canceled flight. Life always happens. That's when perseverance kicks in. Without perseverance you'll be tempted to slip into the old routine of running from one urgent, unimportant task to another. Perseverance is the next vital sign of the 7 Minute Solution.

Are You Persevering?

I will never quit. I persevere and thrive on adversity.
My Nation expects me to be physically harder and
mentally stronger than my enemies. If knocked down,
I will get back up, every time. I will draw on every
remaining ounce of strength to protect my teammates
and to accomplish our mission. I am never out of the fight.
—NAVY SEALs ETHOS/CREED

PLANNING, ENGAGING, LIVING with purpose—it all sounds so easy, so idyllic, until life kicks you in the teeth and knocks you off your feet. Something happens to stop you in your tracks. Suddenly you're scared, angry, exhausted, or all three at once. In such moments, you face a critical choice; will you persevere?

Everyone is confronted with difficult circumstances. Checking the vital sign of perseverance means asking yourself "Do I have the grit and determination to move beyond the hard times life brings? When I'm faced with obstacles, will I push forward, or will I quit?"

Perseverance is a choice. It involves determination and the decision to continue regardless of difficulties. Without perseverance it is impossible to achieve your goals. You need perseverance to start and *finish* each task. It is a skill that very few people master because it is quite difficult, but it is highly prized and greatly rewarded.

GRIT: THE SECRET INGREDIENT

In 2005, I toured the U.S. Military Academy at West Point, New York. The men and women there awed me with their dedication to serve their country and fight for freedom. Reading Dan Pink's book *Drive: The Surprising Truth About What Motivates Us,* I learned a little more about the determined men and women of West Point. Pink shared the following story, which I have paraphrased. In 2010, 12,500 students applied to the academy. Each hoped to fill one of the roughly 1,300 openings to become a cadet. Those who are chosen go through six rigorous weeks of cadet basic training—otherwise known as "Beast Barracks"—before they ever set foot in a classroom. Before the final twelve-mile march that concludes this *introductory* training, one in twenty of the chosen applicants drops out of the program.

You aren't accepted to West Point unless you're talented and dedicated. But not everyone who is accepted stays. Researchers from West Point, the University of Pennsylvania, and the University of Michigan posed this question: Why is it that some students continued on the road toward military mastery and others got off at the first exit? Their study revealed that those who make the cut and stay the course aren't necessarily stronger or smarter than their peers who quit.

The best predictor of success wasn't intelligence, physical condition, or leadership ability. Quoting Pink, "It was the prospective cadets' ratings on a noncognitive, nonphysical trait known as "grit," defined as "perseverance and passion for long-term goals."

You need grit. Grit is the secret ingredient that empowers us to move from where we are today to where we want to be tomorrow. Grit is the difference between saying "I'll try to do it" and saying "I will do it." Hopefully you understand by now that repetition—performing the right tasks and thinking the right kinds of thoughts over and over again—strengthens the connections in your brain. Eventually, all that repetition makes it easier to make positive choices and take positive action. Perseverance is what makes that repetition possible. It is this "stick-to-itiveness" that enables you to do what you say you will do and, as a result, become the person you want to be and live the life you desire.

Perseverance is a choice. It is the commitment to following through on what you say you want to do. It means that:

- If you say you want to be in the best shape of your life, you do what it takes to be in the best shape of your life. You exercise, walk, run, lift weights, do cardio, and make the physical effort to improve your health *daily.*
- If you say you want to renew and restore your faith, you take daily steps to renew and restore your faith. You read, pray, listen, reach out, and serve the world around you.
- If you say you want to be more competent in your work, you work to become more competent. You study, practice, seek out mentors, and hold yourself accountable to your word.

There are people all around you who are doing what you have said you want to do, living the life you dream of, and accomplishing goals you set for yourself long ago. *You can do the same.*

So what's holding you back? Old patterns? Bad habits? Are the piano strings you are accessing no longer in tune with how you want your life to play out? If old cognitive models and bad habits are holding you back, *now* is the time to create new models and more productive habits. It is time to develop new and stronger neuronal connections that support your desire for a better, more rewarding, more fulfilling life. Living out your dreams takes work, and sometimes that work feels impossible and fruitless. But when life gets hard, take confidence knowing that it's the tension-filled times of challenge and pressure that produce the deepest levels of growth—and the greatest victories.

THE EXPEDITION OF THE *ENDURANCE*

I love the story of Ernest Shackleton, a British explorer whose desire to be the first man to walk across the Antarctic turned into a long battle to survive unimaginable conditions. His remarkable perseverance and dedication inspired his crew to do whatever it took to fight for their lives and see the voyage home. I've learned many lessons from Ernest Shackleton and his crew on his ship the *Endurance*. Here are ten key principles of perseverance that may be helpful to you as you develop this vital skill in your own life.

1. Follow Your Passion

The voyage of the *Endurance* wasn't Shackleton's first attempt to make history. In 1907, he failed in his effort to be the first person to reach the South Pole. But rather than give up and decide the time and energy he had spent training to achieve that goal were all for naught, he shifted his driving purpose to becoming the first man to walk across Antarctica. He believed the continent held many scientific treasures, and he wanted to be the man to discover them.

From 1910 through 1914, Shackleton made plans for his next adventure. He created a prospectus, detailing all the provisions and supplies needed. He charted the safest course for the expedition. And, following protocol, he sought the necessary approvals from the British government. He also had to find funding, which wasn't easy since Great Britain was on the brink of war. (In fact, he set sail from London on August 1, 1914, the same day Germany declared war on Russia.) But he persisted. Finally, with all the formalities out of the way, it was time to find his crew.

2. Understand the Odds

Certainly, Shackleton sought personal reward and perhaps glory, but he wasn't blind to the danger and challenges that awaited him. He needed his crew to understand the odds, as well. It is said he ran the following newspaper advertisement to find a crew for the *Endurance*'s voyage:

MEN WANTED: FOR HAZARDOUS JOURNEY. SMALL WAGES, BITTER COLD, LONG MONTHS OF COMPLETE DARKNESS, CON-

STANT DANGER, SAFE RETURN DOUBTFUL. HONOUR AND
RECOGNITION IN CASE OF SUCCESS.

—Sir Ernest Shackleton

Don't you love that honesty? Without fanfare, empty promises, or
trumped-up tales of riches and glory, the straightforward ad worked.
More than five thousand men responded. Why? Because, like you,
they were looking for excitement, adventure, and the chance to be part
of something exceptional.

We all want to feel as if what we're doing matters, as if we're part of
something that is making a difference in the world around us. And like
my friend Karon Fields, who went skydiving for her fiftieth birthday,
we all want heart-pounding experiences that take our breath away and
make us feel fully alive. But it is essential to acknowledge the risk; that's
how we prepare for the journey and succeed despite the obstacles.

Of the five thousand men who applied, Shackleton chose twenty-
six. A stowaway brought the total crew to twenty-eight.

3. Decide Early that You Will Persist

Shackleton came up with the name of his ship, *Endurance,* because
his family motto was "By endurance we conquer." Shackleton knew
the obstacles he would face. He knew the hardships of arctic expe-
ditions. Not in spite of this, but because of this, he named his ship
Endurance.

How many of us need this to be our motto? It's easy to give up
when a task becomes too hard or not to try it at all because the obstacles seem too daunting. Decide from the outset that you will persist
and see your journey through to the end.

Determination is placing a stake in the ground. It involves making
unwavering decisions about what is most important to you in life and
creating mental placeholders for those decisions. Determination is not
a casual occurrence. Determination is life-changing. Determination
requires a sense of knowing and trusting because once you've made
these types of decisions they are permanent.

4. Make the Most of Your Circumstances

The *Endurance* made its final stop on land December 5, 1914, on South Georgia Island. By January 10, the crew could see the continent of Antarctica. On January 18, 1915, ice packed around the ship, only eighty-five miles short of the Antarctic shore.

Pack ice was to be expected, and the ship carried coal to keep the crew warm while they waited for the ice floe to thaw. But it never did. And when the sun set on May 1, the men knew they wouldn't see daylight again for four months. Can you imagine the cold and the feeling of hopelessness? Held captive by the ice, they lived in darkness not for a day, not for a month, but for four long months. Eventually, the sun rose again, but the ship remained stationary in the frozen ocean with ice crushing in on all sides.

As you read this, do you feel the pressure of life's circumstances crushing in on you? Are there times that you feel as though you are lost in a dark world? How do you handle times like this?

To make the most of their circumstances and maintain good spirits among the crew, Shackleton assigned everyone jobs. He believed that the ship would someday soon break free of the ice, so the crew prepared for the best outcome by performing routine maintenance. Shackleton also made sure their bodies stayed in excellent physical condition with a vigorous exercise regimen. And to keep their spirits up, they sang and played tunes on one of the crew member's banjos.

By disciplining himself to focus on keeping the mission together, he was able to remain calm in the face of hazards and difficulties. This enabled him to prepare for success—and survival—in the future.

When times are challenging and life feels bleak, doing the activities you know you should be doing will help you stay on track and keep you mentally and physically sound. There was nothing Shackleton could do to make the sun come up or make the ice thaw, but he kept about his business of preparing for the future—he didn't get overwhelmed by the immediate fact that there were hazards and difficulties, and instead kept the mission together by focusing on how he could better prepare himself for the future he knew would be ahead.

5. Prepare for the Worst

After ten months of cold and desperation, conditions grew worse. The ice that had been pressing in on the ship finally pierced its hull. Although the *Endurance* withstood more than the crew had imagined possible, the pressure from the ice finally overtook the strength of the ship. Cold water rushed in, and the 144-by-25-foot *Endurance* slowly sank to the bottom of the ocean.

But Shackleton had known the day was coming. For weeks the ice had groaned as it scraped and crushed against the boat. The crew had prepared for that terrible eventuality by moving most of the supplies off the ship. They had built igloos on the ice floes for all of the dogs. They had taken the three lifeboats off the ship. They had salvaged as much as they could from their beloved *Endurance,* and when it sank, they moved into tents on the ice.

Constant stress in your life will do to you what the ice did to the *Endurance.* Day after day, the grinding in our lives can become overwhelming until, finally, it threatens to overcome you. There may be nothing you can do to avoid the overwhelming circumstances creating pressure in your life, but you can take steps to prepare for the difficult times.

Grit is the ability to dig down deep into yourself for strength and fortitude. It is completeness of character. Grit carries the idea of an indomitable spirit, courage, and the ability to be resolute in your decisions.

6. Keep the Faith

At approximately six to ten feet thick and up to two miles in diameter, the ice floe that had surrounded the boat was fairly stable. So without the *Endurance,* and with no ability to send word for rescue, Shackleton and his men lived on this large chunk of ice, floating wherever the ocean currents and wind took them.

As the weather warmed, the ice shrank. Periodically, it shuddered and split; huge chunks broke off. Cracks appeared without warning, and the men never knew if one would form directly below their tent and toss them into the ocean. Their lives hung in the balance; if the ice split in the wrong place, they knew they could drift away without any cover or provision. And crack it did. After almost six months, their original piece of ice had decreased to only two hundred yards in diameter.

Imagine: no radios, no communication, no one to swoop in with a helicopter to rescue them. They were in the middle of the ocean on a tiny chunk of ice; they knew the only way out of their situation was to rely on their mental agility, physical skills, and combined experience. Are there times when you feel lonely? Do you ever feel lost, floating in bitter circumstances without direction? Just imagine what it must have felt like to be literally stranded on the ocean with no help coming.

Surely Shackleton's men felt that desperation. But despite the continuous cold and unending wetness, the twenty-eight men remained hopeful that they would find a way home. They could have lost hope. Instead, they took action.

The men had three lifeboats and they decided to put them into the ocean. Considering their options, they knew they needed to leave the treacherous ice floe. So they boarded the lifeboats and set sail. Amazingly, within days of launching the boats, they saw land. The ocean current had pushed them to within thirty miles of Elephant Island. On April 16, 1916, they set foot on solid ground for the first time in more than a year. The island was nothing more than rock and ice, but it was exactly what they needed.

When you feel hopeless and lost, that is when perseverance counts the most. You can act on the belief that a better day is coming, or you can give up. You can keep the faith or give up. But, as Shackleton's expedition illustrates, your miracle may very well be waiting for you just beyond the edge of the horizon.

"Tenacity" is a word that originates with the meaning of adhesiveness. It describes a "stick to it at all costs" quality, a form of glue. Tenacity never gives up, never lets go.

7. Make Small Improvements

Shackleton's crew had escaped immediate danger, and with penguins to eat, they wouldn't starve. The land offered a refuge, but it wasn't a permanent solution, and Shackleton knew it was unlikely that they would ever be found.

After spending only eight days with his crew on Elephant Island, Shackleton decided to set sail in the twenty-two-and-a-half-foot lifeboat, named the *James Caird*. His goal was to sail across eight hundred miles of open ocean to South Georgia Island, the closest inhabited island, where there were whaling stations.

The sides of the lifeboat originally rose barely five inches out of the water. The crew used salvaged wood to extend the sides of the *James Caird* to well over a foot high. They also created a protective wooden covering over the top of the lifeboat. Only then did Shackleton set sail.

The changes they made to the boat may seem small compared to the journey that lay before him. But Shackleton was wise enough to realize that those small changes would significantly improve his odds of success. How can you prepare for your journey? What small improvements could you make to your life? Most of us believe we must take radical steps for change to occur. But this story illustrates that something as minor as adding fifteen inches of wood to the sides of a boat can make all the difference in the world.

Right now there are hundreds of tiny microactions you could take that could enhance and improve your life, your relationships, your health, and your results. You don't have to make huge changes. In fact, one of the core principles of the 7 Minute Solution is that taking tiny steps forward every day quickly adds up to monumental change.

Could you drink an extra glass of water? Could you go to bed an hour earlier? Could you walk for fifteen minutes a day? Could you read ten pages of a book a day? Of course you could! And, as was the case for Shackleton, I know that you'll see great benefit from these tiny actions.

8. Do What Must Be Done

On April 24, 1916, in the bitter winter cold, Shackleton and five men set sail on the open ocean. They left the safety of Elephant Island in a tiny lifeboat with only a compass, fifty feet of rope, a sextant, the stars, and an unquenchable belief to guide them.

Far too many people choose to remain in a "secure" location such as Elephant Island. They realize that the circumstances aren't optimal, healthy, or even safe—but they choose to stay in the same familiar place rather than risk the unknown. They're not willing to get into the lifeboat. They're not even willing to build up their life by making simple changes. Unwilling to take any risks, they slowly die.

Because Shackleton believed it was the right thing to do, he risked the journey to South Georgia Island. Seventeen days later, he and his crew completed one of the greatest navigational feats in history. The lifeboat landed in King Haakon Bay; the whaling station they were trying to reach was on the opposite side of the island, in Stromness Bay. By that time the battered boat was useless. Only three of the men could walk; the other three were near death from exposure. They could have quit, but, again, they persevered. The three healthy sailors removed screws from the wrecked boat and screwed them into their boots for traction. They navigated and started and failed and started again for nine days. Then, with extraordinary fortitude they trekked the final thirty-six hours without a break. Exhausted and pushed to their absolute limits, step-by-step they scaled ice-covered mountains thousands of feet high, using the compass and fifty feet of rope. Ten days after they landed on the west coast of South Georgia Island they found their way across the unmapped island to the Stromness Bay whaling station.

Those men were willing to do whatever it took to accomplish their goal—which at that point was reaching help. Are you doing whatever it takes to save your life? Are you taking the necessary risks? Are you persevering against all odds?

Willpower is an innate drive. Willpower can move you in any direction, for good or for bad. Your will is creative, and it is very persuasive. Willpower is the driving factor that controls the moment-by-moment decisions that impact your behavior. It controls every action you take from what time you get up in the morning to how hard you're willing to focus your attention to the amount of exercise you will incorporate into your life to what you will eat. Willpower does not control what you say you want to do; willpower affects what you actually *do*.

9. Know Who You Are

On May 20, 1916, Shackleton knocked on the door of the Stromness whaling station. When the whalers asked tersely, "Who are you?" He replied, "My name is Shackleton."

Part of perseverance is knowing who you are and what your life's purpose is. Shackleton was a leader. During his journey, his purpose had changed from being the first to cross Antarctica on foot to getting his men to safety. Regardless of challenges, distractions, and even doubts that the odds were against him, he wasn't willing to give up on his goal of achieving safety for his men and himself. Because he was clear about his mission, two of his men were now safe and warm at the whaling station, and the three on the other side of the island were rescued shortly thereafter. Now five of his men were safe. Twenty-two remained on Elephant Island.

Shackleton knew he was the kind of person who would stop at nothing to accomplish his objective. You'll discover that part of persevering is the determination and discipline of keeping your eye on the prize, never losing sight of your goals. That focus will help you keep challenges and distractions in perspective and so you can succeed.

10. Never Stop Trying

Within three days Shackleton headed back to Elephant Island for the rest of his men, but the ice was too thick and he had to turn back. For three months he tried to return. On the first attempt, he made it to within a hundred miles of Elephant Island before the ice stopped him. The second time he was within sixty miles of the island when the pack ice forced him back. After a third failed attempt, Shackleton made it to

Elephant Island on his fourth and final try. Uncertain what he would find, Shackleton was relieved when he found the twenty-two men still there. Amazingly, every man had survived.

Shackleton's original mission was to be the first to journey across Antarctica via the South Pole. The South Pole had already been reached in 1912. He wanted to walk from coast to coast. He failed, but his failure opened the way for an even greater mission. Millions of people have heard his story, and, if you listen to what it teaches, you too can learn the true meaning of endurance. The expedition, which had faced danger and seemingly impossible challenges, became a heroic tale of survival: mission accomplished. In fact, more than simply achieving his goal, Shackleton demonstrated that the courage to focus on a goal can create not only success but an extraordinary journey.

Ernest Shackleton's story is one of perseverance. It is the story of imagining, dreaming, desiring, and doing. Ernest Shackleton dreamed about being the first man to walk across Antarctica by foot, he took action. He was willing to risk his life—literally—to accomplish his dream. His dream almost cost him his life, but his perseverance yielded the adventure of a lifetime and earned him an unforgettable place in history. Pursuing your dreams may come at a price, but the cost of not living out your life's purpose is far higher.

WHY YOU NEED PERSEVERANCE

Unfortunately, life rarely happens as we plan it. Unexpected circumstances rush in at us from every side, crushing our time and energy much like the pack ice that surrounded Shackleton's ship. Often those circumstances push in on your life through no fault of your own. It could be that you experience a serious health problem such as cancer. Or at some point the economy could impact your job or financial situation. Regardless of the circumstances that surround you, you can choose how you will respond to those circumstances. You have the freedom to decide what course of action you will take. You can allow the difficult circumstances to crush you or make you stronger. If you persevere, the challenges you encounter may be the most important and profitable turning points in your life.

CAN YOU LEARN TO PERSEVERE?

Have you ever wondered, "Why do some people seem to have more willpower than I do? What is it about me that keeps me from becoming the person I want to become? I know what I want to do; I've even written down what I want to do. But I can't seem to make myself take the actions that I have said I want to take."

There is a difference between wanting and doing.

Defining your purpose and setting goals often highlight what you want to do. But there must be another step. "Your direction, not your intention, determines your destination," wrote Andy Stanley, the author of *The Principle of the Path: How to Get from Where You Are to Where You Want to Be.* In other words, your actions determine your destination.

There is a psychological process in which every individual decides where he or she is going and emotionally commits his or her whole life to that particular course of action. This is a cognitive process. It is deliberate. You regularly think about where you want to go. The question is, are you only willing to continue to think about it? Or are you ready to make up your mind and take action?

You must *decide on* and *commit to* the course of action to which you will dedicate your life. Perseverance requires you to focus on what is most important to you, no matter what obstacles or distractions might present themselves. But you will be able to persevere only on a path that is deeply embedded in your heart and soul, a path that, no matter how difficult, is one you want to be on, a path for which you are willing to pay whatever price to continue on to the end. Each person chooses his or her own path based on personal values and ideals. Only if the path is something that is deeply connected to your heart's desires will you feel the rewards of perseverance.

Can you learn to persevere? Can you increase your willpower? The answer (and you should know this by now) is yes! The human brain is nothing short of amazing. Psychologists and scientists now believe that willpower can be measured and increased. You can increase your ability to persevere. And as you are learning from every chapter in this book, it is the plasticity of your brain that enables these changes to occur. The speed of the changes is shocking. It doesn't have to take a lifetime to change; it takes only a decision.

Exercising Your Willpower

Some of you may be familiar with the concept of framing and outcome. You see basketball teams do this at the end of their pregame warm-up when they huddle together by their bench, put their hands into the air, and at the top of the circle, joining hands, they begin to jump and shout in unison. As fans, your heartbeat responds to their excitement. They are psyching themselves up for the next two hours of incredible physical effort. They are framing their minds to give them the mental willpower to persevere and to win.

What you may not realize is that how you frame the tasks you persevere through every day matters.

Scientists have not yet discovered where willpower lives in the brain, but they are aware that it is a limited resource. A study done at Case Western Reserve University showed that people who were asked to persevere through one act of will were much less likely to persist when given a second task. In their book *Welcome to Your Brain: Why You Lose Your Car Keys but Never Forget How to Drive and Other Puzzles of Everyday Life,* Sandra Aamodt, PhD, and Sam Wang, PhD, described a study in which there were two groups. The first set of volunteers was asked to eat radishes, while the second set of volunteers were given freshly baked chocolate chip cookies to eat. Then both groups of volunteers were asked to solve an impossible puzzle. "The radish-eaters abandoned the puzzle in eight minutes on average, working less than half as long as people who got cookies or those who were excused from eating radishes," the authors wrote, adding, "Task persistence is also reduced when people are stressed or tired from exertion or lack of sleep."

Recognizing that some simple "pregame" framing for yourself and your team can make a difference in the outcome of your project, why not try serving some freshly baked, hot chocolate chip cookies before your next important staff meeting? Why not play some music to release the creative energy before your team of engineers works on a new project design? Even simple things such as making sure your team is rested before beginning a new project will impact their enthusiasm and commitment.

Aamodt and Wang suggest that willpower is like a muscle: "One possibility is that brain mechanisms for generating active control rely on a resource that can somehow be depleted." Your brain's stamina is limited and can be quickly depleted, leaving you unable to stand up to the circumstances you face every day.

If we continue on with their analogy, the same is true that the more you exercise your willpower muscle, the stronger it becomes. In other words, the more often you utilize your prefrontal cortex, the more time you spend planning and clarifying where you want to go, and the more time you spend actually doing what you say you will do, the stronger your willpower will be. Like muscle, willpower seems to become stronger with use.

Like exercise, it seems that diet may also be important to your ability to exert willpower. Aamodt and Wang theorize that the depletion of willpower is somehow correlated with how the brain synthesizes blood sugar. Blood sugar is the brain's main energy source. "Most cognitive functions," they point out, "are unaffected by minor blood sugar fluctuations over the course of a day, but planning and self-control are sensitive to such small changes." Maintaining proper blood sugar levels may help keep your willpower in much better shape. Something as simple as eating more proteins and complex carbohydrates may help you stay on track with the goals you have established for yourself.

Clearly, there are physical and psychological limits to our willpower. Knowing your purpose, managing your stress level, and eating a healthful diet can help you expand those limits. But before we get to that, you need to understand how stress—whether it is positive or negative—affects the body and the brain.

Is Your Brain Stressed Out?

Lieutenant Colonel (ret.) Dave Grossman is an army ranger and the author of *On Killing: The Psychological Cost of Learning to Kill in War and Society* and *On Combat: The Psychology and Physiology of Daily Conflict in War and in Peace* and a coauthor of *The Warrior Mindset: Mental Toughness Skills for a Nation's Peacekeepers.* He travels about three hundred days a year training members of the military, law enforcement officials, and school safety officials about the reality of violence: how to prepare for it, prevent it, live with it, and deal with the effects of post-traumatic stress syndrome. He is an expert on stress and its effects on the body.

Stress not only plays a major role in our lives, Grossman explains, it also has a significant impact on our brains. When we are frightened or angry, the blood vessels in your body contract and limit blood flow to the external parts of your body. Unfortunately, your brain is one of the first extremities to lose blood flow, and your forebrain—the prefrontal cortex, where our rational thought, planning, and execution occur—shuts down. You have seen this portrayed in movies where the wife goes into labor and the expectant father jumps into the car and heads to the hospital without his wife. Under extreme stress, it's not that you don't want to concentrate, but that you physically can't concentrate. There just isn't enough blood flowing to the front of your brain. That's when the midbrain takes over. Remember, the midbrain is the primal/animal part of our brain. And when you're stressed, this instinct-driven part of your brain takes charge and seeks to protect you. The midbrain is not rational; it cannot think ahead. The midbrain is reactive and driven by emotion.

This limitation of blood flow occurs in part because of vasoconstriction. "Vasoconstriction is a physiological and automatic response to stress," Grossman says. "Interestingly, the outer layer of your body becomes like a layer of armor; you can take a significant trauma on the perimeter of your body, and as long as the enemy does not hit an artery, you won't experience much blood loss. It is a powerful survivor mechanism that shifts into gear in stressful situations."

Though vasoconstriction helps protect the body, another side effect is that the muscles don't receive blood either. If the muscles don't receive blood, they stop working. That's why one of the first signs of stress is the loss of fine motor control. If you've ever been pulled over for speeding, you know the feeling of being unable to sign your name clearly because your hands are shaking. That loss of fine motor control is a result of being stressed about getting a traffic ticket.

If your stress level continues to rise, you will slowly lose your complex motor control. The condition gets worse and worse until you enter into a catastrophic situation that in the military is called "condition black." In condition black, the first thing that shuts down is your sense of hearing. In high-stress combat situations, many soldiers don't hear the sound of gunfire. Tunnel vision is another physiological response to high stress levels. You may have heard people describe experiencing an intense situation as if they were looking through a toilet paper tube. Soldiers say that the tunnel vision can be so intense it's like looking through a soda straw. And if you've ever wondered why movies use slow motion in high-stress battle scenes, the answer may be because that's how we experience such situations in real life. If you've ever been in a car accident you know that it takes only a few seconds, but it feels as if you spin or skid across the road for several minutes. The final effects of condition black are that your memory is distorted and rational thought stops. During intense situations, there is simply no blood supporting rational thought in the prefrontal cortex of the brain; the more severe the stress, the more irrational the behavior. "Under stress your view of the world can become incredibly skewed," Grossman says. "Stress can spin you out of control into a variety of different dynamics."

But, he explains, it is possible to prepare for and limit the effects of stress so we can persevere in any situation. Something as simple as taking deep breaths can restore the oxygen level in your blood and therefore rational thought in your prefrontal cortex.

One More Step

Friedrich Nietzsche said, "What does not kill me only makes me stronger."

"The Bible says the same thing over and over again," Grossman says. He points to Romans 5:3–4: "And not only that, but we also glory in tribulations, knowing that tribulation produces perseverance; and perseverance, character; and character, hope."

The idea of persevering through the difficult times of life is nothing new. We must have faith in the human ability to endure. We must have faith in the human ability to come out the other end as a stronger human being. Change is a fundamental foundation of life and nature. People change every day. People can choose to grow.

When I asked Grossman about his understanding of how people change and grow, it was no surprise that he began to talk about the plasticity of the human brain. "Think of the human brain as a vast meadow. Anytime you walk anywhere in that meadow, you leave a path behind you," he says. "Your brain is the meadow, and your paths are your memories. The more you go up and down a path, the deeper and more pronounced the path becomes."

Those pathways run through your brain, and every action you take every moment of every day reinforces your neuronal networks, digging deeper pathways and making stronger and stronger connections. In short, you become what you think about.

Grossman explains that the military uses neuroplasticity to train soldiers to increase their ability to endure and thrive. "We train them day in and day out in real-life situations. We train them physically. We train them mentally. Every day we give our soldiers a series of challenges. And every day they find out they can meet the challenges they are presented with. Through this training they build confidence, they build physical strength, and, just as their muscles respond to the physical training, their brains respond equally quickly to the mental training," he says.

Tiny challenges, attempted and accomplished on a regular basis, increase your ability to persevere. The thrill of mastering a new skill boosts your self-confidence. Neuroplasticity and training based on challenges and repetition are what makes the military model so powerful in helping young men and women develop positive life skills. It is also why soldiers can persevere even in the face of amazing stress. They learn by building on tiny steps of achievement that they can accomplish great feats.

Grossman honed his own confidence in Army Ranger School, and he describes the experience as one so difficult that it made everything else seem easy. During fierce training exercises the soldiers would go days at a time without food or sleep. He remembers one night of training that was so intensely exhausting he was ready to quit.

"I was exhausted, I hadn't eaten food in days, I hadn't slept in days, and we were on a patrol. We were going up this slick, slick mountain slope. It was steep and high," he says. The route was so steep that he had to use trees for leverage to pull himself up the mountain. His muscles aching, his feet slipping in the mud, the only thing he could see were the two luminous pieces of tape on the back of the helmet of the man in front of him. Darkness surrounded him both physically and mentally.

"As I made my way up the mountain, at every step I would say to myself, 'At the next step I'm going to let go of the tree branch and roll down the hill and get injured and get an honorable way out,' " he remembers. He kept telling himself, "I will just take one more step and then I will let go, just one more step, one more step, one more step."

Of course, those single steps eventually led to the top of a hill and a bit of a reprieve before the next hill. "You go through the process again," he says, "knowing that eventually somewhere down the line there will be sleep, there will be rest, there will be food, and you will be able to recover and say to yourself, 'It will never get that bad again, never in my life will I have to live by taking just one more step.' And then, the next night, you find yourself doing it again."

Not being a soldier, I can't imagine the grit it must take to force oneself through such agony. Why do they do it? The answer is simple, Grossman says: "It reinforces the sense of courage. Courage is just taking one more step."

What type of willpower and perseverance do those men and women have that the rest of us don't? How can they function at that level of mental and physical demands when I cannot even control my exercise routine? Grossman reminds me that willpower is developed simply by taking the steps themselves. Many of his successes came from having experienced previous successes. He knew that when the time came he could take one more step. His courage, motivation, and willpower came from all the previous steps he had taken.

A 7 Minute Microaction to Test Your Perseverance

One simple microaction is to intentionally include a challenging 5 before 11 activity on your calendar every few days. For example, if you are in sales, and your goal is to make three prospective sales calls before 11 o'clock, then just for that day challenge yourself to make ten calls. In sales, activity equals revenue. If you increase your activity by 300 percent, your revenues will grow as well. And, something interesting happens internally as you reach way beyond what you have thought yourself capable of accomplishing in the past. Your confidence increases, your excitement increases, and your overall productivity increases. You feel a renewed sense of purpose in your daily work, because as you see yourself rising to new levels of accomplishment, the intrinsic rewards Dan Pink discussed rise dramatically.

The Value of Perseverance

The book *The Gates of Fire: An Epic Novel of the Battle of Thermopylae* by Steven Pressfield is on the Marine Corps commandant's required-reading list. Early on, it poses the question "What is the opposite of fear? What quenches fear as water quenches fire?"

The answer is love.

"Soldiers will die in combat to save their fellow soldiers," Grossman says. "In the end, that love for others is why people are willing to lay down their lives."

Perseverance is built on this kind of love. Every shred of the concern you have for others, your love for others, your desire not to let people down, the whole dynamic comes together as the key that enables you to persevere and go just one more step.

Perseverance is built on love. The foundation of purpose is love. The 7 Minute Solution is built on love. There is no way to create a life with meaning without love. There is no way to persevere without love.

When you're feeling stretched and stressed, when you feel as though you can't go on, Grossman says, "Never judge yourself by your worst day. Take pride in your good days. Wake up every day, and take one more step up the warrior path. And pray that a lifetime of preparation will be sufficient. At the moment of truth and the hour of need, you will be the one who will lead the others home.

"Love quenches fear as water quenches fire. The greatest manifestation of love is not to sacrifice your life but to live a life of sacrifice—for your family, for others—and to place the welfare of others—people in your business and people in your family—above yourself.

"In the end what matters is love. We are given a spirit not of fear but of love, the most transformational, all-consuming force in the universe. We are given a spirit not of fear but of love: love for others, love for God, love for yourself. The greatest force is love.

"Hooah!"

7 MINUTE SOLUTION PRACTICAL APPLICATION NO. 7: PERSEVERANCE AND WILLPOWER: PUSHING PAST THE ONE-YARD LINE

If you want more willpower, you must build and strengthen the neuronal connections that will enable you to persevere. The military trains. You can train yourself by placing small, attainable challenges in front of yourself every day. This 7 Minute concept is called "Pushing past the one-yard line."

Perseverance in business separates you from where you are today and where you want to be in the future. How many projects in life have you started but not finished? How many times have you been swept away by the novelty of a new marketing concept, only to find the file sitting on your desk six months later untouched?

Why is perseverance in business important? *Because half done is not well done.*

In football, if you are able to run the ball from your own end zone to the one-yard line of the opposing team, you have done a great job of moving the ball ninety-nine yards down the field. Unfortunately, landing on the one-yard line is meaningless unless you have the perseverance to move the ball the final thirty-six inches into the end zone. Over the years I have seen countless football teams return a kickoff to the one-yard line. Lift your right arm, and stretch it out to your side. From your shoulder to your fingertip is how much farther the team would need to go.

From my vantage point in the bleachers, I mentally chastise those six-foot, five-inch, 300-plus-pound men. They are in the best shape of their lives; they have been practicing drills for just this opportunity for their entire athletic lives. I scream, "Dude, just lean forward!"

But as I watch those men struggle with all of their might to move the football a mere thirty-six inches, I feel a deep pain inside my heart. I am quickly reminded of all the times it has seemed that my life has landed just short of the final goal.

Being left on the one-yard line of life is a terrible place to be. You can see your destination. You have overcome all of the obstacles to get you this close. You have persevered to this point, and you definitely don't want to settle for almost making it!

How many of you can relate to this? For years you have done a good job. You know you are competent. You can see how close you are to reaching your goals. You are only inches away from discovering the meaning and purpose you have been looking for.

This is a great time to call a time-out. If I were the coach, I would ask my team to pause and think about the ninety-nine yards of success they had just experienced. I would want them to feel the excitement and the power of what it had taken them to get to the one-yard line. I would want them to reframe their success and their accomplishments, and then, like Karon Fields, I would remind them that they are standing with their toes out the door. And really, it's as simple as pushing past that one-yard line. This last push is where we experience new growth and where we engage in powerful emotions of meeting challenges head-on with everything we have. The one-yard line of life is taking the next step and taking one more step and again one more.

To push through the one-yard line of life, you must begin with recognizing where you are stuck and what is holding you back. You may feel stuck because of your life circumstances. You may feel that you need additional education or a new skill set. Regardless of why you feel stuck, part of becoming unstuck begins with honestly acknowledging what you are thinking and feeling. Only then can you evaluate whether your thoughts and feelings are valid or are simply old, outdated cognitive models that need to be replaced.

Much of what holds you back in life is the self-defeating barriers of inaction, indecision, insecurity, and unpreparedness. The ability to push past the one-yard line usually relies on reviewing the foundational skills that made you so successful in the first place.

Pushing past the one-yard line means breaking out of your habits and ruts and trying a new routine. Like creating an exercise plan or getting to the office first. Or taking a Saturday morning to clean out the physical clutter in your office that has been holding you back.

It is time to adopt the "100-yard mindset." Half done is not done. One-yard-line activities are not just about taking the smallest steps forward, but taking them forward every day. The team that pushes past the one-yard line is the team that put in fifteen extra reps in the gym every day for the last six months. They drank one extra bottle of water. They went to bed thirty minutes early so they would be fully rested, they practiced a play three more times until it was great, not just good enough. If you are ready to push past the one-yard line of life, there are the tiny actions and choices you make every day.

7 MINUTE LIFE™ STORY: THE "ALL THAT" FACTOR

Haven't you met a person who seemed to have it all together? A person who had something you wanted? Who had what is described as the secret sauce, the magic bullet, the "it" factor? Those rare individuals have a magnetic force, a personality with a gravity that pulls you toward them. They simply have "all that." They walk into a room, and the energy level rises. They can be introduced to you, and from that moment you believe them to be your friend and advocate. In a flash, you like them, trust them and hope they will teach you.

Only a rare few people have this force. As an author and speaker, I have the privilege of getting to know many of those people. Steven Spencer is a senior executive with a major pharmaceutical firm. We met several years ago during a training session I was facilitating. He has the "all that" factor. Here are his thoughts about pushing past the one-yard line of life.

"I am a thirty-eight-year-old black man. I grew up in a single-mother household. Neither of my parents, whom I'm still very close to, went to college. Luckily, I was good at playing football, and even though my grades in high school were only mediocre, several colleges wanted me to play for them. I chose Lafayette College in eastern Pennsylvania and finished my degree in psychology in four years. After college I worked full-time during the day as a bank teller, and at night I worked as a personal trainer. I definitely have the work ethic. I started at the bank at 8:00 A.M., finished at 4:00 P.M., then I started my personal training at the gym at 5:00 P.M. and finished at 11:00 P.M. Five days a week, this was my schedule. On Saturdays and Sundays I did personal training from eight until five."

I asked Steve what success secrets make him so different from the average person. "I don't think I'm different from any other person. I think the one thing I do is execute on what I want to do. I think everyone has an opportunity," he says. When Steve thinks about all the salespeople and executives he has known through the years who have had the "all that" factor, a smile creeps across his face as he tries to define what it means when someone has that "secret something": "When one of these people walks into a business meeting, the whole room lights up. You know that person will bring something to the table. I would describe them as people with discipline, perseverance, high levels of integrity, competence, personal awareness, and a deep sense of inner drive. They know exactly where they're going. They know what brings them meaning and fulfillment; they have a purpose, and they know their priorities. They established goals that are important to them.

"But the biggest differentiating factor for these people is not that they had the 'all that' factor, it's that they live it every day. They did what they said they would do. They weren't just talking about it, they *were* it. They didn't have to prove anything to anyone; they just lived their life because that's who they were."

When I asked Steve how he reengages with work, his answer made me smile. "How I reengage with work? I can't even count on one hand the times when I was not engaged with my work. I think that's the difference."

Finally I asked him, "What does living with meaning mean to you?"

"It means two words: I'm happy."

Characteristics of a Person with the "All That" Factor

○ Is driven	○ Is passionate	○ Is fearless
○ Is systematic	○ Is a good listener	○ Is healthy
○ Has focus	○ Is properly assertive	○ Is creative
○ Is a planner	○ Has a good work ethic	○ Has a good sense of humor
○ Has clear vision	○ Is a team player	○ Is a leader
○ Knows his or her purpose	○ Dreams	○ Is a self-starter
○ Is not afraid of risk	○ Maintains proper nutrition	○ Is disciplined
○ Is able to persevere	○ Is fit	○ Is an innovator
○ Is personable	○ Is able to say "no"	○ Is balanced

○ Is charismatic ○ Is self-accountable ○ Is knowledgeable

○ Has a "just do it" attitude ○ Is concise ○ Is resourceful

○ Maintain high energy ○ Is consistent ○ Is confident

○ Is rock solid ○ Is open to new ideas ○ Is competent

○ Is a clear ○ Has good organizational ○ Is intelligent
  communicator   skills

Though the list may seem intimidating, remember that your personal "all that" factor will grow as you prioritize what you spend your time on and fully engage with it in that time. This list illustrates many traits that can be learned or improved through repetition. Some people do seem to be born with the "all that" factor, but we can all choose to be more deliberate focusing on the qualities we deem important.

Best of all, you'll discover that being fully engaged allows you the opportunity not only for success but also for satisfaction, the awareness that being engaged creates brings deeper meaning and fulfillment to your life.

Are You Living in a State of Flow?

*Most important, in flow, the relationship between
what a person had to do and what he could do was perfect.
The challenge wasn't too easy. Nor was it too difficult.
It was a notch or two beyond his current abilities, which stretched
the body and mind in a way that made the effort itself a delicious reward.
That balance produced a degree of focus and satisfaction that easily
surpassed other, more quotidian, experiences. In flow, people lived
so deeply in the moment, and felt so utterly in control,
that their sense of time, place, and even self melted away.*

—DAN PINK,
DRIVE: THE SURPRISING TRUTH
ABOUT WHAT MOTIVATES US

LEARNING TO LIVE IN a state of flow is one of the seven vital signs of living the 7 Minute Solution. From time to time, you have all been there. When was the last time you were so engaged in a specific task that time stood still? When were you so completely absorbed in doing something you love that hunger didn't even matter? Living in a state of flow is choosing to live moment by moment at your optimal level. Living in flow calls out the very best of you, it is being in the zone and living to your highest and best. Flow is only experienced in the present moment. Flow cannot be possessed, it cannot be captured—it can only be lived. When you have experienced flow you will know it. In those moments, you live as you are intended to live, while at the same time reaching just a little bit farther.

From time to time I have asked audiences in my workshops to stand and stretch their arms in the air as high as they can. And, then I asked them to stretch just a little more. To reach just that little bit higher. It is in reaching just that little bit higher that you can find flow in the activities of life. When you have a skill that you take to just the next level, when you break through the new product design problem, or when you run your first 5K and your time is three minutes faster than you have ever run before. That feeling of having all of your resources focused on stretching just a little higher is flow. Let me give you a personal example. I love writing. Part of what I love most is an incredible level of focus, intensity, and concentration that writing an entire book requires. When I am fully engrossed in my work, I'm not distracted by what's going on around me; suddenly I'll realize that I've written ten pages and an hour has passed in what feels like no time at all.

In a state of flow, you use your gifts and talents in a way that stretches your abilities. Your life is filled with purpose, creativity, hope, and the satisfaction of knowing that your work is making the world a better place. In flow, you feel fully alive.

The first five vital signs—awareness, motivation, growing and learning, engagement, perseverance—allow you to know that you are alive. Living in a state of flow is being willing to place yourself just beyond that tiny gap of what you thought you could do and doing just a little bit more. Learning to live in a state of flow is part of the more I was looking for in life. Flow brings a deep and meaningful sense of accomplishment. Flow brings connection to your very best self. Flow challenges you to become more of who you are intended to be. But, when I first learned about living in a state of flow, I didn't know how.

CHOOSING FLOW

In *The 7 Minute Solution,* you've learned to recognize the preciousness of your attention span. You know now that what you allow into your life through what you see, hear, touch, taste, and smell has an impact on the quality of life you experience. But as you read this book, you may wonder, what is the point of all this effort to learn and grow, engage and persevere? The goal is to live in flow—your optimal state of being—so you can feel more, love more, do more, and experience more meaning.

Flow is a cognitive state that can also be referred to as being "in the zone." When you are in flow, you experience the perfect balance between your ability and your dreams. Flow is an emotional and physical experience that pulls you forward and stretches you to the limits of what you believe you can achieve—and then pushes you beyond those limits. It occurs when you are doing something you absolutely love, something that requires every ounce of your skill, yet you feel incredibly full of energy. In flow, it's as if every ounce of energy you exert is instantly replaced with joy and a sense of accomplishment.

You may think that lying in a hammock on the beach is the perfect setting for achieving flow. Doesn't it sound idyllic to relax near the surf, exerting no effort, just enjoying life? Certainly, that sandy experience offers enjoyment, but the reality is that most people experience a state of flow in their work rather than when they are at leisure. Research shows that mindless relaxation is much less likely to allow you to achieve flow. In flow, work may feel effortless because you are enjoying the moment, but it is the effort and challenge of work that make the moment rewarding. As the Tom Hanks character Jimmy Dugan explains in *A League of Their Own*, "The hard is what makes it great." We want life to challenge our full potential.

In his best-selling book *Flow: The Psychology of Optimal Experience*, Mihaly Csikszentmihalyi lists the eight components of flow. They are:

1. The chance to actually complete the task
2. The ability to concentrate on what we are doing
3. Clearly defined goals
4. Immediate feedback or results
5. Intensity that removes the awareness of the worries and frustrations of everyday life
6. A sense of control over one's actions

7. The absence of concern for self
8. A distortion of time that makes hours feel like minutes and minutes feel like hours

"The combination of all these elements causes a deep sense of enjoyment that is so rewarding people feel that expending a great deal of energy is worthwhile simply to be able to feel it," Csikszentmihalyi wrote. When I first read the words describing the components of flow, I wanted to know how I can experience flow on a daily basis. I want my life to be meaningful. I want to experience this conscious enjoyment of life, being fully present and swept away with the gratitude and goodness of enjoying these precious moments.

Understanding how to get into a state of flow enables us to experience it more frequently. Let's review Csikszentmihalyi's ideas about flow one at a time.

1. You have a chance to complete the task.

This goes back to our 7 Minute concept of the one-yard line. How many times have you started a task, only to fall short of finishing it? When we experience that gap of falling short of what we really want to do, we fall short emotionally as well. Setting yourself up to experience flow means that you must recognize the limitations of your abilities. You must also allow adequate time and find the appropriate resources (energy, money, and so on) to complete the task.

2. You must be able to concentrate on what you are doing.

Concentration and attention go hand in hand. Your brain has a limited capacity for attention. Interruptions and distractions pull you away from being able to get "in the zone." When you can remove external distractions and emotional mental clutter from your life, you can focus your energy and attention like a laser beam. In such moments, you will feel the joy of utilizing your personal strengths and skill sets to their highest and best level.

3. Your ability to concentrate is possible because you have clearly defined goals.

Clarifying your goals must be one of the first steps you take in experiencing the 7 Minute Solution. From the very beginning we have talked about the power of being able to "think, write, do." Think about your goals. Distill your thoughts into a crystal-clear image of exactly what you want to do. Put those thoughts into writing or use another tool to capture your goals, and then focus your concentration, time, and attention on accomplishing your goals.

4. The task provides opportunities for immediate feedback.

Feedback is a critical part of learning. Have you ever watched the joy in a child's eyes as he or she learns to walk? With each step the parent lovingly instructs and provides feedback that is gently encouraging: "Come to Daddy!" "Hold on to my hand tight!" "You did it!"

Immediate feedback is what coaches provide athletes, teachers provide students, and managers are supposed to provide their team members. Feedback allows us to learn and become better at what we do.

Feedback may not always be verbal, and it may not be provided by another person. Sometimes our results, the accomplishment of what we set out to do, provide the stimulation that pushes us to keep working, stay focused, and live fully in the moment.

5. There is a deep but effortless involvement that removes you from the awareness of the worries and frustrations of everyday life.

The human brain has a very limited capacity for the amount of data it can hold in conscious thought at any given time. When you consciously focus all of your attention on completing the task at hand, there is no processing capability left to focus on the worries and frustrations of life.

Our innate desire to do more actually sabotages flow. As Csikszentmihalyi explains, we have a limited capacity for processing information, yet we feel compelled to do more than one thing at a time. To a degree, this is possible. For instance, most people can hold a conversation and walk at the same time. But it is ineffective (if not impossible) to hold two different conversations at once—or listen to someone while concentrating on any other mentally taxing task, such as posting a note on Facebook, reading a book, or playing Sudoku. Multitasking, when it means attempting more than one mental task at a time, robs us of the opportunity to achieve flow. "Just decoding what other people are saying, even though apparently an effortless and automated process, interferes with any other task that requires one's full attention," Csikszentmihalyi wrote.

One of the greatest parts of flow is that when your attention is so highly focused and challenged, your brain maximizes the amount of information it processes at any given time. You cannot have positive and negative thoughts at the same time. When you focus intently on accomplishing a high-value task, no processing power remains for focusing on worries or other pressures. You are able to use your entire mental processing power for good.

6. You can exercise complete control over your actions.

Having a sense of control over our time and our actions is one of the most important psychological parts of emotional health. The freedom to spend your time doing exactly what you want to do—to use your skills in a way that aligns perfectly with your priorities and values—is a powerful motivator.

7. Your concern for self disappears.

Many people experience the deepest state of flow when they look outside themselves and experience life with the purpose of using their gifts and talents to serve others. I've known doctors on mission trips using their healing hands to meet the physical needs of more patients in a single day than they typically see in a week. Despite long hours and limited resources, their work fills them with energy and pushes them to help as many hurting people as possible.

During flow you lose self-consciousness as you become more engrossed in the activity. Your attention can become so intense that there is no additional conscious process or capacity left to experience the normal mental chatter of self-doubt and worry.

8. Your sense of time is changed.

The reality of time is that we always have enough time to do everything we choose to do. When we are in flow, time seems irrelevant. When I am working in flow and lose myself in the challenge at hand, I sometimes blink and wonder where the time has gone.

You have the ability to experience the psychological state of flow often. The more you learn about flow, the more you will recognize which activities in your life are apt to give you the opportunity to experience this depth and richness of being.

Now that you have been introduced to the eight intellectual concepts of flow, it is time for you to understand the power of experiencing flow on a daily basis and realize the depth of richness that flow brings to choosing to live in the present moment.

CROSSING THE LINE, STEPPING INTO FLOW

When Steve Cox was eight years old, he had a dream: he wanted to be a kicker in the National Football League.

In the evenings after work, Cox and his dad would walk to the high school football field to practice. "We had three footballs and lots of time. We would line up thirty yards away from the field goal, and my dad would pretend to snap the ball and hold it with his finger and I would kick it," Cox says. "The goal post stood at the edge of our elementary school playground and when the ball would go through the goal posts it would roll sixty or seventy yards down a hill into the parking lot. What I remember most is not the kicks, but the conversations we had walking together—talking together. Time is what my father gave me. He gave me his afternoons, his weeks, his months—he gave me his attention in hours, and in minutes, and in seconds."

What began in his hometown of Charleston, Arkansas, eventually led to a trip to the Super Bowl. "My life has been nothing less than a miracle. I love to tell children, 'Great things have small beginnings!' I was tiny, but I had big dreams," he says.

Those dreams were fueled by the joy of playing a game he loved. The love of a devoted father and the experience of meeting NFL kicker Tom Dempsey fed the impressionable now-eleven-year-old boy's dreams. Dempsey, who was born with no toes on his right foot and no fingers on his right hand, played for the New Orleans Saints. He still holds the record for longest field-goal ever kicked—sixty-three yards. "I wanted to be just like him," Cox remembers.

Through years of dedicated practice, Cox developed a powerful leg and earned a place in the NFL. "God made me with a leg. I could generate a leg speed of a hundred miles an hour. That's what made me different." The Cleveland Browns drafted Cox in 1981, and he was traded to the Washington Redskins four seasons later.

"In the NFL I had three roles. I was a punter, I kicked off, and I was brought in for the long field goals," he says. In 1988, the Washington Redskins made it to the Super Bowl. Cox was thirty years old.

By that time, Cox had mastered the ability to work in a state of flow. "Every day you have to be great, but as game day grows closer, you have to take your performance to an entirely different level," he says. "Being 'in the zone' was so much of the reward for playing professional football. There were times where our team was just working together at an entirely different level. There's nothing like it." And then there were the moments when the team relied solely on him. Each time he stepped onto the field, it was a now-or-never moment. Cox explains that getting into flow was a mental state of "crossing the white line": "It's not about crossing the hash mark to kick the ball. It's about crossing the sideline. From the moment you step across that white line, you have to have already decided in your mind that you had *made* that kick. The moment you step over the sideline—that's when the kick is made or missed."

Being in flow is not something Steve Cox had to think about. When he lined up to kick a field goal or kick a punt he had between 1.1 and 1.3 seconds to react. Tens of thousands of people yelling, every moment captured in front of a nationally televised audience of millions—1.3 seconds. Steve described those intense moments, "I was so fully focused in the moment, so *not* thinking of anything else. I didn't hear the crowd. I didn't fear the threat of the defense. I experienced complete tunnel vision and I felt overwhelming calm in exactly that moment."

Aside from the thrill of playing in Super Bowl XXII, one of his career highlights was making a sixty-yard field goal in a 1984 game against Cincinnati. When the coach signaled him to go in, Cox's heart pounded with excitement. "I knew this was the time. I took that single step across the white line, and that was all it took. I had dreamed about this moment. I had made hundreds of sixty-yard field goals on the practice field, and I had made thousands of sixty-yard field goals in my mind. The moment I stepped across the white line, I was 'in the zone.'"

The seconds ticked by in slow motion as the ball hung in the air, but, Cox says, "I already knew the outcome of this kick. I had decided the moment I stepped across the white line." That day, in a moment of flow, Cox became the second man in the NFL to kick a sixty-yard field goal. Today, only seven men hold that record.

Flow happens when the challenges you face are just slightly higher than the skills you possess. Flow is constantly calling you to be more in life. Steve Cox began his career kicking sticks in his back yard when he could barely walk. He spent two to eight hours almost every day of his teenage and adult life practicing and perfecting the sport he loved. He kicked tens of thousands, if not hundreds of thousands of kicks. Living in flow has a price that most people are not willing to pay. Flow requires practice, and learning, and effort. It requires looking a new challenge in the face and saying, "Bring it on."

FINDING FLOW

Flow rarely happens by chance. The graphic below illustrates how challenge, when met with skill, leads to flow. If the challenge is greater than your skill set, you'll experience a sense of excitement, or what Csikszentmihalyi labels "arousal," which can drive you to stretch your personal skill sets to their very limits. For example, when runners compete in their first 10K, painters place a blank canvas on their easel, or college freshmen walk into their first lecture. It is the moment that Steve Cox describes as stepping across the "white line": the hair on the back of your neck stands up, your breathing becomes shallow, and you feel a sense of excitement.

If the challenge is high and your skill set is low, you will feel anxious. A common example is walking into a staff meeting to make a presentation without being properly prepared. In situations like that you feel out of control and overwhelmed.

The flip side of this chart shows that if your skill set is very high and the challenge is moderate, you will feel in control of the situation. However, if you are faced with too many such experiences and the challenge remains too low, you will become bored.

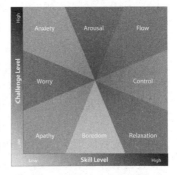

Chart Source: Mihaly Csikszentmihalyi, Finding Flow

The worst place of all, according to Csikszentmihihayi, is where your everyday challenges are low and your skill set is also low. This is where you experience a disconnect with life and you simply don't care. Living a life of apathy day after day, month after month, year after year is what I described as living a life unaware. Life passes you by, neither good nor bad, neither hot nor cold. That is not life, it is torture.

OPTIMAL EXPERIENCES

You have the ability to create an optimal experience for your life—and you are the only one who can decide what that means for you. You must clarify what is most important to you; you must determine and articulate how you would want to live an ideal life. What is your optimal experience?

As you purposefully head into your optimal experience, you're going to discover that facing down challenges and conquering even the smallest obstacles is exhilarating. Your life will no longer be about the humdrum existence of endurance but about taking risks and receiving rewards for what really matters to you.

Just getting through another day rarely inspires us to conquer giants, but for your heart's desire you'll be willing to rush forward, armed and determined to win. Expect a rush of adrenaline and joy as you battle for what really matters to you. Your belief that you can win is integral to your success.

HOW TO RAISE YOUR BELIEF LEVEL

"As human beings we don't perform at our best level; we actually perform at our belief level," says former Blue Angel pilot John Foley. Only the best of the best are chosen to be Blue Angel pilots. They must be in the top one-hundredth of the top 1 percent of all navy pilots in the country. John Foley was one of those men. In his first Blue Angel training session, he was charged with the task of radically improving his competency level; he had three months to raise his performance level by 300 percent. But before he could make a change in his performance, he knew he needed to raise his belief level by 300 percent.

He had to be able to fly an airplane five hundred miles per hour within eighteen inches from wingtip to cockpit. He had to withstand g-forces of seven times that of Earth, far more than needed to make a human being unconscious in seconds. He was subjected to hours of physical training. The "stick" in the jet produced forty pounds of constant pressure on his hands.

How many of us are working in our jobs with the same level of competency and skills we had ten years ago? It's time to draw a line in the sand. It's time to increase the challenges you seek out each day. And to meet those challenges, you will need to improve your skills and mind-set.

When I heard John Foley speak and watched the videos with the booming lyrics of the *Top Gun* movie playing in the background (yes, he was one of the real pilots in the movie!), I wanted to stand up and say, "I want to raise the bar 300 percent in three months. I want to be in the top one-hundredth of the top 1 percent in my industry. I want to be in the best physical shape of my life. I want to believe I can be different!" Let me tell you, John Foley is one of the best speakers I have ever heard. Why? Because he helped me see what an optimal life could be like.

Today is the day to decide what your optimal experience looks like. Today is the day to decide to raise your personal belief level. You get to make those decisions. You get to make those choices. Now is the time. Why not now?

What would you need to do differently to increase your performance? What kind of focus would you need to develop? How could you restructure your schedule to make time to take hold of this new and exciting life? What would your physical health have to become to give you the energy to support this type of existence?

Just as your heart is designed to deliver the correct amount of blood to your body, life is willing to give you exactly the skill sets you need. What are you demanding of your life?

YOUR BRAIN IN FLOW

The psychology of flow is about being in the right place for you. If you are not in the right place, working toward your purpose, all the action in the world won't bring about flow or fulfillment.

Even if you love what you do, not all activities lend themselves to a state of flow. There are times when mundane or less meaningful work—such as cleaning your office—is required. Getting into your optimal focus zone can make even those moments feel less like drudgery. Dr. Lucy Jo Palladino, a psychologist and the author of *Find Your Focus Zone,* says that when we are faced with accomplishing such tasks, it can be helpful to prime ourselves first. For example, she created a music playlist for this type of chore. The music has very few lyrics but definite drumbeats that bring a sense of energy and adventure to otherwise boring tasks. She breaks larger activities into smaller chunks to improve her ability to focus her attention more intensely.

Much of life involves devoting our time and attention to exactly those types of tasks. But with our limited attention span, we often find ourselves starting and stopping the same tasks over and over again, wasting much of our precious time. Placing yourself in the proper focus zone, using flow triggers such as music and intense attention, there is no doubt that you could more efficiently and more easily conquer many mundane tasks in a shorter period. And when you accomplish even the tiniest of those tasks, you feel better about yourself.

"Every time you complete a task, no matter how small, your brain will receive an instant jolt of dopamine," Dr. Palladino says. "Nothing succeeds like success."

Dopamine is the chemical responsible for your brain's reward system. It is also a key factor in achieving optimal focus. When you cross something off your list, it not only feels good, it's good for you. Dopamine is a biological fuel pump for motivation. Dopamine is one of the neurological reasons that creating and accomplishing your 5 before 11 list is so important. Remember that the brain is plastic and responds to the chemical and electrical signals that repetition creates. When you create a daily written plan of action that is focused on accomplishing high-value activities—every time you mark a single item off your list as done—your brain is rewarded with one of the most powerful, positive chemicals humans can experience—dopamine, one of the chemicals responsible for placing you mentally into a state of flow.

As you utilize the 5 before 11 concept in your daily life, it will become one of the strongest neural connections you experience. You will seek out the feeling of accomplishment, and you will become more and more self-motivated to focus your limited attention on accomplishing your most important tasks.

Unfortunately, there is an activation cascade that can quickly move from a positive feeling of motivation to overdrive. This feeling of overdrive is chemically induced by the addition of too much norepinephrine. Flow is intended to be a pleasurable but not stressful competitive state. But norepinephrine is only a molecule or two away from dopamine in its chemical compound. The chemicals in your brain are much like a soup: too much norepinephrine in your body, and you shift into stress; too little dopamine, and you shift into apathy. Flow is the perfect blend of the two at the perfect time. When you move beyond enjoying an activity for its own sake into a more competitive mode, your brain can pump too much norepinephrine, bringing you out of flow.

"Your thoughts elicit feelings, and your feelings elicit thoughts," Dr. Palladino explains. "As you experience this cognitive process of thought and feeling, your cognition pumps chemicals at exactly the same time the chemicals induce cognition. They actually cause each other."

When you feel safe and have thoughts of well-being, you generate a chemical called serotonin. And when you generate serotonin, you have a greater sense of well-being.

Success breeds success. As you succeed, your brain releases the chemical dopamine; as the dopamine is absorbed at the receptor site, you feel motivated, until there comes a point of overstimulation through the production of too much norepinephrine, and then you can feel scared or overwhelmed, which can completely shut down your sense of motivation. Norepinephrine functions at the basic neurological level of your brain. This chemical is one of the most important to human survival. It is the jolt of adrenaline that hits you when you see a snake. Unfortunately, it is also the same neuronal reaction as when we are overloaded at work or feel stress in our lives.

Dr. Palladino uses a great analogy: Think of these chemicals as accelerators and brakes in your life; dopamine and norepinephrine are accelerators. Norepinephrine motivates us to survive, while dopamine motivates us to thrive. Serotonin reminds you to slow down. It helps you acknowledge the value of life and relax long enough to enjoy it.

These chemicals are functioning every moment of every day. They act like switches on a train track: if you get too relaxed, you can get a small jolt of norepinephrine to bring you back to clarity and focus. Even as you are in the process of accomplishing a task you love, a dose of dopamine releases in your brain. This reward chemical is a pat on the back for doing what you said you would do, and that tiny dose motivates you to continue working. Your body desires, hopes, it will get another dose of dopamine. Then there comes a time to slow down; serotonin is released, and you experience a sense of meaning and accomplishment. In such moments you know your life matters, and you experience an abiding understanding of purpose.

Then you remember that you have a project deadline, and, like drinking two cups of coffee, your body fills with adrenaline due to the norepinephrine that is released, and you are back to your daily activities. With the simple realization that there is a deadline, your heart begins to beat a little faster, you breathe a little more rapidly, your clarity returns. Dopamine is released, and you return to that perfect blend of focus, excitement, and purpose.

It's important to note that norepinephrine is both our friend and our foe. From the beginning of time, norepinephrine has been essential to our survival, instantly jolting our attention to awareness of danger that looms. But today, this adrenaline-based stress chemical surges unchecked far too often. When we are overexcited and overstimulated, we are stressed and anxious and cannot focus on accomplishing even the simplest of tasks. Everything becomes urgent, and we cannot move forward.

However, in small doses norepinephrine is the powerful awakener that we need to move through the day; it acts like the bumps on the shoulder of a highway, so that when we lose our focus and drift away, norepinephrine wakes us up and puts us back onto the right path."

GETTING INTO THE ZONE

Can you get to where you want to go from where you are today? If the work you're doing isn't the right fit for you or isn't aligned with your purpose, working harder or more efficiently will not bring satisfaction. If you are in the right place, you'll be happy to know that experiencing flow seems to be fairly consistent, regardless of whether you are a businessperson, a top-level athlete, a stay-at-home mom, a teacher, or an artist. When you are able to fully engage in what you love, when you spend time focusing on your true passions in life, the activity itself becomes the most meaningful reward.

Flow is the perfect balance of taking on the highest challenges possible and calling on all of your skill sets to accomplish them. In flow, your attention is focused like a laser beam, filtering out everything unimportant to accomplishing the task at hand. You are driven, devoted, intrinsically motivated, and inspired.

The more I learned about living in a state of flow, the more I realized I was experiencing this optimal state on a daily basis in my current work. The vital sign of living in flow is absolutely not intended to make you think you can only experience flow when you run, or paint, or are involved in your favorite hobby. This vital sign has been written to challenge you to discover what steps you can take to find yourself in a state of flow more often every day. Go back and look at the eight components of flow:

1. The chance to actually complete the task
2. The ability to concentrate on what we are doing
3. Clearly defined goals
4. Immediate feedback or results
5. Intensity that removes the awareness of the worries and frustrations of everyday life
6. A sense of control over one's actions
7. The absence of concern for self
8. A distortion of time that makes hours feel like minutes and minutes feel like hours

You'll discover that your flow occurs only on purpose, when you push beyond what you may think you can do. Rather than relying on chance or serendipity to create flow, consider setting aside time to think, time to crystallize your drive and your effort. Two great American thinkers spoke about those concepts. Henry Ford believed that "Thinking is the hardest work there is, which is probably the reason so few engage in it." President Abraham Lincoln advocated spending time on the preparation that makes drive and effort effective, noting that a sharp ax was more crucial than sheer strength when it came to chopping down a tree. Flow rarely happens by chance. Clarify your values, understand your priorities, give yourself time to prepare for success.

As you seek out your best you may find yourself asking, "What do I believe will call me to create a life with meaning?" This takes us to the final vital sign, are you living with faith?

VITAL SIGN 7:

Are You Living with Faith?

Faith is deliberate confidence in the character of God whose ways you may not understand at the time.
—OSWALD CHAMBERS, AUTHOR OF
MY UTMOST FOR HIS HIGHEST

THIS VITAL SIGN MAY feel different from the other characteristics and strategies we've discussed. You might have been surprised when you opened this book to find a chapter on faith. On the surface, the 7 Minute Solution may appear to be mostly about goal setting, productivity, and time management. But ultimately, the 7 Minute Solution is about meaning.

For many, faith is an anchor to a meaningful life. As with the word "faith," each person defines the word "meaning" in his or her own way. We all believe in something. The exploration of this vital sign is intended to help you gain a deeper understanding of exactly what it is that you have faith in and how connecting with what you believe to be true can bring more meaning to your life. As with most 7 Minute ideas, I believe we must consciously recognize that what we have chosen to have faith in directly impacts our life. Think back to the seven vital signs of the 7 Minute Solution:

Are you aware?
Are you motivated?

Are you growing and learning?
Are you engaged?
Are you living in the state of flow?
Are you living with faith?

As you reflect on each one of these vital signs, they reflect on you. They reflect where you are in life; they reflect the priorities, values, goals, and dreams you have; and they reflect where you are in this present moment.

When we surveyed 592 people about happiness and meaning, many of the responses to the question "What aspects of life are most meaningful to you?" came through again and again. Overwhelmingly, the participants indicated that the priorities they value most are:

Family
Love
Friends
Faith
Making a difference in the lives of others

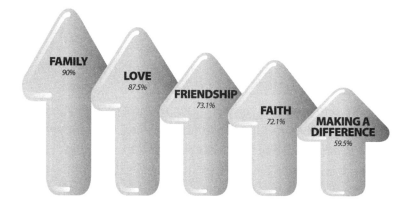

In February 2011, we conducted an online survey, and out of 592 total respondents, those five values were most important. 72.1 percent of all those who took the survey said faith was one of the top five things they valued most in life.

Take a look at a sampling of the responses to the question "What aspects of life are most meaningful to you?"

Family relationships
Fulfilling His purpose
Relationship with God and the community of faith and all that entails
Family, faith, and friends
Family, helping others to be better
My faith, my relationships, my friends, and my work
Health, children
My faith in God is the most important and the rest follows from
    Him. I love family, friendships, and especially laughter because it
    helps heal the soul.
God, my husband, my children, my family
Impacting others' lives
Children, grandchildren (legacy), and faith are being created,
    inspiring others, reaching my full potential, loving and being loved
Relationships with others, making a difference
My children and grandchildren
My relationship with God and my children
Faith, family
Family, God, determining what God created me to do and using
    my talents to benefit others
Children, family, friends, work
Faith, health, love, family, and friends
The love of my family
The memories made and moments spent with my family
Being cared for and being able to care for others
Family, love, friendships, growing and sharing my gifts

I am not surprised by the consistency of the answers we received. At forty-one, when circumstances shocked me into the awareness that my life lacked the meaning I desired, I quickly learned that the more I longed for couldn't be found in self-development and personal-growth programs. The more was not—could not be—all about me.

The aspects of life that are most meaningful are bigger than ourselves. And faith is the thread that connects us to what matters most.

TYPES OF FAITH

Cynthia Kersey, the author of *Unstoppable: 45 Powerful Stories of Perseverance and Triumph from People Just like You,* asked John Maxwell to talk about faith, and this is how he answered:

> Faith is the willingness to believe in God, believe in yourself, and believe in people. . . . Faith in God to do the impossible, to go beyond human strength, human ability, human ingenuity. Faith in yourself . . . you believe in yourself, you are willing to bet on yourself. It allows you to do things others would be unwilling to do, to take that risk, to step out. . . . Faith is also believing in others. Why would you take the risk? Why would you do the unthinkable? Because you believe that people have (the ability) to make a difference in the lives of other people. You believe in others. You have faith in them.
>
> —www.johnmaxwellteam.com/faith

Faith is the deep-seated conviction that invisibly anchors us to God, to the people around us, and even to ourselves. It is not a product of reason or of tangible evidence. The New Testament describes it this way:, "Now faith is the substance of things hoped for, the evidence of things not seen" (Hebrews 11:1).

Faith is an essential element of creating a life of meaning because it is the foundation of conviction that keeps you true to your path— regardless of circumstance. Faith is the bridge that allows us to believe we have been created for a specific reason. Faith allows us to embrace life at a much deeper level . . . believing even in what we cannot see or fully understand. It is the inner quality that enables you to persevere. Faith empowers you to take decisive action. It allows you to see past today's trials, pain, and busyness so that you can envision a life filled with meaning. Knowing life can be better, believing in yourself, believing in others, and believing in God are the defining difference between meaning and futility, hope and hopelessness, confidence and fear, and action and surrender.

As I pondered John Maxwell's definition of faith and his concept of having faith in God, faith in yourself, and faith in others, I wanted to more fully explore each type of faith and how we might learn from each one.

Faith in God

In the Old Testament, Moses meets God in the burning bush.

> There the angel of the LORD appeared to him in flames of fire from within a bush. Moses saw that though the bush was on fire it did not burn up.
>
> So Moses thought, "I will go over and see this strange sight—why the bush does not burn up."
>
> When the LORD saw that he had gone over to look, God called to him from within the bush, "Moses! Moses!"
>
> And Moses said, "Here I am."
>
> —Exodus 3:2–4 (NIV)

In that encounter Moses was given a mission and a purpose. He was called to deliver a tribe of people, the Israelites, out of the slavery of the Egyptians. It was a task that defied reason. Where would they go? How would they survive once they left slavery? What would they do with their freedom? It would take forty years of trust and struggle before Moses fully understood the answers to those questions. But his faith fed his willingness to continue forward despite seemingly insurmountable odds.

The good news is that God comes to us. God knows our name. God makes Himself apparent; God meets us where we are. If we are living with faith, our response should be to simply say, as Moses did, "Here I am." Faith assures us that once we say those words God will continue to meet us and provide for us. An old adage comes to mind: "God does not call the equipped. God equips the called." People with faith continue forward, knowing God will equip them to fulfill their purpose.

Faith in Yourself

Can you imagine leaving a five-year-old at home alone for two weeks at a time? You probably cringe at the thought, but that's exactly what happened to my friend Sean Phillips. His father, who married eight times, left Sean at home alone when he was just a tiny boy—and charged him with the responsibility to care for his baby brother.

Not surprisingly, Sean struggled in school. With a D average, he tested out of his senior classes and graduated a year early so he could join the army. After leaving the army, he eventually became an officer with a local police department where he worked in vice and narcotics.

Sean has a high need for challenge. He pushed himself to the physical limits not only in his work, but by competing in the Panama City, Florida, Ironman—a 2.4-mile swim, a 112-mile bike ride, and a 26.2-mile run. In 2000, at the age of thirty-four, Sean finished the race in fourteen hours, fifty-eight minutes.

He also pushed himself mentally and is what I call a self-educated man. He decided he wanted to become a financial adviser. He interviewed with one of the largest financial services firms in the country and made the first cut. He completed the Panama City, Florida, Ironman two days before his final interview with the firm. When he told the manager that he had just completed the Ironman, he was hired on the spot without a college degree. Through the years, he has continued to push himself to learn and grow and has been promoted accordingly. Today, Sean manages a team of two hundred people, and he uses his drive and motivation to help others find the best in themselves.

When Sean and I met during a recent 7 Minute training workshop, he told me that the principles he had learned that day surprised him. "Most of these business training workshops are geared towards only focusing on our work," he said. "You made us step back and focus on our life. I wasn't expecting that. I wasn't expecting emotion in the room. I wasn't expecting to feel the depth of what I felt. I wasn't expecting it to be so personal, to be so much about what was really important to me."

Sean has come such a long way in his life—from a neglected child to a teen on a mission to serve in the military to a young man who took on the challenge of developing a new career to a leader who helps people accomplish more than they thought possible. He understands that you get what you focus on and that being sure of your purpose is a key to overcoming physical, mental, and emotional challenges.

In November 2011, Sean will compete in the Panama City Ironman, but he knows it will be different this time. "It won't be that the race has changed. The amazing part is the insight I have gained in the last eleven years," he says.

Sean shared three insights with me: "First, it's not really how you view the world, or the circumstances you have faced in life; instead, take responsibility and focus only on the things you can control.

"Next, what are the questions you ask every day? When you ask bad questions, you get wrong answers. Your questions should be, 'What action do I need to take to become more valuable to my children, to my coworkers, and to my company?' 'What can I do today to be better?' 'What do I value most in life?' These are the questions we should ask every day."

Finally Sean made a declaration: "Have less rules about what it takes to be happy. If the rules are simple, and all it takes for you to be happy is to wake up breathing, then, it is likely you will be happy.

"From a child left at home to a grown man, I have survived and thrived."

Sean Phillips has faith in himself.

Faith in Others

Esther Silver-Parker's story illustrates the miracle of what can happen when other people have faith in you. Growing up in a very poor area in eastern North Carolina amid tobacco and cotton fields, Esther was one of seven children. Her parents had a deep belief in education and repeatedly told her, "Study hard and work hard. Somebody will notice you, and you will get scholarships." "So I studied hard," she says.

Esther went to undergraduate school at a small, historically black college. "I had clothes (our clothes always came from somebody else), but I had nothing to take them in to go to school." That's when the "front-porch ladies" of her community stepped in to help. These women, so named because they watched the neighborhood's comings and goings from their front porches, rallied together and bought her luggage. "Blue Samsonite luggage. I remember like it was yesterday. That piece of luggage was a symbol of the faith and hope these women had in my future," she says. "These ladies, who were just as poor as my family, periodically sent me a dollar here and a dollar there. I knew it was a sacrifice for them, and those dollars were precious gifts to me."

Esther was surrounded by people who believed in her. "In college one of my teachers, Mrs. Farrison, pulled me aside and said, 'I am not going to permit you to become too caught up in only the social aspects of college. You're too bright for that. You stay focused on your work. If you don't, I'll make it a point to have you moved out of the dormitory and into my house.'

"Throughout my entire life I just had incredible examples of other people who were very focused on me and on my success. I would be less than a person if I did not do something to celebrate their investment in me."

Esther Silver-Parker continued her education and graduated from Columbia School of Journalism. She worked as a journalist with *Essence* magazine. She then spent twenty-eight years at AT&T, working in the areas of corporate social responsibility and corporate affairs, ending her career there as president of the AT&T Foundation.

In December 2003, she went to work for Wal-Mart in the area of diversity. In 2010, at age sixty-three, Esther retired from her position as senior vice president of corporate affairs for Wal-Mart.

Now in retirement, she is president and CEO of the Silver-Parker Group, a branding and strategy company that donates 25 percent of its profits to helping others. Esther travels the world to teach women about entrepreneurship and business. The women she works with use the principles she teaches to improve their lives—and the lives of others in their communities.

As an example of one of hundreds of success stories, Esther tells of a woman farmer she worked with in Rwanda who had an epiphany after going through the leadership training program. The farmer wasn't getting the productivity she needed from the women who worked on her farm, so she asked herself, "How can I make this better?"

With Esther's help and insight the farmer gave land to each of the women and had them work as a cooperative. As owners of the land, their entire mind-set changed, and it has positively affected all of the women in the community. One person can make an incredible difference.

"That blue Samsonite sticks out in my mind because it is a symbol of kindness, it is a symbol of uplifting, and it is a symbol of giving back. It is also a symbol of loving and caring," she says. "The fact that these women had such faith in me has given me a desire and a purpose to have faith in others."

Others had faith in Esther Silver-Parker, and it made a defining difference.

You can make a difference by having faith in others.

Faith in God. Faith in ourselves. Faith in others.

Everything in life is connected through faith.

So where does faith come into the 7 Minute Solution?

As you read these pages and go through the worksheets, you may feel the desire to rediscover and reconnect with your personal faith. It only makes sense that as you write about what you value most and spend time deciding what your purpose in life is, your spirituality and your personal faith will surface at the top of your list.

My pastor, Dan Reeves, who challenged us in the introduction to consider what are you asking of your life, added another element that may help us think about life, "Why am I here?" and "What makes my life meaningful?"

Dan said, "What gives a hammer its value is understanding why it was created. The design it was made for dictates its meaning. A hammer is a valuable tool when you are driving nails, but it is meaningless without the proper context. As a human, do you know what you have been designed for?"

In order to connect with your meaning in life, I believe you must know what you have been designed for. Do you have a clear understanding of why you are here?

For most of us, engaging in and finding meaning in life reaches far beyond our human bodies. We simply want more. Throughout history mankind has searched for meaning.

I created the 7 Minute Tools because my life was chaotic and disconnected. I was out of line with my values, I was uncertain of my purpose, and I felt distracted and unfulfilled. One of the most significant effects of utilizing these tools has been reconnecting with what is most important. How can we be sure we are following the right paths and setting the right goals? This is part of where faith comes in.

There are only so many hours in the day, and each one of us chooses how we will spend those precious moments. The more organized I am and the more attentive I am in accomplishing specific tasks in the most efficient manner, the more time I will have to spend exploring God's goodness, loving my family, and enjoying the fullness of who I am. Let me repeat that: *The more organized I am and the more attentive I am in accomplishing specific tasks in the most efficient manner, the more time I will have to spend exploring God's goodness, loving my family, and enjoying the fullness of who I am.* Pause and think about this. Attention to the management of your life determines the life you experience.

We have covered so much in this book, and the vital sign of living with faith is a common thread. What is often misunderstood is why it seems so difficult to give ourselves the time and freedom to think and discover more meaning in life. I would like to put forth one more neurological concept. I believe life is less meaningful if you don't use both hemispheres of your brain. The left brain and the right brain function in completely different ways. It is generally believed rational thought is generated from the left side of your brain, and we have spent a great deal of time talking about how to use the 7 Minute tools and systems to make your left brain more efficient.

In this last vital sign, "Are You Living with Faith?" I would like you to consider that no matter how efficient you become at dealing with tasks, what have you gained if your life has no meaning?

It is not in speeding up that we find meaning, but in slowing down. Your right brain takes life in stride, it experiences life in broad brush strokes and is always about understanding the bigger picture. The right brain is much more sensory based. It allows you to experience life as you smell something sweet, as you hear music that inspires your soul and as you see beauty in the world around you. The right brain is about connecting with what you believe to be most true in life.

EXPERIENCING MEANING BY CONNECTING WITH YOUR RIGHT BRAIN

Part of the reason I became so lost in unawareness was that for years—perhaps most of my adult life—I was absorbed in managing my life without experiencing it. I survived by doing what needed to be done. I was incredibly driven, but I wasn't present in my life. Like vital sign #1, I was completely unaware, and life was passing me by.

It is likely that you have focused so intently on developing one side of your brain—the left side—that you may not be aware of the importance of strengthening the right side of your brain. And, the ideas you are about to read will resonate with you instantly.

The human brain is divided into two distinct hemispheres, the left and right. They are virtually equal in size and in the number of neuronal connections. The left brain controls the right side of your body, and the right brain controls the left side. This is why, when someone has a stroke on one side of the brain, he may have significant damage on the opposite side of his body. In both hemispheres of your brain you have amazing neural circuits—hundreds of billions of perfect connections waiting for your instructions. However, the two sides of your brain interpret and distribute information radically differently.

As a left-brain-dominant person, I am in good company. The vast majority of the human population is left-brain-dominant, which can be seen by right-hand dominance (roughly 90 percent of people are right-handed). But hand dominance does not definitively predict brain hemisphere dominance. According to Jill Bolte Taylor, PhD, "Dominance in the brain is determined by which hemisphere houses the ability to create and understand language."

Studies indicate that based on where the language centers are located, 96 percent of the population is left-brain-dominant. The left brain is logical, linear, sequential, organized, critical, judgmental, methodical, and structured. For the bulk of the population, the left brain is the center of language skills. Ninety-six percent of the world has placed value on these left-brain personality traits and preferences. Ninety-six percent of you reading this book believe that to be successful you must choose to think logically, linearly, and sequentially. You believe it is good to be organized and plan out every detail for every project. You are seeking structure in life, because structure brings familiarity and the comfort of routine.

Unfortunately the left brain functions so well, it can function at its best on automatic pilot. If you remember the cognitive models we described earlier, you remember that when we allow our lives to be run completely by subconscious thought, life can become stale and unchallenging.

In direct contrast to the left brain, the right brain is artistic, flowing, emotional, vibrant, intuitive, and in the moment. The right brain sees the big picture, experiences all of the senses of life. The right brain is adventurous, and imaginative. It is creative, full of ideas, boundless in energy, hopeful, and expectant. It is exuberant. The right brain can be almost childlike with its lack of boundaries, high ideals, and big dreams. The right brain seeks connection. The right brain begs for engagement with life.

For much of your life the world has judged you, or at least you have perceived the world judging you, based upon your left-brain skills. The workforce (up to this point) has rewarded the ability of increasing productivity, efficiency, and time management at the expense of living a life with meaning. The left brain can get things done on time and under budget. The left brain functions as a giant project manager: planning and executing, planning and executing, planning and executing.

The left brain seeks out the details of what needs to be done and quickly falls back on how you have accomplished such tasks most efficiently in the past. (Again, remember how the brain utilizes cognitive models.) Rather than determining if how you accomplished them before is the right method for the task at hand, the left brain looks for models and frameworks from past life experience and projects forward expected outcomes regardless of what the reality may be, regardless of what the true costs may be. In contrast, the right brain inspires new solutions and looks for new ideas. The right brain is constantly telling the left brain to slow down and take a second look, let's go to lunch and eat and talk about this, let's sleep on this, let's write it out and see what it feels like . . . why rush?

In short, the left brain works at managing and ordering life, while the right brain is busy experiencing it. If you are living predominantly in your left brain, you may feel as if you're in a constant mental scurry to keep track of the different parts of life while seldom being fully present at any of them. You may be exceptionally efficient, but you also wonder why life lacks flavor and vibrancy.

We must do a better job of slowing down and tuning in to the right brain. The right brain knows how to engage in life using emotion, as well as your senses of smell, touch, taste, hearing, and seeing. That's what brings excitement to life!

You can tune in to the right brain by using your nondominant hand. If you are right handed, write your name with your left hand, brush your teeth with your left hand, dial the telephone, or type a text with your left hand. The more you engage your nondominant hand the more you are physically waking up the connections with the right side of your brain.

You might be asking yourself why am I including this vital information on gaining access to your right brain at this point in the book?

WHAT DO ALL OF THESE BRAIN FACTS HAVE TO DO WITH FAITH?

Faith is experienced primarily through the right side of the brain. The right brain opens us up to faith, to believing in what we cannot see. Without faith, it is impossible to imagine that our lives can be different tomorrow. Your left brain latches on to disbelief and uses its doubts as reasons not to attempt to achieve your goals. Faith is not necessarily logical, linear, or tangible (characteristics appealing to the left brain). Faith has often been described as "caught, not taught," because faith is something we apprehend or experience rather than comprehend. Faith is a feeling of assurance and a sensation of conviction.

The left brain wants to make sense of good and bad. The left brain wants to believe that there will always be order in life: if I do this, I can expect that. Our left brain wants to reason. It asks why bad things happen to good people. If we rely solely on our left brain, we tend to feel hopeless and lost in times of grief or stress.

That is where faith steps in. Faith is something bigger and better than human understanding. It is our right brain that allows us to experience faith, hope, and love. Our right brain allows us to trust in a world where everything does not always add up. It allows us to open ourselves up to the best and worst life offers while knowing that our purpose is part of a much larger plan.

So much of our life is processed with our left brain, trying to find order in chaos, looking for ways to fill the voids in our lives, looking for meaning and purpose with equations and routines. The left brain finds solace by finding patterns and by participating in activities that are comfortable and familiar.

As we finish this section regarding how the right and left hemispheres of your brain can make your life more meaningful, I would like for you to also consider how you experience meaning in your whole self. I would like for you to think about your heart, your body, your mind, and your soul.

THE 7 MINUTE SOLUTION: YOUR HEART, BODY, MIND, AND SOUL

Meaning encompasses more than one aspect of life. In fact, because humans are uniquely and intricately created, fully experiencing life involves drawing on every aspect of your being: your heart, your body, your mind, and your soul.

Your *heart* enables you to understand love, relationships, and friendships. The heart plays a large role in what you experience as meaning, purpose, significance, and fulfillment. The heart is where we connect with our family and friends.

Your *body* enables you to experience life physically. It controls what you touch, see, smell, taste, and hear.

Your *mind* is the body's hard drive. It is the chemical and electrical source of life. The brain enables you to process and express thoughts. It is where our conscious and, more importantly, subconscious thoughts reside.

Your *soul* is where you find the inexhaustible fuel that fills you and renews you.

Engage Your Heart

The human heart is amazing. In the introduction of this book, I talked about the fact that it is ready to deliver exactly the right amount of blood at exactly the right time to meet the needs of your physical body. Then, I began to think about what the heart does. It receives blood and then it gives blood. It receives and then it gives.

That is when it occurred to me that, if I want to create a life with meaning, I need to be ready to receive love and give love, receive compassion and give compassion, receive courage and give courage, receive gratitude and give gratitude. The heart gives and receives.

When something is said to be at the heart of the matter, it is at its very center and core. Your total personality is said to be revealed from your inner heart. The words you speak are spoken from the heart. Your heart is the center of your emotions and your feelings.

Meaning is not just something you do, meaning is something you feel. I encourage you to take time to open your heart. To find more meaning, you must slow down long enough to listen to your heart.

Engage Your Body

The human body was designed to be in motion. We have legs to walk, run, and dance. We have arms to lift, carry, embrace, and serve.

It is time to engage your body and its senses in the physical activities of life.

Go. Live. Breathe. Feel. Move.

Change is difficult. It is almost impossible to change how you feel emotionally until you have the physical strength and stamina to support that change. While I was working through this exercise with Jessica Miller, a friend from work, she pointed out that it is difficult to engage her mind when her physical body is exhausted. She works full-time, has two small children, had just finished sitting for a major exam that her job depended on her passing. Forty hours of family, forty hours of work, and twenty hours of study each week left her little time to sleep. "I realized my body must come first," Jessica says. "It's like putting myself on a physical and psychological bill-pay plan. I need to pay myself first. I need eight hours of sleep. I need thirty minutes of exercise. When I looked at my life, I was already doing more. I didn't want to just do more. There was no time to do more. I wanted to *be* more. I wanted to be different, better. I wanted life to be more meaningful.

"When you choose to put anything new on your calendar, whether you recognize it or not, something else is by default coming out of your calendar," she remarks. Unfortunately, too often what comes out is sleep and exercise. Step one of reconnecting physically with life is to make a written plan for how you will consciously choose to engage your body.

Engage Your Mind

Engaging your mind works like the gears of a bicycle. There are so many images of the brain functioning like gears. We often speak of "getting the wheels turning."

During one family dinner, our then eleven-year-old son, James Mark Lewis, Jr. (who goes by J—as he says, "Just the letter J"), was in the middle of telling the family a very detailed story about what happened at school that day when he stopped in midsentence. Right in the middle of the story, he just stopped talking. He had gotten so excited about telling us what happened that he completely forgot what he was talking about.

When he couldn't remember where he was in his story, suddenly he said, "Oh, well, I guess Freddie fell off the wheel!"

We asked, "Who is Freddie?"

Without missing a beat he answered, "Freddie is the hamster who lives in my brain and keeps the wheels turning so I know what I am talking about. I guess Freddie fell off the wheel."

We all cracked up. And while we were still laughing, J continued, "Don't worry, when Freddie falls off, his cousin Twinkle takes over!"

How many times a day does Freddie fall off of the wheel in my mind? And there are plenty of times cousin Twinkle never shows up!

As funny and true as that story is, it illustrates that our human attention spans are so fragile that we can't even hold on to an exciting idea long enough to share it.

Your mind is a neurological work of art, but your cognitive processing ability is limited. By understanding that you can change your brain, you can begin to believe in (or have faith in) the idea that the life you are experiencing can change if you are willing to change your perception. The mind sees what it wants to see and experiences what it wants to experience. And, if you have lived by walking in the same cow paths for forty or fifty years, it may take significant fortitude of your will and your mind to change the way you *think*.

Engage Your Soul

Right now, do you feel a connection stirring in your soul? Do you feel completely connected to your faith? Or are you realizing that you've been too busy focusing on getting the laundry done and on projects at work? Are you one of the 72 percent of people who say they know beyond a shadow of a doubt that faith brings meaningful life? As you plan your day, consider making time to reconnect with your soul.

Much of the 7 Minute Solution involves doing, but reenergizing at the soul level also involves being. It involves being present in the moment, deciding to breathe in life. Make sure you have time to simply be.

I asked Dan Holmes, the psychologist who introduced the idea of creating cow paths to help me explain the concept of neuroplasticity, to help me understand the psychological difference between the mind and the soul. Dan said, "I see the mind as the storehouse of memory and thoughts. I see the soul as pure consciousness. In counseling sessions I often hear people speak of events in their life in a personal form of plurality. They will say something like, 'I felt sad, when I let myself speak so harshly.' Notice the two people in that statement, I and myself. Who are the two people in that narrative and how are they different?"

I asked him to pause so I could process where he might be going. He continued, "When I am counseling this person I believe that the 'I' they are speaking about is their soul. The 'I' is their pure connection with who they want to be. Their 'I' lives in the present moment, is fully awake, and fully aware. Their 'I' feels meaning and depth and richness in life. The 'myself' in this internal dialogue comes from the mind. The mind assigns a label to everything. Every action is either good or bad. Many thoughts are tied to past memories, and if those memories are negative, your mind may lead you to a path of depression. If your mind puts too much energy into focusing on the future, your mind may lead you to a life of anxiety."

As I listened, it became more and more clear that the I or the soul—the present moment—is experienced in the right brain. And the mind—our storehouse of memories and thoughts, the myself—is tied intricately to the left brain.

In order to find faith and meaning, I need to be able to connect to my soul.

It is impossible not to reconnect with your soul when you connect with your values and your purpose in life.

It is the right-brained moments in life when we feel the hair on our skin rise with goose bumps, our breath becomes deeper, and we feel a sensation in our chest that makes us feel alive again. It's like seeing the Grand Canyon for the first time. The beauty of the intricately carved expanse fills you with awe and reminds you just how small and finite you are. But like the river that cut its way through the rock to reveal a beautiful design, you have a purpose to fulfill. Your faith will help you stay the course, even when the progress is slow. Your faith reminds you at the soul level—your innermost being—that your purpose is part of a much bigger plan.

The activities listed above will help you strengthen your faith and reengage your soul. Make sure to make time for them in your daily life.

7 MINUTE SOLUTION PRACTICAL APPLICATION NO. 8: RECONNECT WITH YOUR BODY, HEART, MIND, AND SOUL

Now it's your turn. As you look at the illustration simply take a few minutes to stop and think about how you would like to reconnect with your heart, your body, your mind, and your soul. What brings meaning to your life? How will you live a more meaningful life? What will you do?

Heart . Body . Mind . Soul

How will you choose to live a more meaningful life:

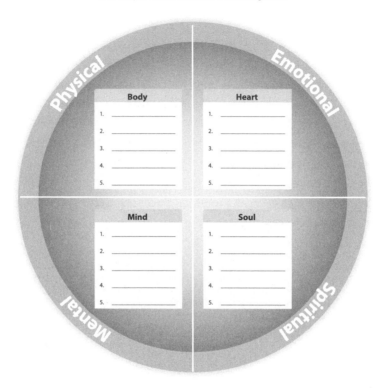

Finding Faith

In 1999, Jim Gramling's wife, Valerie, was killed in a tragic car accident. Her death left him heartbroken, devastated, and hopeless. At the time my daughter was three years old, and I asked her to draw a picture of encouragement for him. I mailed Jim her drawing with a simple note of sympathy.

Not long ago, Jim shared with me how much small acts of kindness had meant the most to him over the last decade. Jim remembers seeing his college roommate getting out of his car to go into his wife's memorial service. Jim hadn't seen his roommate in almost ten years and knew he lived more than two hours away. Although Jim never even got to speak to him, he remembers how much his friend's presence comforted him. On the one-year anniversary of his wife's death his friend Price Marshall left a single rose and a handwritten note on his doorstep. It was another small act of kindness that touched his grief-stricken heart.

Jim is very honest about how losing his wife has made him wrestle with his own understanding of his faith. Jim said, "Anyone who knew me at that time would tell you I *did* allow anger and confusion to overtake me, at least for a while."

Jim quit his job and was unable to do anything other than run. He ran miles and miles hoping the exhaustion and physical pain would dampen his heartache, but his downward spiral continued until, on the third anniversary of his wife Valerie's death, he hit rock bottom. Jim's story of faith is really a story of losing faith in everything. Jim still has questions he hasn't been able to reconcile. He lost his father when he was only twenty-six and his wife at thirty-two, and both of his sisters have battled cancer. His anger, grief, and sadness caused him not only to question God, but for a period to turn from God.

Then, nineteen months ago Jim and his new wife, Lacey, celebrated the birth of their twin girls, Annabel and Madeline. Jim says, "It's not a magic bullet, but it has certainly softened my heart. I mean, who wouldn't melt when you walk into your house and hear two voices singing the sweetest sound of all: 'Daaa . . . dy!' "

Jim and Lacey prayed to have those children and went through in vitro fertilization. "And, just as you hear so often, nine months later we found out Lacey was pregnant again." On May 10, 2011, they gave birth to their son, James F. Gramling III!

Jim Gramling is now forty-two years old. He has gone through trials no one wants to go through, and when I asked him about his life and his faith today he admitted that even twelve years later, there really is no way to get back to "normal."

"Life is a hard path, and there are still parts of me that show the effects of grief. Because of the pain I've endured, I have been reluctant to be as open and vulnerable as I should have been," he says. "However, as the father of our twins and with the birth of our son, I feel an increased urgency to be a spiritual leader for my wife and children."

Isn't that what we all should feel? Shouldn't we all have an increased urgency to know and be known by God? We are looking for answers to unanswerable questions. Like the man in Mark 9:24, we cry out for faith: "Help me overcome my unbelief!"

But faith itself is a gift of grace.

The greatest irony is that when we are at our weakest point, we can know that God is at His greatest.

Jim, like so many of us, is looking for answers to life's hard questions. He wants to reconnect with faith. He wants to trust in God. His children's unconditional love has touched him at the deepest level of his soul. Perhaps their love reminds him not only of his love for them but of the unconditional love of a heavenly father.

Every day Jim's brain is bombarded with millions of bits of sensory information, and he has to choose how he will weave it together and process it into what makes the best sense for him.

Faith, like every other vital sign of life, can be learned. It is shaped by our thoughts and experiences and by our responses to those experiences. But faith can't be acquired by completing checklists. It is developed over time. It is tested by circumstances such as losing loved ones or a job or facing bankruptcy.

Patrick Overton, a playwright and poet, wrote, "When you have come to the edge of all light that you know and are about to drop off into the darkness of the unknown, faith is knowing one of two things will happen: There will be something solid to stand on or you will be taught to fly."

Take a step forward in faith. Your life is waiting for you.

PART III

Creating a Life with Meaning 7 Minutes at a Time

So much of our time is spent in preparation,
so much in routine and so much in retrospect,
that the amount of each person's genius
is confined to a very few hours.
—RALPH WALDO EMERSON

USING THE 7 MINUTE SYSTEMS AND TOOLS

THE STACK OF PAPER on the top left-hand corner of my desk measured more than six inches high. Another stack almost two feet high was hiding under my desk. Every drawer oozed disorganization. Business was booming, but I was crumbling.

The physical clutter in my life overwhelmed me, as did my overloaded schedule. As much as I worked, I never felt I was doing enough. Guilt and frustration consumed me: I didn't have time to finish it all, to hang out with my growing kids, or enjoy my relationship with my husband.

I desperately wanted:

Order
Simplicity
Balance

The idea for the first 7 Minute Tool grew out of an attempt to solve the problem and reduce my stress level. I needed a simple written daily plan of action, so I divided a single piece of paper into a few sections:

- Top Priorities
- Tasks (this was like a primitive to-do list)
- Voice Mail Messages
- Notes

Each afternoon at the end of my workday, I took a few minutes to create a simple written plan for what I wanted to accomplish the next day. And I left it on my desk, so it was the first thing I saw the next morning.

Slowly, this simple process helped me *prioritize* the actions that needed to be tended to first. As time passed, I found I was able to *organize* all of the tasks that had seemed so overwhelming. Though some days I still couldn't complete every task on my list every day, the clarity the list gave me helped me accomplish more than I had before. And finally, after several months of dedicating myself to writing down what I wanted to do, I learned to *simplify* my time and focus my efforts and attention on what mattered most.

This planning empowered me to reconnect with my life. It enabled me to capture the "highest and best" use of my time each day. It freed me to spend more time with my family at home and to accomplish more productive work in the office. Using a single sheet of paper and taking literally seven minutes each afternoon to create my daily written plan of action changed my life forever. Through this life system I was replacing chaos with order.

Through the years, that piece of paper has morphed into one of the most effective 7 Minute Tools in the 7 Minute Solution. This section explains how to use what is now called the Daily Progress Report, as well as a number of other powerful tools you can use to bring more meaning to your life. But you don't have to wait until you read the entire section; go to www.The7MinuteLife.com, click on the Member Tools link, and print out your first daily worksheet. Take a few minutes to write down a few of your day's top priorities, or what we call the 5 before 11 List. This is the first step to living the 7 Minute Life™.

USING 7 MINUTE TOOLS
TO HELP LIVE A MEANINGFUL LIFE

By now you're well aware of the problem: We live in a too-busy, information-saturated world. The nonstop pace distracts our focus and keeps us from paying attention to the aspects of life that bring deeper meaning: our relationships, our faith, our ability to make a difference in others' lives.

The seven vital signs we've discussed—awareness, motivation, growing and learning, engagement, perseverance, flow, and faith—are the keys to bringing the meaning we desire back into our lives. Making a conscious decision to focus our attention on what really matters is the only way to achieve that meaning.

So you are aware of the problem, and you know the solution. In the next section, you will learn how to implement the solution. The tools and ideas there will give you something solid to stand on, as well as the time and inspiration to fly. Life does not have to be an either/or choice; you can be firmly rooted and still experience the thrill of creativity and adventure. We've designed the systems and tools in this book (which you can download free online) to appeal to your left brain's need for structure and order. But equally as important, by implementing them you will free up time and mental space, and you will gain access to your right brain so you can dream, create, and fully feel life.

Throughout *The 7 Minute Solution*, you've been learning how your amazing brain works. My prayer and hope is that you'll use this knowledge and the 7 Minute Tools—worksheets, exercises, and strategies—to improve your life and your results. Specifically, the tools will help you focus your attention on what matters most to you. You must choose what you will pay attention to so you can experience your best possible life. The ability to attend to a task and to concentrate your full attention on something means that you are consciously choosing not to attend to something else. Every choice carries a significant price; what you pay attention to determines the life you will experience.

Your mind is the filter that determines what you will pay attention to. The good news is that you can control that filter. The 7 Minute Solution and the tools we will discuss in this section will help you learn first how to create the boundaries of a meaningful life and then how to create the neuronal pathways to execute that plan seven minutes at a time.

Choice by choice, task by task, the 7 Minute systems, processes, worksheets, and tools act as peripheral brains. Like concrete "rumble strips" on the interstate that alert you when you drift onto the shoulder, these peripheral brains will jolt you into the awareness that you need to make a slight adjustment to your direction. The tools are tangible. You will be able to see them and hold them in your hand. They will act as sensory cues to remind you what is most important to you. They will help your reticular activating system tune in to the activities, circumstances, people, and resources you need to experience a life filled with meaning.

So let's get started! Examples of the tools and worksheets pages of *The 7 Minute Solution* are included in this book, but you'll want to print out copies of the following exercises. Download them free at www.the7minutelife.com under Member Tools. (Feel free to share this website with your friends, family members, and coworkers!) You can begin using the tools immediately, but to get the most out of your efforts, start by investing one day in planning for your next ninety days, and then give yourself seven minutes each day to create a daily action plan.

THE 7 MINUTE TOOLS INCLUDE THE FOLLOWING:

Mental Clutter List
Unfinished Tasks List
Daily Progress Report
90-Day Focus Kit

The Mental Clutter List

Earl Nightingale, Napoleon Hill, and Zig Ziglar, along with countless other personal-development teachers, as well as cutting-edge neuroplasticity research, have taught us that our thoughts shape our reality. That fact can work to our benefit or to our detriment. When our thoughts keep us from focusing on what we want, they are working against us. Such thoughts are what I refer to as "mental clutter."

Mental clutter is any thought that takes up your time and emotional attention. Mental clutter—worry, doubts, fears, and stress—can easily divert you from the path of success. The four primary causes of mental clutter are:

1. Avoidance
2. Procrastination
3. Distraction
4. Indecision

The emotional cost of mental clutter is significant. If you choose to allow these issues to persist, you'll experience stress, distraction, worry, and fatigue.

You can download the full-size version of the Mental Clutter Worksheet at www.The7MinuteLife.com.

What can you do to battle these problems? The first step is awareness. Once you're willing to admit that you have allowed mental clutter to be a part of your life, you can use your brain to overcome it.

Use the Mental Clutter List to make a list of the things that are bothering you. Are you aware of how much emotional energy this mental clutter pulls from you? What are you tolerating in your life? From the tiniest of issues, like cleaning out your closet, to the monumental problems, like honestly evaluating any financial issues, alcohol abuse, or true mental concerns. Now is an excellent time to become aware of the mental conflict you are struggling with.

The most amazing part of being honest about what bothers you is that you don't have to have a solution. In fact, some of the concerns you list may not have a solution. For example, if worries about the nation's economy consume your thoughts, by acknowledging that worry, you will likely also recognize that there may be nothing you as an individual can do to change things on a national level. But by writing down your concerns, your mind, your heart, and your soul will begin their search for answers. For example, your concern about the economy may lead you to take actions to help create personal financial security. Clearing out mental clutter is critical to your success. These mental obstacles stand in the gap between where you are today and where you want to be. (You might want to go back to "Vital Sign 2: Are You Motivated?" and review the section on gaps on page 97.)

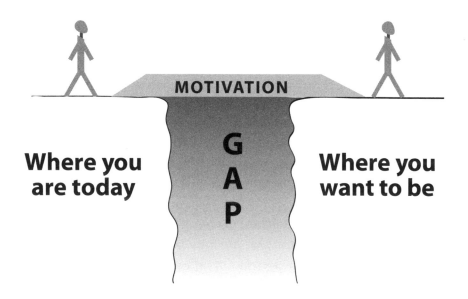

When you clean out that gap, you can move closer to your goals. In the process of completing your Mental Clutter List, you may identify unfinished tasks that you need to complete. Which leads us to the next tool: the Unfinished Tasks List.

The Unfinished Tasks List

Written goals are powerful. But when I first started using the 7 Minute Tools in my own life, I became aware of a deep problem I had with my personal goal attainment. Even as I looked at the goals and action steps I had written for the next ninety-day segment of time, a gnawing feeling in my stomach told me that something was very wrong. It took me several years to understand why I experienced discomfort when setting my ninety-day goals.

Each time I wrote down my new goals—goals that were intended to inspire and move me forward—I heard a voice inside my mind saying "Allyson, why do you even feel like you have the right to set new ninety-day goals? You have so many unfinished goals and commitments in your life right now! Look at yourself, you already have fifty to a hundred unfinished tasks and commitments on your to-do list that you haven't done. Exactly when do you think you'll have the time to work on these new goals?"

Every ninety days I made emotional commitments with myself by setting new goals. When I didn't accomplish those goals, I experienced a sense of breaking commitments with myself. And when you break a commitment, you feel bad. By not having done what I'd said I would do in the past, every time I set new goals I experienced negative emotions. Every one of my unfinished tasks and broken commitments held me back like the heavy rock Dan Reeves talked about in the introduction of this book. Dealing with your unfinished tasks is one of the most important 7 Minute Solutions you have the opportunity to consciously attend to.

As with any to-do list, it is important to actually do what you set out to accomplish. However, for a variety of reasons, some tasks just don't get done. David Allen, in his book *Getting Things Done: The Art of Stress-Free Productivity,* calls unfinished tasks "open loops." As the name suggests, open loops circle continually in your subconscious mind, periodically popping up into your consciousness. As soon as you remember an incomplete task, your brain focuses on it and prompts you to do it—immediately. Your brain believes that all unfinished tasks in your life need to be completed *right now*! You might be able to successfully bat away a reminder like a pest, but it will continue to send out pesky distress signals from your subconscious, making you miserable until you finally stop whatever else you are doing and finish the task.

Regardless of the size or scope of the tasks to be completed, unfinished business causes constant stress and distraction. Open loops perpetually interrupt concentration, pull at your focus, induce anxiety, and drain your energy. That is why it is so important to write unfinished tasks on a master to-do list. By placing them in a single, safe place you stop the open-loop process and put your mind at ease. It is tantamount to your conscious mind reassuring your subconscious that it need not worry, as the task will be done in a timely manner.

The left brain is a constant source of mental chatter. Even as you read this section on unfinished tasks, your left brain has been incessantly chattering to remind you of what you have not accomplished. Like a gnat buzzing in your ear, you hear a barrage of chatter that sounds something like this: "You need to change the oil in your car, you need to get your teeth cleaned, your shoes need to be shined, you have a staff meeting at 10:45 today, you have a report due at that staff meeting, you need to pick up the dry cleaning, you need to call Sarah about lunch, you need to clean up your e-mail box, you need to get a drink of water, you need to lose twenty pounds, you need to go back to college and get a master's degree, you need to create your ninety-day goals, you need to create five-year goals, while you're at it list the top ten things on your bucket list, why haven't you scheduled time for that difficult conversation that you

You can find the full-size version of Unfinished Home Tasks worksheet on page 346.

have needed to have for more than six months? You need to change the oil in your car, you need to get your teeth cleaned . . ."

Whew! It's exhausting, isn't it? And the mental chatter never ends. It disrupts, interrupts, and pulls your attention away from whatever you are trying to focus on at the current moment. We can focus our attention on accomplishing only one task at a time, and the better we become at training our brains to focus on starting and finishing one task at a time, the more efficient and productive we will be.

There is a way to quiet mental chatter and better handle all of the unfinished tasks and open loops that are constantly circling in your mind.

David Allen recommends that you set aside time to do what he calls a "Mind Sweep." A Mind Sweep is where you write down every Unfinished Task and open every loop in your life. On pages 346–47, we have provided Unfinished Home Tasks and Unfinished Work Tasks Lists for you to complete your Mind Sweep.

Every ninety days, I set aside time to go through the exercises shown in this book. One of those exercises is writing down every unfinished task in my life. Every one of them. I separate my unfinished work tasks and my unfinished home tasks. I want to see everything that is unfinished, because when I can see it, I can do something about it. Then my brain can quit trying to remember it, and mental capacity is freed up for higher thinking.

Stop, Thief!

Your productivity is being silently stolen every day. You have thieves in your house. Every unfinished task in your life is an energy and productivity thief.

From the button missing on your suit coat to the mess in your garage, every unfinished task is robbing you blind. These thieves don't steal in big obvious ways. They tug at your attention for only a few moments at a time. Not a big deal. Right?

Wrong.

Their cumulative effect is staggering. You may have as many as fifty of them consciously or unconsciously nagging at you.

Do you realize how much of your life is stolen in a year by fifty unfinished tasks? Even if each task occupies your attention on average for only thirty seconds a day, that's 1,500 seconds, or twenty-five minutes a day of distraction. Twenty-five minutes doesn't sound like much, but . . .

25 minutes x 365 days = 9,125 minutes

That's approximately 152 hours, or almost four full forty-hour workweeks, stolen from your attention each year!

What would your business look like if you had four extra weeks of creative attention, rather than distraction and stress?

What would your relationships with your family and friends be like if you could be mentally and emotionally present with them for an extra four workweeks a year?

What would your sense of peace be like if for four full workweeks a year your mind was filled with gratitude rather than worry?

You must stop those thieves. Your business, your family, your health, and *you* deserve to be free of them.

I have some good news! I am going to help you get rid of them for good. Your productivity thieves are going to be identified, arrested, and removed from your life starting today.

Let's start with an audit. If you haven't already printed out the Unfinished Tasks Lists shown on pages 346–47, you can do so at www.The7MinuteLife.com.

Or grab a notepad and write the words "Unfinished Tasks" at the top of the page.

Now list every single unfinished task you can think of. Think about work and home. Write down every disorganized drawer you have wanted to get to, every project you keep thinking you will complete, every phone call you have intended to make. Write down things as small as sewing on a button to as big as finishing a home renovation. Anything that isn't finished, write it down.

Just by writing those things down, you have begun to stop the embezzlement. The mental and emotional deficit they are causing you has just been reduced. Congratulations!

Get Rid of the Thieves for Good

1. Next to each unfinished task, write the first action step you must take to get moving.
   These action steps can be microactions.

YOU KEEP meaning to take your car in to the shop because of an annoying rattle. Write down: Call and set up appointment for car repair.

YOU WANT to store a bunch of keepsakes in the attic. Write down: Pick up packing boxes on way home from work.

You get the idea.

Writing down the first step is important for two reasons. First, many people procrastinate because they are overwhelmed by the big picture of what needs to be done. Second, people who write down goals and action steps are much more successful than people who don't.

2. Identify the five easiest tasks, and complete them immediately.

   You have been stuck on this stuff forever. Completing five tasks right away will give you a sense of accomplishment and some immediate momentum. Don't make things hard on yourself. Start small and build on that success. You are building dynamic momentum that is going to change your life one microaction at a time.

3. Every time you complete a task, schedule the next action step you will take to complete the next task.

   The biggest mistake people make after writing their list is shoving it to the side and never looking at it again. You can avoid that mistake by using the completion of one task as a trigger for action on the next task. The magic key is scheduling. Never allow yourself the luxury of not having your next action scheduled. This simple step is the defining difference between stressed-out people with furrowed brows and lengthy lists of unfinished tasks and peaceful people who are playing with their family because their tasks are done.

4. Check off every task as you complete it.

   A checkmark may seem trivial. It's not. Every checkmark conditions you to want closure on the other unfinished tasks. Every checkmark releases dopamine and endorphins, which create a compelling internal motivation.

Why not take a Saturday and see how many of these unfinished tasks you can complete in one single day? Many of them may take only minutes. Keep track of everything you accomplish. As you complete an item on your list, mark it off with a checkmark. Don't underestimate the mysterious, motivating power of a checkmark.

Many people tell me that using the Unfinished Tasks List is a significant turning point in their lives. Why? In a sense, this list serves as a written contract you make with yourself. By creating your list, you are making an emotional commitment to complete the tasks you write down. The moment you write down everything in your life that is unfinished and you put that list in a safe location, the mental chatter in your brain turns off. You'll experience something amazing: peace and quiet! Without the distraction of mental chatter, you'll be able to focus better and complete more tasks faster. As straightforward as it may seem, there is an incredible power of emotional accomplishment each time you finish a task and mark it off your list.

Of course your list of unfinished tasks is never-ending, but it can become manageable. When you physically work through one or two of the unfinished tasks on your list every day, you will not believe the feeling of internal organization and control you will experience. Those small steps will help you understand that your personal actions really do matter. And as you reduce the clutter in your mind, you will find new energy to focus your attention rather than feeling constantly pulled and interrupted by what was unfinished in your life.

Every piece of paper on your desk is an unfinished task. Every piece of clutter in your home is an unfinished task. Every unreturned phone call, every unfinished project, even every pound you need to lose—all of those unfinished tasks are heavy rocks that weigh you down and keep you from accomplishing your goals. By using the Unfinished Tasks List, you have the opportunity to work your way through your demoralizing to-do list and begin to learn how to keep your commitments to yourself and to others. By keeping your commitments and doing what you say you will do, you will experience many tiny daily "wins" in life.

It is the tiniest of steps forward that will help you accomplish monumental change.

7 MINUTE LIFE™ STORY:
GETTING RID OF THE IRRITANTS

John Arnold is a raving fan of the 7 Minute Solution. Within thirty days of learning about these tools and strategies, he increased his productivity tremendously. Like most of you reading this book, he had an endless to-do list. At any given time he had twenty or thirty items written on legal pads. Sticky notes, envelopes, and scraps of paper cluttered his office and home. The lists and notes were reminders of everything he thought he had to do, that he should do, that would be good to do—but it was a list that never got done.

As he worked through the process of planning rather than reacting to life, John was amazed by his reaction to creating his complete Unfinished Tasks List. As he held this list in his hands, he realized the mental burden it had become. He called the list "the irritants."

As an example, two years ago John and his wife, Susan, moved into a new house in Texarkana, Arkansas. Not long after they moved in, the light in the laundry room went out. It was a big fluorescent box on the ceiling. John had to climb up on a ladder to reach the light. When he opened the box, the entire fixture tore out of the ceiling, ripping jagged holes where the toggle bolts had been.

For eighteen months John and his family lived with a lamp sitting on the washer and a hole in the ceiling. You can imagine the irritation he felt every day when he walked through the laundry room. John jokes, "For a year I kept flipping the light switch even though it didn't work." For a year and a half he bumped into that irritant.

From broken light switches to buttons off of suit jackets to dirty closets to unspoken conversations to starting your exercise program, unfinished tasks are definitely irritants.

As John worked through the 7 Minute Tools, his first Unfinished Tasks List contained twenty-five items. He got the ball rolling by completing five of the easier unfinished tasks on his list. He refers to starting with the easy tasks by associating it with a principle he learned in physics: the coefficient of friction. He explains that whenever two objects come into contact with each other, there is friction between them. A different coefficient (amount) of friction exists depending on whether those things are at rest or in motion. If you've ever moved a heavy piece of furniture, you've experienced this concept in action. You push and push and push—and the furniture doesn't budge. Then, all of a sudden, the once immovable object starts moving, and once it's in motion, it requires a fraction of the effort to keep it moving. "Mentally, I had to pop my Unfinished Tasks List loose to get it moving," John says. "That's why I chose to do the five easiest tasks on my list first." As he experienced success, he felt the emotional and psychological benefits of doing what he said he would do. Within thirty days he had completed eleven of the tasks, meaning he had eleven unfinished tasks out of his mind and marked off his list. Making his list of unfinished tasks—and being serious about changing his life—was all it took to make a huge difference in his attitude and outcomes.

Fixing a light fixture that has ripped out of your ceiling is not easy, and it requires several steps. John broke down the tasks in "Fix ceiling light" into smaller steps such as "Find Spackle." Finally he transferred his unfinished task to his calendar when he scheduled, "4:00 P.M. Tuesday—find Spackle." It was a simple step that he could commit to and accomplish.

At 4:00 P.M. on Tuesday, he went into his garage and found Spackle, grabbed a ladder, and patched the holes. But it was "fast-drying" Spackle, and once it dried he thought, "I wonder if I have paint that matches?" Then he thought, "That paint is going to be dry in one hour, and I can hang the light." And by ten that night he had a new light fixture in place. He was thrilled! His whole family gathered to watch him flip the switch on the wall. Nothing happened. The bulbs were burned out. But there was no stopping John at that point. He told his family to go to bed; he was going to the store. After waiting a year and a half, he was so excited to have the light fixed that he was going to make it work that night. And he did.

My guess is that if John had written down, "Spend six hours fixing light fixture," nothing would've happened. But his only commitment was to find Spackle. Once he had "popped" through that coefficient of friction, he was able to finish a project that had bothered him for eighteen months.

John shared another amazing insight from his experience of living out the 7 Minute Solution and using the Unfinished Tasks List. "I expected to experience a reprieve of stress and a sense of accomplishment that gave me confidence to do more, and I did," he said. "But marking the eleven unfinished tasks off of my list within the first thirty days of using your tools shifted my thinking about how I paid attention to the unfinished tasks in my life. I find myself now recognizing when something is about to become an unfinished task. I can choose to deal with the task right then rather than let it even get on my Unfinished Tasks List. That change has been huge, and I never saw it coming. I was elated just seeing eleven things drop off my list, but I didn't realize that the discipline of getting rid of them would change my relationship to them."

For John, completing the unfinished task of fixing that light began by scheduling "Find Spackle" for 4:00 P.M. on a Tuesday on his 7 Minute Life™ Daily Progress Report. And that's the next 7 Minute Tool we're going to learn about.

The 7 Minute Solution in Daily Life

Utilizing The 7 Minute Solution in your daily life is a process of stepping back every 90 Days to decide who you will become and what you will focus your attention on. As Mimi Bock said, it begins with the Big Picture.

This illustration captures how the process works. In each chapter we have given you the concrete 7 Minute Solution Practical Application tools and worksheets. But, you must do more than read about them. If you have not done so already, now is the time to go back to each section and write down your priorities, rediscover your purpose, and create your written 90-Day goals, and then focus on TODAY. If your TODAYs have been passing by without meaning, consider if you have been using the six-step process shown in the illustration.

The amount of time you have left on this earth is limited. Just as nature does, the process of The 7 Minute Solution encourages you to reflect on what is most meaningful in your life every 90 Days. Life changes. You change. Don't let life pass you by, not even for a single moment.

The 7 Minute Solution Flowchart

Priorities

Step 1: Rank Your Priorities
What is most important to you?
What's the point?
What do you value in life?
What makes your work meaningful?

Purpose

Step 2: Rediscover Your Purpose
Purpose is how you serve others
Purpose is how you use your gifts and talents to change the world
Love is the foundation of purpose

Life Goals

Step 3: Understand Your Life Goals
Where are you in life?
What life goals do you want to accomplish?
What has been keeping you from taking action?

The Timeline of Your Life

Step 4: Where Are You in Life?
You can't do everything right now
Choose when you will take action

90 Days 90 Days 90 Days 90 Days

Step 5: Create Written 90-Day Goals
Present Tense Specific
Quantifiable Goals

Today

Step 6: Today - 5 before 11™
Know what you want to accomplish
You need a written daily plan of action
Focus on accomplishing 5 high value activities before 11 o'clock

But, life is not lived in 90-Day increments. Life can only be experienced *today*. Today is all we have. As we move into the next section, we will tie this solution together into a repeatable system for you to use every day.

I have spent so much time repeating the key concepts in this book, because repetition and association is how the brain learns. And, learning actually changes the brain. However, if you want your behaviors to change you have to do more than learn, you have to choose to take action.

I encourage you to implement The 7 Minute Solution in your life for a 90-Day period of time. As you reflect on your priorities of faith, family, health, friendships, and meaningful work you will see your priorities appearing more often in your life. Your reticular activating system will act as a huge net capturing those moments in your life and making you aware of the tiniest things you might have been missing before. When you take the time to write down your purpose, and then in 90 Days you write it down again, your written purpose becomes more than just words; it beats into your heart and your soul. As you understand your purpose, you see it in action, and simply living from a foundation of purpose you find more meaning in your life.

And then, every 90 Days you set new goals for your personal life and for your work life, and where you may have been afraid to set goals in the past, you are now filled with anticipation and excitement as you hold them in your hands. They are not just meaningless goals, now they are goals tied to Your Bigger Picture. They are meaningful goals. You believe they will make your life better and the lives of others better when you accomplish them, and you find new-found drive and passion surrounding your work.

And finally, every afternoon, take 7 Minutes to reflect. There are multiple 7 Minute ideas in this book, but taking 7 Minutes every day to think is one of the primary 7 Minute Solutions.

Stop and you think about what is meaningful in your life. Pause and make deliberate decisions for what you will and will not let into your time and into your mind. Be careful about which meetings and projects you agree to become a part of—do so only if they are in alignment with your priorities and purpose. Be careful what you let into your mind. Be aware of what you hear, what you read, what you watch and even who you spend time with.

Take those amazing 7 Minutes and use your Daily Progress Report to focus your high-value activities, and as you write them down, you make a mental commitment to complete 5 high value activities before 11 o' clock the next morning.

And, day by day you execute on the plan you have laid out before you.

You Think. You Write. You Do.

Every step you take draws you closer to a more meaningful life.

Time is a huge element in meaning. Are you experiencing a life with meaning right now? Are you breathing in life? Or, are you longing for more time, more meaning, and more purpose?

Change happens in an instant.® It happens the moment you *decide* to change.

THE 7 MINUTE LIFE™ DAILY PROGRESS REPORT

There is nothing brilliant nor outstanding in my record, except perhaps this one thing: I do the things that I believe ought to be done. . . . And when I make up my mind to do a thing, I act.

— THEODORE ROOSEVELT

'M NOT EXAGGERATING when I say that this one page of paper can change your life. Of all the tools I've discussed to this point, the 7 Minute Life™ Daily Progress Report has made the biggest difference in my life. The human brain craves structure. Most people are seeking order, simplicity, and balance in life. I've found that this simple, one-page tool has done more for my productivity and efficiency and for achieving my major goals than any other time management system.

We've learned that repeating behaviors allows you to physically change your brain. Repeat the right behaviors often enough, and over time success will be inevitable. If you use this page daily, ninety days from today you will be functioning with a different brain—a brain that is hardwired to accomplish what you set out to do each day so you can achieve your dreams.

The 7 Minute Life™ Daily Progress Report is *the* foundational daily tool for the 7 Minute Solution. This tool will help you prioritize, organize, and simplify your life both at work and at home. Many organizing tools help you manage the tasks and projects you need to complete, but the 7 Minute Life™ Daily Progress Report helps you manage not only your tasks but your relationships, communications, spending, and physical and mental health as well. Each of these plays a critical role in your sense of purpose, meaning, and fulfillment.

My friend Donna Feyen offers this description of what the 7 Minute tools, processes, and strategies have meant to her: "At a granular level, I redefined what my priorities were for *each day*." I love that!

The clarity she gets from writing down her ninety-day goals, identifying her purposes, and using the 7 Minute Life™ Daily Progress Report has helped her get and stay on track with her goals. "The biggest outcome for me is having everything in one place," Donna says. "No more Post-it notes, no more torn sheets of paper. I have one location for everything, and the 7 Minute Life™ Daily Progress Report is that location. Having everything in one safe location greatly reduces anxiety and stress."

Let's take a closer look at how the 7 Minute Life™ Daily Progress Report can help you manage all the critical areas of your life.

MANAGING TASKS

Three sections of the Daily Progress Report give you control over the tasks in your life:

- What to do first (5 before 11)
- Unfinished tasks
- Appointments

These sections help you feed, weed, and order the tasks in your life. The 5 before 11 List sows the seeds of what is most important to you; accomplishing unfinished tasks will weed out open loops that are siphoning off valuable energy that could be used on your high-value tasks; and your appointment section provides order to your day so you can be in control of your time.

Donna says that she and her team experienced a huge breakthrough using the 5 before 11 concept. "Our projects are big, and it can be hard to break them down to the simple question of 'What's the very next step we need to take?' By focusing on high-value activities, it is easier for us to clarify what we need to do next."

Almost everyone creates to-do lists, but, as Donna points out, "My 5 before 11 List prioritizes what is most important so I can focus on accomplishing my high-value tasks first. This single change in my daily routine has dramatically increased my productivity and the productivity of our team."

If you commit to completing five high-value activities before 11 A.M. each day, in the next ninety days you will taken 450 steps forward. Those 450 small actions will help you become the person you would like to be. Four hundred fifty small victories, emotional accomplishments, and wins. Four hundred fifty small steps—microactions—combine to create massive change. That's why the 5 before 11 List is an integral part of the 7 Minute Solution.

MANAGING RELATIONSHIPS AND COMMUNICATION

Four sections of the Daily Progress Report challenge you to develop your relationships and monitor your communications on a daily basis:

- Daily Contacts
- 7 Minute Life™ Connections
- Thank-You Notes
- Voice Mail

Daily Contacts

If you are in sales or business, you know that building relationships is absolutely essential. The Daily Progress Report pages are designed to help you track the people you contact and speak with daily. On the left-hand side of the Daily Contacts section, you will see a series of dashes. These dashes allow you to track how many people you attempt to contact. You have no control over the number of people you actually reach, but you do control how many people with whom you try to get in touch. The Daily Contacts section is a visual reminder that will challenge you to invest in personal relationships. (*Note:* Mass e-mails don't count. Your Daily Contacts section should be filled in with the names of people you call or send personal e-mails to.) You can read more about how to use a point system to increase the effectiveness of your contact efforts by visiting www.The7MinuteLife.com. Even if you're not in business, becoming intentional in connecting with others can help you lead a more engaged life.

7 Minute Life™ Connections

People who lead exceptional lives are often experts at partnering. They're always looking for relationships that will enhance their lives. Your list of 7 Minute Life™ Connections is your opportunity to become intentional about developing essential relationships. Your list might include prospective customers, mentors, colleagues, and friends. If you are struggling with whom you should have on your 7 Minute Life™ Connections list, go back and read your ninety-day goals. Ask yourself, "Who could help me achieve these goals better or quicker?" Also, consider whom you can help. Is there someone you could be mentoring right now? Who could benefit from a relationship with you? There is a lot of living to be found in giving.

Thank-You Notes

It almost goes without saying that expressing gratitude through handwritten thank-you notes is an invaluable investment in your relationships. We all know the warm feeling that comes from being appreciated. There is an invisible value to the Thank-You Notes section that you might not have considered: when you are prompted every day to consider for whom you are grateful, you are actually hardwiring your brain to be more grateful. Because of neuroplasticity, as you practice gratitude daily, you will actually begin to have a more positive experience in life. You are physically changing the structure of your brain so that it is easier for you to have a daily attitude of gratitude.

Voice Mail

The Voice Mail list is included on your Daily Progress Report to offer you a peripheral brain to manage your communications. No more forgotten calls, Post-it notes, or "Don't forget to call James" scribbled on the back of an envelope. How many times have you racked your brain to remember where you jotted down a message? Those days are over if you track them on the one sheet you need to manage all of your activities.

MANAGING YOUR SPENDING

Having a conscious grasp on your spending is a basic financial skill. In fact, when helping clients resolve debt, some financial advisors ask people to monitor their spending. If you do not already record your purchases and you begin to do so, you may be shocked by the amount of impulse spending you're doing. Again, the true power of this tracking tool isn't so much in the list as it is in the neuronal connections that will form when you're visually prompted to consider what you spend. Over time, awareness will develop into adopting conscious, smarter spending habits.

MANAGING YOUR PHYSICAL DEVELOPMENT

On the bottom left-hand side of the 7 Minute Life™ Daily Progress Report, you'll see icons for tracking your water consumption, sleep, exercise, and meals. A conscious effort around even one of these areas can dramatically enhance your energy level and your ability to handle stress. Sleep deprivation and dehydration have an enormous impact on your productivity. Improvement in each of these areas can be achieved with microactions such as:

- Drinking a bottle of water rather than a soda
- Turning off the television and going to bed thirty minutes earlier
- Taking fifteen minutes during lunch or after work to take a brisk walk
- Not having seconds at dinner or passing on dessert

Again, just by tracking what you're doing, you will raise your awareness and change your behavior.

MANAGING YOUR MENTAL DEVELOPMENT

How many minutes a day do you take to reflect on your life? On the lower-right-hand side of the Daily Progress Report, you will see several blank lines that you can use for notes that you want. One user of the Daily Progress Report uses those lines to evaluate his day. After answering the one question needed to evaluate the day—"Did I do what I said I would do today?"—he takes a few minutes to reflect on why he did or didn't. He records what worked well and what didn't. Those few minutes of reflection enhance his planning for the next day.

Even a single insight from a conscious period of reflection can radically transform your next day. For example, realizing that you didn't get your 5 before 11 List done because your administrative assistant kept interrupting could result in your asking her to hold any questions or calls until after 11 A.M. That simple request could make the difference between success and failure in accomplishing your high-value tasks.

How many minutes a day do you spend reading, listening to audiobooks, or soaking in a webinar? If you're uncertain on where to start, look at your ninety-day goals. What knowledge do you need to arrive at those goals? What book could make you more knowledgeable? Is there a biography about someone who does what you do that could give you valuable insights? Search online and see if there are webinars that address your goals.

As you can see, the 7 Minute Life™ Daily Progress Report is broken into many different pieces and gives you one location for all your notes, ideas, and goals. The more you use its pages, the more familiar they will become to your brain, and over a few weeks you will actually create mental connections with its layout and design. You will create neural pathways that make executing your daily written action plan possible. Remember the cows in the pasture of your mind. Repeating positive behaviors is how you train them to create a path to exactly where you want to go each day. As the pathways become more pronounced, your thoughts will naturally take the path you want with very little prompting. You are hardwiring your brain so that success becomes inevitable.

Donna Feyen has been to several 7 Minute workshops and has facilitated our online 7 Minute course for her mentoring circle. Although she knows the material very well, she says, "Every time I attend a workshop or reread the materials, I learn new things." Donna isn't alone. Every time we reteach the 7 Minute ideas, they wake people up. When people write down their priorities, discover their purposes, set ninety-day goals that they believe they can achieve, create a master list of unfinished tasks, and acknowledge the mental clutter that has been holding them back, a great deal of emotion is unleashed. Are you ready to experience the emotional uplift for yourself?

Are you ready to live a 7 Minute life? It doesn't take long to plan for success. Planning is a tiny step—a 7 Minute step. But when you take even seven minutes to create the next day's 5 before 11 List each evening, you will take another step toward the life you desire. When you write down the tasks you are committing to accomplish by 11:00 the next morning, the mental chatter revolving around those activities will subside. Once you place your thoughts into a safe location somewhere, your brain realizes it no longer needs to constantly remind you about what you need to do. As the mental chatter slows, you have more capacity to focus your attention and energy on what you need to accomplish rather than listening to your brain's constant reminders. Each morning your goal should be to come in to work and find one single piece of paper on your desk. That piece of paper will be your 7 Minute Life™ Daily Progress Report, with your 5 before 11 List written in the top-right-hand corner. Your only job will be to accomplish those five high-value tasks before 11 A.M.

I created the 7 Minute Life™ Daily Progress Report to help me prioritize the specific tasks I wanted to accomplish on a given day so I could focus on accomplishing my newly established high-value activities. Rather than relying on mental chatter to constantly remind me of what needed to be done, I wanted to rely on a written daily plan of action. Ultimately I found that when all was said and done, my day could be simplified down to one question: **Did I do what I said I would do today?**

prioritize.   organize.   s implify.

THE 7 MINUTE Solution encourages you to *prioritize* what is most important to you, *organize* what you want to accomplish on a single piece of paper, and *simplify* your life down to one question: Did I do what I said I would do today?

Asking this question prompted me to explore why I didn't. I cannot describe the feeling of accomplishment you will have the first time you are able to answer, "Yes, I did everything I said I would do today." A tremendous sense of freedom and peace arises when you say "Yes" to this one question, because you no longer feel that the nagging sense of "I should have done more."

What about you? Are you ready to hardwire your brain so that success is inevitable? Are you ready to say "Yes" at the end of the day? It's time for strategy. It's time for some new tools. This one tool has forever changed my life, and it can change your life, too. All the instructions for how to use this simple but extremely powerful tool are available online when you download the PDF at www.The7MinuteLife.com. The first thing I hope you'll schedule on your calendar is a day to personally walk through the 90 Day Focus Kit, which, by the way, is the next 7 Minute system we'll discuss.

You have an opportunity to change tomorrow today. The 7 Minute Life™ Daily Progress Report can help.

90 DAY FOCUS KIT AND PLANNING MEETING

You can download this *free* kit at www.The7MinuteLife.com. It is filled with the actual questions, worksheets, and checklists to walk you through our strategic planning process.

Why 90 days? Broken into four pieces, a year is much easier to manage.

So how do you do it? We believe that you need to take the time to tune everything else out and Prioritize, Organize, Simplify® your work life. How can your team take it to the next level if you don't all understand what that next level is? Maybe *you* see the big picture, but do you have to clarify it for others? The downloadable tools can help you do that. We hope you will use it over and over again at your regular team meetings to plan where you want and need to go. It is important to revisit these topics again and again to make sure you are in line with your goals and objectives both at work and home.

Planning for the Meeting

THINGS YOU NEED FOR THE MEETING

- A full day to meet with yourself or your team
- A quiet off-site location free from distractions
- Pens
- Calendars
- Blank paper
- A written agenda
- Printed copies of your sales figures, prospect lists, to do lists, etc., so you can see where you are now
- Printed copies of The 7 Minute Life™ 90 Day Focus Kit for each team member

TIME LINE FOR THE MEETING

- Plan to spend the first four hours focusing on completing the worksheets and talking through ideas for where you want to go.
- Continue to talk during a working lunch about ideas for how you can reach your goals.
- Spend the second part of the day focusing on how you can execute your ideas. Who does what? Who needs to be involved? When are the deadlines?

FOCUS WORKSHEETS

You should spend about four hours working through these worksheets together. Everyone should work to fill out the worksheets individually.

8:00   Arrive
8:15–8:45   Eat breakfast and share expectations and desired outcomes for the meeting; complete brief business assessment

Step 1: Prioritize

8:45–9:00   Priorities Page (7 minutes)
9:00–9:30   Highest and Best Use of Your Time (20 minutes)
9:30–10:00   Who Do You Want to Be 90 Days from Now? Health, Home, Work, Family, Friends, Faith, Finances, Learning (30 minutes)
10:00–10:15   Purpose (15 minutes)
10:15–10:30   Break

Step 2: Organize

10:30–11:15   Unfinished Tasks (45 minutes)
11:15–11:30   Mental Clutter (15 minutes)

11:30–12:30　90 Day Work Goals (1 hour): What are our goals for the new year? What are the concrete action steps we will implement to achieve these goals? Who is responsible? What are the timelines?

12:30–1:30　Lunch

1:30–3:00　Open Discussion of Strategic Questions: What is our core business? Who is our target market? What differentiates us from our competition? What is our compelling story? What is our crushing offer? How should we focus our attention? What additional skills and knowledge do we need to acquire? What is the highest and best use of each member of our team based on our personal strengths? What are our personal driving values and priorities? What is our purpose?

What brings life meaning for each team member? Have we clearly defined specific service model roles? Are we most effectively utilizing the strengths of each team member?

What worked best? What didn't work? What will we change? What will we do more of / less of?

Step 3: Simplify

3:00–4:30　Translate all goals into tactical action steps in a 90 Day Calendar. Assign specific task responsibilities to individuals.

We continually have people tell us they don't have the time to commit to taking a full day each quarter to plan. Our response is that if you take the necessary time to clarify and commit to a plan of action that is realistic and in alignment with your priorities, your purpose, your strengths, and your goals, you will be able to focus your attention on accomplishing what is most important and the revenues will follow.

Today is the day to schedule time for your first 90 Day Focus planning meeting.

7 MINUTE LIFE™ STORY: CREATING A LIFE WITH MEANING 7 MINUTES AT A TIME

I first met Rhonda Horne during a training session I was facilitating for a major corporation in 2009. She later shared with me that although she had always had an idea of her purpose, the training that day had compelled her to articulate it.

"It took another year for me to be able to translate my thoughts into a written format," she says. Finally, in October 2010, she clearly identified her purpose. "From that moment on, my purpose has become the point of energy in my life. I have come to understand that it is from my purpose that I live," Rhonda says.

As I interviewed Rhonda about the impact her written purpose statement was making in her life, her voice cracked with emotion. She paused before she read this:

> My purpose in life is to allow myself to be the person I am meant to be. I am first a wife and mother, my love knows no boundaries. I'm a person of action, influence, and forgiveness, constantly striving to serve and inspire others through service, teaching, encouragement, and collaboration. I am a person of faith, a believer in God, myself, and those that surround me. I am a person of learning, building my knowledge so that I share it with others. I am a person of experience, learning how to execute and live with integrity and passion. I am a person of enthusiasm, believing that the work you do is the work you love, and is willing to share that enthusiasm with others.

As I listened to Rhonda read her purpose to me, I felt the depth of what they meant to her. Then she said, "I have something to strive for every minute of every day."

Even before she could define her purpose, Rhonda began to use the 7 Minute worksheets and systems. She says that prioritizing her life and her daily actions empower her to accomplish the ninety-day goals she set for herself. "I choose to focus my time and attention on completing actions that are making a difference in my company. There are plenty of times that I still get busy; in fact, there are times that I am absolutely swamped. But being busy is no excuse for being overwhelmed. We can manage through the interruptions and distractions when we have a plan. When we know where we are heading, we can manage through to the ultimate goal.

"I am using the Daily Progress Report to prioritize what I need to do every day. I no longer have to wonder if this task for this project is what I should be focusing my time on right now. I have a plan of action, and my job is to execute that plan. Step by step, moment by moment, I am executing at my highest and best ability. I write it down, and I do it. I know I'm working toward meeting the expectations of my team members and my directors. I'm helping drive the bottom line."

Learning to use the 7 Minute tools and systems on a daily basis took time and persistence. Rhonda notes that she had to change her beliefs and embrace new ideas. But she was willing to try. "I was ready for change. In fact, I was longing for change. What I was doing simply wasn't working. If something isn't working, why should we continue to do it?

"As I began the process, at first it was hard. Not that the actual exercises were hard, but holding myself accountable to a new system and remembering to create my 5 before 11 List . . . all of this was very new to me. But I worked my way through the first ninety days, and then I started the process all over again."

Today, Rhonda uses the 7 Minute tools and life system to enhance every area of her life. Not only has she been able to achieve her work goals, she and her husband use the system's principles to map out their financial and family goals. She uses the reminders on the Daily Progress Report to track her food intake and make sure she's drinking enough water each day. And at the office, it's not uncommon for one of her colleagues to send out an e-mail asking what's on everyone's 5 before 11 List. The tools have helped her bring order and clarity to her life, but defining her purpose made the greatest impact on her level of happiness and fulfillment.

"Knowing my purpose has given me an entirely different level of confidence in myself as a person. My purpose has put my life into perspective, and my purpose sets the right direction for every decision I make."

LIVING THE 7 MINUTE LIFE

If we all did the things we are capable of,
we would literally astound ourselves.
—THOMAS EDISON

WHAT IS LIFE?

What is the point of a meaningful life?

If you had to define your life at this very instant, how would you define it?

There is no scale of life that can rank good versus bad. Life is not good or bad, easy or too hard, fun or dull, challenging or boring. Life is all of those things. The only thing that can make life good or bad, easy or too hard is your perception of it. Regardless of your circumstances today, they will change tomorrow. You can't always change your circumstances, but you definitely have choices as to how you will react to what is happening in your life and how you will respond to what you are perceiving.

Having served as a senior executive for an international pharmaceutical company for fifteen years, Amy Tyler understands the challenges and pressures of the current economy and work environment. As a business leader, she experienced incredible business success while overcoming unbelievable obstacles. But she lives a vital life. She embodies the principles of conscious awareness, motivation, growing and learning, being engaged, persevering, living in flow, and having a deep understanding of what it means to live a life of faith. I asked Amy to share one practical way that she works to live out each vital sign we have discussed in this book.

THE 7 VITAL SIGNS	PRACTICAL WAYS TO LIVE A VITAL LIFE
Conscious Awareness	Begin by putting your dreams on paper. If you don't write them down, there's little chance you'll ever achieve them.
Motivation	Interact daily with at least one person who motivates you. This may be face-to-face or through a CD or Internet download.
Growing and Learning	Read a book that challenges your values. Have a friend read it at the same time; call each other to share AHAs. This multiplies learning!
Engaged	Begin every day with positive affirmations about your faith, family, and work. Speak them aloud. They will engage your soul.
Perseverance	When times get tough, make lists of what you are grateful for. This is the best cure for pushing through the greatest challenges.
Living in a State of Flow	Determine one skill you are good at and determine to be great at it! This can be done through one simple microaction per day, giving you the slight edge, which is all it takes to be great.
Living in Faith	Proverbs 3:5–6 says, "Trust in the Lord with all your heart, and lean not on your own understanding; in all your ways acknowledge Him, and He shall direct your paths." Put this into practice and watch peace abound.

By living with purpose, she has accomplished what many sales leaders set as their goal: under her leadership, her regional team was number one in sales for the entire country three years in a row. This incredible consistency testifies to an amazing amount of teamwork. Her goal was to ensure that every person on her team:

- Understood his or her purpose, *beginning with the end in mind*
- Knew his or her skill sets *and consistently worked to master them*
- Was continually inspired by the group's goals

As a result, her team worked at its optimal level for three straight years. That's incredibly impressive. What does it take to be number one for three years running? It takes a great deal of planning and communicating, it takes compassion and caring for your team, and it takes loving what you do. But for Amy, winning was not the prize; the journey, the process of growing day by day, was the prize.

Winning was only an outcome.

"Every day may not be exciting and joyful and exactly the way I want it to go," she says, "but that does not mean it doesn't have meaning. I think each day I can grow from what I experienced that day, whether overcoming the challenges or reveling in the positive and great experiences. So meaning for me is how I have grown through that day."

Life is loud, disruptive, and messy. Life is chaotic, and for the years we are blessed to breathe, we spend our days seeking to find order in it. We want life to make sense. We want to believe that our life matters and there is purpose in the chaos.

We must push through the noise. Throughout this book I have used phrases and metaphors to compel you to understand the importance of life:

- Vital signs
- Wake up

- Put your toes out the door
- Push past the one-yard line
- Lean forward into life
- Take one more step
- Breathe in life
- Be present

In the Middle Ages scientists and philosophers believed that the soul resided in the human heart. I believe the soul resides in every conscious and subconscious thought you have.

Picture yourself in a dark auditorium. A video of a human heart appears on the screen, and you begin to hear the familiar sound: *boom-boom, boom-boom.* Let the sound of the heartbeat fill you. The rhythmic beat reminds you that you are alive. But it is not really your heart that gives you life; it is your brain that tells your heart to beat. Second by second, your neurons connect and reconnect, until they ultimately create the path to your success. The microactions you take, the priorities and goals you set, the ideas you pay attention to all work together to shape your life.

If you've learned anything from this book, I hope it is this:

- You can control your thoughts.
- You can create massive change by taking small, repetitive, posi-tive steps every day.
- You can experience a life full of meaning by making a con-scious decision to focus on the aspects of life that matter most to you.
- And, perhaps most important, faith, love, family, friends, and making a difference in the lives of others; as you focus your at-tention on meaningful things, you are connecting pathways in your brain to create a life with meaning.

Life is experienced in minutes—not years. The 7 Minute Solution is about taking time—just seven minutes a day—to recalibrate your life, to bring your actions into alignment with your values, priorities, and purpose. It's time to become aware of what you are devoting your precious minutes to. Because when you focus your attention—moment by moment—on what really matters to you, you will experience a life of meaning.

EPILOGUE

I WROTE THIS BOOK because I wanted more out of life. I wanted more hope, more joy, and more meaning. I believe life can be different tomorrow than it is today. The seven vital signs of awareness, motivation, learning and growing, engaging, persevering, living in a state of flow, and faith for me were merely the beginning of awakening to a new life.

As I live out The 7 Minute Solution I gain a deeper understanding that having a meaningful life is not a destination, rather a meaningful life is the daily journey. It is living up to your highest and best every day. The 7 Minute Solution is enjoying every moment of every day.

Realize that every 7 Minutes is an opportunity to reinvent the world. Every 7 Minutes is an opportunity to reinvent your world. We must choose never to let another 7 Minutes go to waste again. The energy and enthusiasm and depth life has to offer does not have to end: the 7 Minute Solution can help you find meaning in every 7 Minutes for the rest of your life.

In life I was sensing I was on the edge of something incredibly new. Something exciting, a little scary, and completely exhilarating. I hope I've shared that sense of expectation with you. My hope is this book has made you feel something.

I'd like you to think back to the story of Karon Fields. At the age of fifty she decided to jump out of a perfectly good airplane. It was something she had always wanted to do. She went to Bolivar, Tennessee, she listened to fifteen minutes of instruction and then she made a decision to get on the plane. As you finish reading these final pages, it is time to get on the plane. And then once the plane gets to the correct altitude, the door will open and you will feel the cold, invigorating air come rushing in. Just as Karon did, I recommend you surround yourself with a wise and talented community of encouragers.

With her tandem instructor, Karon slowly walked toward the door of the airplane. One step at a time—that is how you live out The 7 Minute Solution.

Staring down at the ground below, Karon felt completely alive again. To compensate for the noise her instructor yelled, "*Put your toes out the door!*"

And, she did.

It's time to ask more of your life—life is ready to deliver what you ask of it. It's time to live with your toes out the door. With the wind in your face, and the challenges in front of you, choosing not to be afraid of the energy or the risk, but ready to embrace a life with meaning.

The 7 Minute Solution Fast Start Guide:

A 31 Day Action Plan

The greatest amount of wasted time
is the time not getting started.
—DAWSON TROTMAN

The 7 Minute Solution Fast Start Guide: A 31 Day Action Plan is a way to keep you on your path. It is designed to be used over a thirty-one-day period to help you take tiny steps forward every day. To fully utilize this book, it will be important to make some emotional commitments to yourself.

We believe that change happens in an instant®; it happens the moment you decide to change. The decision is to change, but that decision is only the beginning; real change is a process, just as in nature you plant seeds, you tend them, and you wait for the harvest. Real change takes time. To produce in life, to grow, takes time. This thirty-one-day guide is designed to give you practical tools and steps to help you grow in a way that will best suit your needs.

Put Your Thoughts into Writing

As you implement The 7 Minute Solution Fast Start Guide you will see that many of the daily activities involve writing out your thoughts and answers in great detail. As you progress through each day, we will explain some of the theories regarding how the brain functions and the importance of translating subconscious thought into conscious activity. To receive the full benefit of this guide, we strongly recommend that you translate your daily activities into writing.

Every time you pick up a pen and write down your thoughts, you are etching them into deeper and deeper neuronal pathways and thus gaining clarity and insight into what you truly believe; somehow you validate your thoughts as you write them down.

You will also notice that certain key ideas are repeated. Repetition is one of the ways the human brain creates new neuronal pathways. Repetition is how we learn and grow, it is how we become familiar with new concepts, and it is what allows sustainable change to occur in our daily lives.

These daily written activities will help you gain a deeper understanding of who you want to become, and over the next thirty-one days, we hope to deliver concrete ideas for you to implement many of those changes.

There are thirty-one sections in this guide, one for each day going forward. It will be structured with a title, it will then have a Today's Key 7 Minute Takeaway, it will have the content, and then it will conclude with a 7 Minute Solution Action Step. It is our hope that this easy-to-follow guide will help you transform your life from where you are today to where you want to be. Life is a journey; this is just part of the process.

All of the tools we discuss throughout this book can be downloaded for free through the Member Tools section of www.The7Minute Life.com.

For convenience, we have created an ancillary tool that many of the members of the 7 Minute community find helpful. *The 7 Minute Life™ Daily Planner* consolidates many of the tools into a single bound book. Its primary benefit is that it contains 90 days of the Daily Progress Reports in a single book. You can find out more information about *The 7 Minute Life™ Daily Planner* on our website.

Day 1: Assess Your Life

Today's Key 7 Minute Takeaway: Know your vital signs.

In order to start the 7 Minute Solution, you must first check your vital signs. You must make a full assessment of your life. You must know your strengths, your personal gifts, your current challenges; you must understand where you are mentally, and much of this begins with the question "Why?" or "What?"

At the basis of this is "What are the most important needs of life?" What is it that you are looking for as you begin this journey? What many people are looking for is self-worth, meaning, and fulfillment. The basis of much of life is understanding the need to love and the need to be loved.

The 7 Minute Solution Action Step:
Make a full assessment of where you stand in life today.
Use this scale, with 5 being the best.

	1	2	3	4	5
Are you aware?					
Are you motivated?					
Are you growing and learning?					
Are you engaged?					
Are you persevering?					
Are you living in a state of flow?					
Are you living with faith?					

Your thoughts about where you are in life today: _____

_____

_____

_____

_____

_____

_____

_____

Day 2: Begin with the Outcome

Today's Key 7 Minute Takeaway:
Who do you want to be thirty-one days from now?

Who do you want to be thirty-one days from now? What does that person look like? Where do you want to go? You must understand the beginning of the journey, but you must also clarify where you would like to go.

The thirty-one days to a brand-new you help you clarify where you want to go, but only you can clarify the outcome of this journey.

One of my friends, Cozy Dixon, has a saying: "Play the movie to the end." I really love this statement because I really believe we are all living in a movie—and we can choose the ending. Much like a famous painter, you can start with a blank canvas and partially create the future that you would like to see.

Today, I'd like you to take a look forward. Imagine your health. Imagine the weight you would like to be. Imagine the types of foods you would like to eat. Imagine your ideal day: What time did you get up? What did you do? What time did you go to bed? Can you gauge your own level of personal energy? What brings you strength, excitement, and courage? What would that day look like?

Imagine if I handed you a paintbrush and asked you to paint your perfect life. Could you articulate it in a way in which all you would have to do was hang the canvas on your wall, look at it every day, and day by day slowly take one step forward toward it? You must begin with the outcome.

Today's action step is to paint the canvas of your life in words. Be as specific as you can; describe yourself in great detail as the person you want to become, look inside your heart, find out what awakens your soul, and listen to that person. Take time now to paint the canvas.

The 7 Minute Solution Action Step:
Paint the canvas of your life in words.

_____

_____

_____

_____

_____

_____

_____

_____

_____

_____

Day 3: What Motivates You?

Today's Key 7 Minute Takeaway:
There is a bigger question than "What motivates you?"
The bigger question is "What motivates you not to change?"

Dr. Dan Holmes explains that understanding what motivates you not to change is essential. "The question is not 'What motivates you?' The bigger question is 'What is motivating you not to change?' "

His question made me realize that there are many actions and behaviors that I am simply not willing to change because I am receiving benefits from those negative behaviors, from not receiving enough sleep to not eating healthful foods to not exercising. What is it that motivates you not to change?

In order to understand motivation properly and to be able to live the 7 Minute Solution where you're willing to step into change, you must be willing to change. We definitely believe that change happens in an instant®; it happens the moment we decide to change. Are you ready to decide to change? It is a simple mind-set, but only you can make that decision. When you decide to change, you will be motivated to eat the right foods, to get the right amount of rest, to create time in your schedule for an exercise program, and to try new things.

Why do you want to change? What is it that you believe you need to be motivated toward? More learning? More competency? What is it that you need? What will make you feel better, look better, and be better? Are you looking only for external motivations? At Seven Minutes, Inc., we believe we must find the internal motivation of what drives us. We must believe that change is right for us, that it's the right time to change, and that we are in a safe place to be able to change. Lasting motivation comes from a sense of rightness in your life. When the activity itself motivates you, you will find internal reward from living out that lifestyle.

The 7 Minute Solution Action Step:
List everything that is motivating you not to change.

_____

_____

_____

_____

_____

_____

_____

_____

_____

_____

_____

Day 4: Prioritize Your Values

Today's Key 7 Minute Takeaway: Priorities are inexhaustible fuel.

Your time and energy are both finite; therefore you must consider carefully which activities and emotions to spend your limited amount of time and attention on. You may be surprised to learn that you are squeezing out things that are most important to you, while lavishing huge amounts of attention on unimportant things. That is why you must know your priorities.

If you already use *The 7 Minute Life™ Daily Planner,* turn to the "Prioritize" page or download the page free at www.the7minutelife .com. Now is the time to prioritize your values. On this page you will see seventy-five values listed; these are foundational values including love, friendships, freedom, learning, influencing others, laughter, and many others. As you look at the list, it is important to decide which things you value most. What is your inexhaustible fuel? These foundational values are at the core of your being; they are your soul; they are what will drive you forward.

The Key 7 Minute Takeaway is to discover your inexhaustible fuel by taking the time to prioritize your values.

The 7 Minute Solution Action Step: Rewrite your top ten values.

Review how you are spending your time, compare it to your priorities, and see if they are lining up authentically with how you would like to live your life.

At the bottom of the page, take some time to review your findings and create some action steps for how you can do a better job of saving time so you can focus on what is most important to you.

1. _____

2. _____

3. _____

4. _____

5. _____

6. _____

7. _____

8. _____

9. _____

10. _____

What did you discover regarding how the life you are living is aligning

with your stated priorities? _____

_____

_____

_____

_____

Day 5: Think, Write, Do

Today's Key 7 Minute Takeaway:
We must move from subconscious thought to conscious activity.

At Seven Minutes, Inc., we believe that there are three words that can change your life forever: think, write, do. First you must slow down long enough to think about what's most important to you. You took the first step yesterday, when you took the time to think about your priorities. Now you need to move from the subconscious thought activity and bring those thoughts into conscious thought.

It is very interesting that the mind uses language to bring ideas from subconscious thought to conscious thought. We think in words, and we can articulate what is most important to us in words. Words are very powerful, but they are fleeting. So the second step in capturing your thoughts is to put your words into writing. Write down what you would like to accomplish in life. Think, write, and then the third step is do.

One of the most important parts of utilizing *The 7 Minute Life™ Daily Planner* is that it enables you to have one safe place in which to keep all of your notes. It's important to keep a journal of your progress. It's important to keep notes on all of your creative ideas, all of your goals, and what you will do to achieve them in one place; *The 7 Minute Life™ Daily Planner* is that place. You don't want to just think about what you want to do, you want to write it down. Then you must translate those goals and thoughts into action by doing them.

Life is full of choices; it's time to get onto the bus, it's time to start taking action.

The 7 Minute Solution Action Step: Make a list:
What will you think? Write? Do?

Think _____

_____

_____

_____

_____

Write _____

_____

_____

_____

_____

_____

_____

Do _____

_____

_____

_____

_____

_____

Day 6: Show Up Ready

Today's Key 7 Minute Takeaway: Expect a call to greatness.

To be brand-new, you have to believe that you have a call to greatness. Can you feel a deep stirring within your heart and soul that says "I am ready to be different tomorrow than I am today"? The key takeaway of today, to show up ready, is much like what the football players I see coming to practice at Arkansas State University, the Red Wolves, have to do. I have learned at least fifteen things about the 7 Minute Life™ from football:

1. You must show up ready. Every day you must wake up ready to experience life in a way that you've never experienced it before. You have to change your mind-set, you have to believe bigger, you have to raise your level of personal belief.

2. It's important to find a coach who believes in you. Who can you go to that will give you the rules and skill sets for what you need to learn?

3. You must play to the strengths of your roles. On a football team there are many roles to play, each one is different, and each player has different strengths, depending on his role. Be willing to play to your role.

4. Life requires a lot of training and preparation. Are you ready for the life of someone who is called to greatness?

5. You have to play through pain. Football hurts, and there's no doubt that life will hurt as well. You must be willing to play through the hurts of life.

6. Football players have a strategy. Do you have a plan?

7. You must execute the playbook. You must know what works and execute from that place of strength.

8. Football players have a mind-set backed up by their skill set. Are you determined to succeed? Are you improving your skills?

9. Sometimes it helps to be in the right place at the right time. As when a receiver catches a well-placed pass, you must be ready and in the right place.

10. In football the players work toward continual improvement. They have daily practices in which they become stronger, faster, and more in tune with one another.

11. Team players trust their teammates. Do you work with a team? Does everyone on the team know his or her role?

12. Football players have the full force of effort behind them. Inertia constantly moves them forward.

13. Football players have to be all in. It is rare that you will see a football player who is not totally in the game.

14. Football players play with greatness.
15. Win or lose, they play. They are in the game. And they come back for the next game. Sometimes things don't go your way, but you have to try again.

The key takeaway is to be in the game; just showing up is half the battle. Be ready.

The 7 Minute Solution Action Step: Answer the following questions.

1. What is your mind-set? _____

_____

_____

2. Who are your coaches? _____

_____

_____

3. What are your strengths? _____

_____

_____

4. How will you train and prepare for greatness? _____

_____

_____

5. What hurts? Can you fix it? _____

_____

_____

6. How are you executing your strategy? _____

_____

_____

7. What is your plan? _____

_____

_____

8. How are you improving your skills? _____

_____

_____

_____

9. What is the right place? _____

_____

_____

10. How are you experiencing continual improvement? _____

_____

_____

11. How can your team improve? _____

_____

_____

12. What provides you the energy and motivation to live a full-force life?

_____

_____

13. Are you all in? _____

_____

_____

14. Are you living with greatness? _____

_____

_____

15. Are you showing up? _____

_____

_____

Day 7: The Reality of Time

Today's Key 7 Minute Takeaway: Time is a finite commodity.

It is important to realize that time is finite. Each day we have twenty-four hours, sixty minutes in an hour, sixty seconds in a minute; time is finite. Look at the calendar below and realize that next week, and the outcome of that week, depend completely on what you do. Every decision you make and every moment you spend is a choice. When you choose to spend your time and attention on one thing rather than on something else in life, that something else never exists for you. That call was not made, that task was not done. Deciding how you will spend your time and what you will focus on is one of the key elements of the 7 Minute Solution.

The choices you make for how you spend your time are how you experience life. The minute-by-minute decisions you make every day create your experiences. Whether you are happy or sad, fulfilled or unfulfilled, whether you are finding meaning in life or not, is defined, executed, and experienced according to how you spend your time. Positive choices fill you with energy and meaning; negative ones fill you with stress, distraction, chaos, and confusion. Take a look at the calendar on the following page. How are you spending your time?

○ Amount of sleep	○ Time spent with friends	○ Time spent on computer
○ Amount of water consumed	○ Time spent reflecting	○ Time spent at office
○ Amount of exercise	○ Money spent	○ Time spent on hobbies
○ Amount of food consumed	○ Television watched	○ _____
○ Number of books read	○ Time spent cleaning up clutter in office	○ _____
○ Time spent with family	○ Time spent cleaning up clutter in home	○ _____

The 7 Minute Solution Action Step:
Using this calendar, learn to manage your time.

Take this calendar and begin to block out the big items—based on your priorities—that you want to schedule time for: time to sleep, time to eat, time to shower and dress, time to spend with your family, time to exercise, time to relax, reflect, and restore. Introduce only those big items into your calendar. You will also want to block out your time for work, then see how little time you have left for other activities. Choose to use the remaining time wisely. Make sure that you have scheduled time for the things that are most important to you. Time is finite, and the decisions you make every day matter.

Day 8: Schedule Time for a 7 Minute Life™ Personal Retreat

Today's Key 7 Minute Takeaway:
You've probably wanted to make real change for years.
Now is the time to take action.

You can think about changing; you can even talk about changing; but there comes a point when you must take action to change. You must take the physical step to actually begin to change. There are 365 days in a year; at Seven Minutes, Inc., we want to encourage you to take 1 percent of that time—or 3.65 days, one day per quarter—to plan your life. This plan begins by scheduling time to walk through the 7 Minute Life™ 90 Day Focus Kit as a personal retreat.

To prepare for this, it's important to get a good night's sleep and go into the retreat expecting to understand new things. We recommend that you schedule time to get away from your regular surroundings. Use this time to update your priorities, to rediscover your purpose, to set ninety-day personal and professional (work) goals, to create a master Unfinished Tasks List, to review your mental clutter list (coming later), and to ask yourself all of the important questions in life. For example, what do you need to do differently over the next ninety days? Who do you want to become? Who do you need to reconnect with? How will you put the next quarter's ideas and strategies into place?

The 7 Minute Solution Action Step:
Schedule a day to walk through the 7 Minute Life™ 90 Day Focus Kit.

Date: _____

Time: _____

Location: _____

Day 9: Discover Your Purpose

Today's Key 7 Minute Takeaway: Develop congruence.

Purpose is what you do for others. Purpose is how you serve the world around you. Purpose is how you use your gifts and talents to change the world. Love is the foundation of purpose.

Take the time to go to this web page and watch a three-minute video on discovering your purpose in life: www.youtube.com/watch?v=5AxMvKjv7sA.

What are you meant to do in this life? What do you enjoy doing? What are your strengths? What things do your friends like most about you? What are you doing that helps you find the most meaning in life? You will begin this exercise by writing down what you love in life.

When I was discovering my purpose, I paused to think about what I love in life. At the top of my list was my faith in God. Numbers two and three are my husband and my children. Number four is growing, learning, reading. Five is sharing through writing. Six is creating. Seven is doing fulfilling work. And I wrote down an additional one of peace. Those are the things that I love in life. What do you love in life?

If you use *The 7 Minute Life™ Daily Planner,* turn to the page entitled "Discovering Your Purpose" on page 18, or download a free PDF of that page at www.The7MinuteLife.com. My purpose unfolded in less than seven minutes. Yours may take longer, but take out a pen and a piece of paper and give yourself permission to answer "My purpose in life is . . ." and then write from your heart about the things you love.

The 7 Minute Solution Action Step: Discover your purpose words.

Boil your purpose down into words that you can easily understand. What do you love in life?

1. _____

2. _____

3. _____

4. _____

5. _____

6. _____

7. _____

Day 10: Set Ninety-Day Goals for Your Personal Life

Today's Key 7 Minute Takeaway:
Who do you want to be ninety days from today?

Whether you like it or not, ninety days is coming. Ninety days will come and go whether you have goals or not, but you have a much better opportunity to become the person you want to be by having thought about what you want to become and by instituting "think, write, do": think about what you want to become, write down your goals, and then create action steps so that you can translate those goals into doing. Think, write, do.

Turn to page 19 of *The 7 Minute Life™ Daily Planner,* entitled "90 Day Personal Goals," or download the 90 Day Personal Goals Worksheet at www.The7MinuteLife.com, and write down at least seven personal goals that you would like to accomplish in the next ninety days. Personal goals should be written in the present tense, as if they've already been accomplished. Goals could include, for example, "I am in the best physical shape of my life. My relationships are healthy and fulfilling. I spend quality time with the people I love. My home is clean and clutter-free. I read a book every month."

For many people whom we coach and consult, one of the top personal goals is to be in the best physical shape of their life. So you would want to write down—in the present tense—"I am in the best physical shape of my life." But consider that a goal cannot be accomplished; the only thing that can actually be accomplished is the task that will take you closer to achieving that goal. Therefore, you will notice on the 90 Day Personal Goals Worksheet that under each goal there is room for up to five action steps. Under that action step I have written:

> Action 1: I walk 30 minutes, 4 times a week.
> Action 2: I do calisthenics two times a week.
> Action 3: I walk the dogs.
> Action 4: I eat healthy foods.
> Action 5: I drink 60 ounces of water per day. (Under "the best physical shape of your life," you could also include the amount of sleep you want to have every day.)

The 7 Minute Solution Action Step: Take each action step and translate it into an appointment on your calendar.

You can see that on the 90 Day Personal Goals Worksheet, you will be able to write down seven goals that are each followed by five action steps. For example, if I write, "I walk four times per week," I physically need to put those thirty-minute sessions onto my daily schedule so that I will find the time to walk four times per week.

What are the first five actions you will take?

Goal:_____

Action step:_____

Action step:_____

Action step:_____

Action step:_____

Action step:_____

It is exciting when you clarify and write down the action steps; however, you might have known the actions you need to take for years. The difference is in transferring what you want to do into time on your calendar to accomplish those actions.

Day 11: Set Ninety-Day Goals for Your Work Life

Today's Key 7 Minute Takeaway:
Communication about work goals is essential.

Setting goals is important in your job. Having goals set for you is very different than setting goals for yourself. As you set your ninety-day work goals, make sure that these goals are in alignment with your priorities and your purpose and establish goals that will ignite your energy for work. Your personal ninety-day work goals don't necessarily have to be what someone is imposing upon you. Your ninety-day work goals should align with what drives your internal motivations.

Please turn to the page of *The 7 Minute Life™ Daily Planner* entitled "90 Day Work Goals" to see how the page is laid out, or download it at www.The7MinuteLife.com. There is room for seven goals, each followed by five action steps. However, with work goals, if you are the team leader, we believe it's important for you to use the page in two separate ways. Not only will you set your own personal work goals, but if you are creating teamwork goals we find it helpful to create only one, two, or three goals for each ninety-day period. They need to be clearly articulated and then followed by specific action steps that can be easily understood. The key element of work goals is to communicate them to every member of your team and continue to communicate them every day for the next ninety days.

People working on your team want to understand what is expected of them and how they can be most in alignment with accomplishing the goals that have been set out. Communicating and accomplishing ninety-day work goals will bring fulfillment and meaning to your work.

7 Minute Solution Action Step:
If you are the team leader, create clearly defined ninety-day work goals that are followed by action steps.
If you are a team member, request that your supervisor work through this exercise at the next staff meeting.

Use this time to brainstorm fifteen action steps you can take to accomplish your top personal and work goals. Be creative.

You may be surprised that the last ideas on your brainstorming list may be the best ones—because they may not be the most obvious.

Day 12: Create Master Unfinished Tasks Lists for Work and Home

Today's Key 7 Minute Takeaway:
Making a list of your unfinished tasks will help you move forward.

As with any to-do list, it is important to actually do what you have decided to. However, for a variety of reasons, some tasks just don't seem to get done. David Allen, in his book *Getting Things Done: The Art of Stress-Free Productivity,* calls unfinished tasks "open loops." As the name suggests, "open loops" circle continually in your subconscious mind, periodically popping up into your consciousness. As soon as you remember that you have not completed a task, your brain focuses on it and prompts you to do it—immediately. You might be able to successfully bat it away like a pest, but it will fester and send out distress signals in your subconscious, making you miserable. The cycle continues until the job is done.

Now consider this. On any given workday you may have anywhere from thirty to fifty unfinished tasks. Regardless of the size or scope of the task to be done, they are stressing you. These incomplete loops perpetually interrupt your concentration, pull your focus away from what you are doing, and induce anxiety. That's why it's so important to put unfinished tasks into a master to-do list. By placing them in a single, safe place, you stop the open-loop process and put your mind at ease. (To your subconscious mind, it is sufficient to have everything in writing and in one safe location. Once you have put your tasks into written form, your brain understands that it need not worry; the tasks will be done in a timely manner.)

Use the pages of *The 7 Minute Life™ Daily Planner,* or download the Unfinished Tasks Worksheet, to create your master list of unfinished tasks at work and at home. You will find space for 120 unfinished work tasks and 60 unfinished home tasks. Write down every project or task in your life that needs to be completed.

The 7 Minute Solution Action Step:
Create a master list of unfinished tasks.

Create your master list of unfinished work tasks in *The 7 Minute Life™ Daily Planner.* Your key action will be to go back to your Unfinished Tasks Lists and choose to finish two tasks per day. Translate your unfinished tasks to your weekly calendar, and make a commitment to mark them off your list.

Unfinished Work Tasks			
Task		Action	
1.			
2.			
3.			
4.			
5.			
6.			
7.			
8.			
9.			
10.			
11.			
12.			
13.			
14.			
15.			
16.			
17.			
18.			
19.			
20.			
21.			
22.			
23.			
24.			
25.			
26.			
27.			
28.			
29.			
30.			

Unfinished tasks cause stress and chaos in your life

www.The7MinuteLife.com   © 2011 Seven Minutes, Inc. All rights reserved.   870.897.0845

You can find the full-size version of the Unfinished Work Tasks on page 347.

Unfinished Home Tasks			
Task		Action	
1.			
2.			
3.			
4.			
5.			
6.			
7.			
8.			
9.			
10.			
11.			
12.			
13.			
14.			
15.			
16.			
17.			
18.			
19.			
20.			
21.			
22.			
23.			
24.			
25.			
26.			
27.			
28.			
29.			
30.			

Unfinished tasks cause stress and chaos in your life

www.The7MinuteLife.com   © 2011 Seven Minutes, Inc. All rights reserved.   870.897.0845

You can find the full-size version of the Unfinished Home Tasks on page 346.

As you start and complete the items on your list, make sure you keep track of all the things you accomplish by marking them off with a checkmark. A checkmark is a mysterious and motivating power. In a sense, these lists are tantamount to a written contract that you make with yourself. By creating these lists, you are making an emotional commitment to complete these daily activities. As straightforward as it may seem, there is an incredible feeling of accomplishment each time a task is finished completely and marked off your list.

We also recommend you read the book *Getting Things Done* by David Allen.

Day 13: Learn How to Utilize Your Unfinished Tasks Lists

Today's Key 7 Minute Takeaway:
Unfinished tasks drain you of energy and capacity.

Your mind has a limited capacity. Even now as you think about the unfinished tasks list that you created yesterday for work, you are now full of a sense that there is a lot to be done.

Now, on Day 13, you will be creating your Unfinished Tasks List for home.

While packing for a trip recently, I had stuffed my bag so full that the zipper almost burst. That is a clear picture of what my mind must look like with all the unfinished tasks that I have in it. My mind must be jammed full of things, creeping and bursting to come out and be completed. If your brain is filled to capacity, how can you have the energy or the time to do new and creative things that will bring you fulfillment? Now is the time to create your Unfinished Tasks List, both at work and at home, so that you can begin to slowly unpack the bag.

Now that you have created a master Unfinished Tasks List for work and for home you are realizing that those lists are like the bags that I have described. Your brain is so full of previous commitments and unfinished items that you lack the strength and energy to complete any of them. Many people feel overwhelmed by these tasks and they begin to understand that they are living in a state of constant chaos and distraction.

The 7 Minute Solution Action Step:
Prioritize the first ten unfinished tasks and translate them to specific days on your 7 Minute Life™ Daily Progress Report.

The power of the 7 Minute Solution is in giving you the framework, processes, and systems to know what you need to do, help you prioritize what to do first, and then translate what you want to do into action. We want to help you prioritize, organize, and simplify your life at work and at home.

Your master task list may have fifty to a hundred items; it may have more. It is possible that some of the items on your Unfinished Tasks List have been on your list for months or possibly for years. Your next job will be to prioritize the list down to your top ten items. Now that you know everything is in a safe place and you don't have to accomplish them all at once, choose your top ten. Once you have your top ten, translate them into two unfinished tasks that you will make an emotional commitment to complete every workday for the next five days. Remember, the 7 Minute Solution is about committing to take small steps forward every day. Part of what is so overwhelming about unfinished tasks is that there seem to be so many of them. By prioritizing them and committing to complete only two per day, you will find it easier to not be overwhelmed. Schedule them in *The 7 Minute Life™ Daily Planner* under "Unfinished Tasks," and then schedule them on your calendar for the amount of time you anticipate it will take to complete each one; make an actual appointment on your calendar to start and completely finish the task. Beside the unfinished task, create the next action you need to physically take to begin the process of completing these tasks. As you finish each task on your Unfinished Tasks List, you will find that you have greater capacity and new energy to bring on new and creative ideas that will again help you discover your meaning in life.

If you completed one or two of your unfinished work tasks every day, within a month or two your list would be completed and you would find you have time and new mental capacity to focus on new projects that are more in line with your goals and objectives.

Day 14: Do Away with Mental Clutter

Today's Key 7 Minute Takeaway: Mental clutter is a barrier.

Mental clutter acts as a barrier between where you are today and where you want to go. As you begin to work through your mental clutter, you will want to ask yourself, "What am I tolerating in life? What am I procrastinating on? What are the things that are holding me back from becoming the person I want to become? What is circling in my brain?" This is slightly different from your Unfinished Tasks Lists in that it may contain emotional items as well.

When initially addressing your Mental Clutter List, you don't have to take action to decide what will get rid of these things. You simply have to take time to become aware of what you're tolerating. Mental clutter often involves things that are nagging at you, that bother you, and that cause you stress and distraction.

The 7 Minute Solution Action Step:
Write down what you are tolerating in life.

Mental clutter vies for our attention. We can focus on only one thing at a time. But as you write down what is bothering you, you may find that your subconscious mind slowly begins to work these things out on its own. You will come up with new solutions and new ideas for how to clear the mental clutter from your life. Be willing to take action when such ideas occur.

Whether it's a relationship that needs to be repaired or a difficult decision that needs to be made, take the time to create a written Mental Clutter List to identify exactly what is keeping you from reaching your full potential.

MENTAL CLUTTER LIST

1. _____

2. _____

3. _____

4. _____

5. _____

6. _____

7. _____

Day 15: Neuroplasticity:
The Brain Is Plastic, or Changeable

Today's Key 7 Minute Takeaway:
Science is proving that the brain is plastic or changeable.
You really can be different tomorrow than you are today.

Neuroplasticity refers to how your brain can be rewired. Our brains are made up of physical structures and neuronal pathways. We make new connections through these neuronal pathways, which are called synapses. According to the book *Find Your Focus Zone* by Lucy Jo Palladino, the connections are formed in direct response to what you pay attention to; they are formed through repetition. Neuroplasticity is a concept that has been around since the 1800s but has become better recognized by science through the understanding of CAT scans, SPECT scans, and functional MRIs (fMRIs). Scientists are now able to see into the physical structure of the brain to understand its "wiring."

To understand neuroplasticity, imagine that on the way home from work today you are somehow involved in a tragic car accident and you lose your ability to see. Immediately, the physical structure in your brain that surrounds the optic nerves, and affects your capacity to see, would begin to shrink due to lack of use. Much like real estate, your brain has a limited capacity. The brain cells—real estate—that help you see would begin to shrink physically. At the same time, because you are not using that space, other cells would begin to use up that space that just moments before had been used for sight. The brain is a use-it-or-lose-it circuitry. The more you rely on specific connections, the stronger they become, but when you don't use those connections—for whatever reason—your brain will immediately use that "real estate" for other processing needs.

The cells that manage your sense of hearing would begin to expand physically and take up more "real estate." The same is true of your sense of touch, your memory, and your sense of smell; all those things would begin to take up additional space in your brain. Through neuroplasticity, the things that you do most often are the things that would begin to be utilized by your brain.

The 7 Minute Solution Action Step:
Choose what you will focus on and learn about,
and repeat positive behaviors.

1. What will you focus on? _____

_____

_____

_____

_____

2. Learning changes the physical structure of your brain. You focus

on what you learn. What will you learn this week? What will you read?

_____

_____

_____

_____

3. You can modify your behaviors through repetition. What behavior do you want to modify? Exercise, sleep, becoming more proficient at a skill or hobby? _____

_____

_____

_____

_____

The most exciting part of neuroplasticity is that thought creates new connections or synapses. What you think about leads to change.

Day 16: Attention!

Today's Key 7 Minute Takeaway:
You can pay attention to only one thing at a time.

In 1890, in his textbook *The Principles of Psychology*, William James remarked:

> Every one knows what attention is. It is the taking possession of the mind, in clear and vivid form, of one out of what seem several simultaneously possible objects or trains of thought.

When is the last time that something actually took possession of you in a clear and vivid form? Are you ready to pay attention to your life in a fashion that will take possession of your heart and soul?

To pay attention, you must focus your attention on one out of many things. As you can see in James's statement, attention implies withdrawing from some things in order to deal effectively with others.

Attention has the opposite effect from distraction. As we can focus on only one thing at a time, my question to you is: what will you pay attention to today?

Attention is one of the things that you must begin to take advantage of. Attention will be the key to your success of living the 7 Minute Life. We have only a limited amount of time and capacity—both in our brain and in our calendars—and every decision you make will impact what you can pay attention to. Also, as you learn to start and complete one task at a time, you will become much more productive and efficient.

The 7 Minute Solution Action Step:
List the things you will pay attention to.

WHAT WILL YOU PAY MORE ATTENTION TO?	WHAT WILL YOU PAY LESS ATTENTION TO?
1.	1.
2.	2.
3.	3.
4.	4.
5.	5.
6.	6.
7.	7.

Day 17: Concentrate Your Attention

Today's Key 7 Minute Takeaway: Focus your attention.

Choosing to focus your attention fully on one task at a time is a skill that will immediately improve your personal time management and productivity. Just as focusing a light beam produces great power, as you narrow your focus you will greatly intensify your ability to accomplish individual tasks and projects.

In the previous sixteen days, you have become much more consciously aware of what's important to you. We make choices based on our values, our priorities, and the goals we set. We must also understand our purpose to determine what to pay attention to.

Now that you have these things outlined, you can direct your attention much like a radio. You can turn up the volume on the things that are most important to you, such as faith, family, and health. You can turn down the volume on things that are less important, such as negative thinking, distraction, and clutter.

According to William James in *The Principles of Psychology*, we can focus our attention on only one thing at a time. My question is: what will you concentrate your focus on today? That is why we created *The 7 Minute Life™ Daily Planner*. Starting tomorrow, we will begin to help you understand how to utilize these tools more fully.

7 Minute Solution Action Step:
Make a list of five high-value activities. What are the things you will consciously focus your attention on every day? How will you do so?

1. _____

2. _____

3. _____

4. _____

5. _____

Day 18: The 7 Minute Life™ Daily Progress Report

Today's Key 7 Minute Takeaway:
Repetition will make you successful.

The Daily Progress Reports will give you the framework you need to create a structure for your day, from the 5 before 11 List to having and knowing the 7 Minute Life™ Connections to having a safe place to put two unfinished tasks every day to being able to track everything else in one place. We believe that you can increase your productivity with this single sheet of paper.

Time management is a skill you can learn that enables you to efficiently use the minutes in your day to focus on achieving high-value priorities. Remember, life is a series of choices. You can choose to live with order, productivity, effectiveness, excitement, and less stress.

All this begins with learning how to structure your daily activities by deciding what is most important for you to accomplish on a daily basis. The Daily Progress Report takes your personal values, your purpose, your ninety-day goals, and your unfinished tasks and gives you a place to record the daily activities that you would like to achieve first and the action steps that you believe will enable you to achieve your purpose and find meaning in life.

It's important to go back to "think, write, do." The Daily Progress Report requires you not only to think about what you want to accomplish ahead of time but to write down your 5 before 11 List and then do the things on that list. By making an emotional commitment to accomplish the things that are most important to you—and then end-

You can find the full-size version of the Daily Progress Report on page 340.

ing the day having accomplished all the things on your list—you will begin to have a feeling of fulfillment. The feeling of authenticity that comes with this process is eye-opening. It allows you to live in congruence with the life you desire.

The 7 Minute Solution Action Step:
Learn how to use The 7 Minute Life™ Daily Progress Report.

Watch three short videos to more fully understand how to use *The 7 Minute Life™ Daily Progress Report*. It is the framework or guideline for helping your brain find the structure it needs and craves in order to function most efficiently.

> Link 1: www.The7MinuteLife.com/DailyProgressReport1
> Link 2: www.The7MinuteLife.com/DailyProgressReport2
> Link 3: www.The7MinuteLife.com/DailyProgressReport3

Day 19: 5 before 11

Today's Key 7 Minute Takeaway: If you complete five high-value action steps before 11 A.M. every day, you will complete 450 proactive steps in the next ninety days.

Completing your 5 before 11 List is one of the activities you should do on a daily basis. Just before you leave the office in the afternoon, turn to tomorrow's Daily Progress Report and make a prioritized list of the five highest-value activities that you are willing to commit to completing before 11 A.M. the next day. Your life will be radically different if you start every day knowing what five specific action steps you must take to get closer to reaching your goals. This process takes only seven minutes a day but can make every day count.

Imagine walking into an office that is clean and uncluttered and placing only one object on your desk. That thing is *The 7 Minute Life™ Daily Planner*. Open it to today's date with your five highest-priority tasks listed. Your job is to complete those tasks before 11 A.M. That means beginning and finishing each one.

This single concept will keep you from living in a constant state of reaction by giving you a daily written plan. At the end of each day you will look at your 5 before 11 List and answer "yes" or "no" for each item on it. It's that simple.

The first step in changing your life is choosing to change. When you do, you will find yourself on a new path to a better life. But after taking that giant leap, you must take small steps to meet your goals. We call these small steps "microactions." The power of this one tool—the 5 before 11 List—cannot be overstated. Because people live in a constant state of reaction, there is little time to determine which daily activities are advancing your goals. Microactions are tools that turn your ninety-day goals into daily activities.

The 7 Minute Solution is about taking small steps toward your goals every day. It is the *every day* part that is the most difficult. The 5 before 11 List enables you to commit to small, daily activities that will propel you toward success. *The small wins will keep you motivated.*

The 7 Minute Solution Action Step:
Clarify the high-priority action steps for your life at work and at home that you would like to accomplish in the next ninety days.

When we consult with executives, we often find that they have been so busy with fire drills that they have forgotten the basic actions that originally made them most successful.

Day 20: 7 Minute Life™ Connections

Today's Key 7 Minute Takeaway: Life connections bring meaning.

In this segment of the 7 Minute Solution process, you will find a page that asks you to list thirty 7 Minute Life™ Connections in business and thirty 7 Minute Life™ Connections in your personal life.

The sad part of technology is that it often isolates us from the parts of life that have made it most meaningful. Through texting, tweeting, and Facebooking, we have isolated ourselves from one another. Many people also spend hours each day in front of a television rather than connecting with people face-to-face. The 7 Minute Solution involves making sure that you spend time with other people both at work and at home. These are two things that can make your whole life more successful.

The 7 Minute Solution Action Step:
Create two lists of people—one for work and one for your personal life—whom you would like to connect with over the next thirty-one days.

Connections
business

Friends . Network . Prospects.
Who do you know that you need to stay in touch with?

Connection	Phone	Comments	Stay Connected
1.			
2.			
3.			
4.			
5.			
6.			
7.			
8.			
9.			
10.			
11.			
12.			
13.			
14.			
15.			
16.			
17.			
18.			
19.			
20.			
21.			
22.			
23.			
24.			
25.			
26.			
27.			
28.			
29.			
30.			

Connections
personal

Friends . Network . Prospects.
Who do you know that you need to stay in touch with?

Connection	Phone	Comments	Stay Connected
1.			
2.			
3.			
4.			
5.			
6.			
7.			
8.			
9.			
10.			
11.			
12.			
13.			
14.			
15.			
16.			
17.			
18.			
19.			
20.			
21.			
22.			
23.			
24.			
25.			
26.			
27.			
28.			
29.			
30.			

You can download the full-size version of the 7 Minute Life™ Business Connections at www.The7MinuteLife.com.

You can download the full-size version of the 7 Minute Life™ Personal Connections at www.The7MinuteLife.com.

Day 21: Track Your Progress

Today's Key 7 Minute Takeaway:
You will become what you do and what you track.

Tracking is one of the first steps to personal accountability. Are you aware of the level of exercise you do on a daily basis? Are you aware of the amount of water you consume? Are you aware of what you eat? Are you aware of how much sleep you get? How much you reflect or pray? How many books and how many minutes you spend reading? Do you know how much money you spend?

At the bottom of every page of the Daily Progress Report are several boxes for you to track your activity. We encourage you to drink at least eight eight-ounce glasses of water per day. We encourage you to increase the amount of sleep you get, the amount of exercise you do, the amount of time you spend reflecting, and the amount of time you spend reading, and even to track what you put into your body as fuel. The boxes at the bottom of the page will act as psychological triggers to remind you of the things that are physically important to you.

Your spending plays a part in how you experience life. Staying hydrated plays an important role in making sure you have the energy you need. Sleep and restoration are key elements of the 7 Minute Solution. Certainly doing physical exercise and making sure that your body has the amount of energy it needs to aspire to greatness every day are important. Also important are reflection and taking time to take inventory, to practice faith, to reflect on the things that are most important to you, and to continually learn by spending time reading. The fuel that you take into your body both physically and spiritually is key.

The 7 Minute Solution Action Step:
Begin to track your daily actions to bring into focus
each of your activities and track your improvement.

- By tracking in writing, you instantly become aware of your progress.
- Track one or two items a week to become more aware of your habits.
- Choose what you will track from the following list.

○ Amount of sleep	○ Time spent with friends	○ Time spent on computer
○ Amount of water consumed	○ Time spent reflecting	○ Time spent at office
○ Amount of exercise	○ Money spent	○ Time spent on hobbies
○ Amount of food consumed	○ Television watched	○ _____
○ Number of books read	○ Time spent cleaning up clutter in office	○ _____
○ Time spent with family	○ Time spent cleaning up clutter in home	○ _____

Day 22: Send Thank-You Notes

Today's Key 7 Minute Takeaway: Be thankful.

The first thought that I have about thank-you notes is: are we truly thankful? I can count how many thank-you notes I received last year through the mail on my fingers. Fewer than five of those were hand-written. It's amazing the impact a handwritten thank-you note makes. I save many of the handwritten thank-you notes I receive simply because they are so personal in nature.

The 7 Minute Solution Action Step:
Today, buy thank-you cards and stamps and take the time
to write three thank-you notes to three people.

Examples of thank-you notes:

Dear _____:
There is absolutely no reason for me writing this letter other than to say THANK YOU. Thank you for your business and for the confidence you have placed in us. It is a pleasure doing business with you, and I consider you one of my most valued clients.

I am here to be of service to you. Thanks again for the opportunity to earn your trust and confidence.

Sincerely,

Dear _____:
I just wanted to write you a quick thank-you note for your time today. We appreciate your confidence, your friendship, and your business. Please let us know whenever we can be of service to you.

Thanks again,

To whom will you write?

1. _____

2. _____

3. _____

Day 23: Prioritize, Organize, Simplify

Today's Key 7 Minute Takeaway: Simplify.

This graphic is a visual representation of applying The 7 Minute Solution to your life. So many people find themselves in a swirl of chaos, confusion, and constant distraction. They feel the emotional stress of being pulled in so many directions. The 7 Minute tools give you the structure to organize your thoughts and your daily actions to live a more congruent and meaningful life.

But, for me the most important element has been the understanding that I truly do not have to do more every day. Rather, it is when I know exactly what I need to do and that it is in simplifying my life that I can become more effective.

At the bottom left of every page of the Daily Progress Report, you will see one simple question: Did I do what I said I would do today? The answer is "yes" or "no." Look back over your last week. Are you taking steps to meet your goals? Are you growing? Are you spending time on the items you said are your priorities? Is your life congruent with what you hope to achieve? Are you living in alignment with what you value most, or have you become distracted? Continuously read through your ninety-day goals for home, your ninety-day goals for work, your priorities, and your purposes, and make sure you focus on what's most important to you.

At the end of the day, the purpose of the 7 Minute Solution is to help people get rid of the chaos in their lives and to organize them in a fashion in which they can clearly see where they want to go. The purpose is to be able to simplify it down to one page where they can accomplish five things before 11:00, stay connected with the people who are most important to them through their 7 Minute Life™ Connections, encourage them to clear the decks by checking off unfinished tasks from work and home every day, and monitor how much they're spending, how much water they're drinking, how much they're sleeping, exercising, praying, and reading, and even what they're eating. So at the end of the day you can ask yourself a simple question: "Did I do what I said I would do today?" You can simplify all of that down to a "yes" or "no" question. The power is in doing what you said you will do. Nike made the idea famous when it said, "Just do it"; at Seven Minutes, Inc., we want to help you simplify your life down to "Did I do it?"

The 7 Minute Solution Action Step: Create your ideal day.

Reflect on what an ideal day at home and at work would look like. Describe it in detail. What time do you get up? What do you wear? What do you do? Who are you with? What do you accomplish? What do you say you will do?

DESCRIBE YOUR IDEAL WORKDAY	DESCRIBE YOUR IDEAL DAY AT HOME
_____	_____
_____	_____
_____	_____
_____	_____
_____	_____
_____	_____

Day 24: Creating Your Optimal Life

Today's Key 7 Minute Takeaway: Understand the definition of "flow."

In 1990, Mihaly Csikszentmihalyi published the national best seller *Flow: The Psychology of Optimal Experience.* Flow can be defined by saying that athletes are in the flow or you feel in the flow of life or you're in the zone. Flow is when you experience this optimal life. As I understand flow, there are many things involved in creating flow in your life. Flow is reaching just beyond what you can do on your own.

Human beings crave learning, growing, and expanding. Goals are incredibly important in experiencing flow; they must be realistic yet still able to pull you forward. Having clear goals is essential to having flow. Concentrating and being able to pay full attention to something are the essence of flow. When you are in flow, time ceases. You are so in the moment, so swept away by what you are doing, that the activity itself is the reward. I find it amazing that when you are experiencing flow, life seems so effortless, so purposeful. When was the last time you had that feeling of flow—a feeling of purpose, unconscious excitement, and enjoyment?

Flow pulls us beyond ourselves; flow draws us out. What is so amazing is that flow makes us feel utterly in control of our calling, yet most often when we experience flow we are serving others. It is very interesting to see that time and self disappear in flow.

The 7 Minute Solution Action Step: Describe your optimal life.

When was the last "best day of your life"? _____

_____

_____

_____

How did you feel this morning when you woke up? _____

_____

_____

_____

_____

What would it take to make you wake up feeling a sense of anticipation

that life could be amazing? _____

_____

_____

_____

_____

Do you have a deep understanding of your purpose in life? _____

_____

_____

_____

Do you know what drives you? _____

_____

_____

_____

Why are you willing to work so hard, and when do you feel that you are

in the zone? _____

_____

_____

_____

Are you living an optimal life? _____

_____

_____

_____

Day 25: Read

Today's Key 7 Minute Takeaway:
Reading books changes the physical structure of your brain.

Due to neuroplasticity, what you put into your mind changes the physical structure of your brain. Reading the right books will change you into the person you want to become.

Imagine that your brain is a suitcase; everything you stuff into it will become part of that suitcase, which is bulging with unfinished tasks. What if you could finish the unfinished tasks that are in there and have an empty suitcase? What would you choose to fill your mind with? If you actually created capacity in your brain and increased your free time, how would you choose to fill that case? I want to fill it with books that stimulate my imagination and make my soul soar. I want to read books that teach me about people whose lives inspire confidence, who teach me courage, and who make me want to persevere through the most difficult times in life. I want to read books of history, books about greatness, books about people's mistakes so that I won't repeat them, and books by people who have created great servanthood.

You can see our recommended reading list at www.The7Minute Life.com/reading/index.html.

The 7 Minute Solution Action Step:
Decide which book you will read next.

The best way to read is to have a disciplined approach, reading ten pages each day. Though this isn't necessarily a 7 Minute microaction, we believe that reading ten pages each day can change your life. If you can read ten pages each day and there are thirty days in a month, every thirty days you could read a three-hundred-page book that could change your life. Reading books that will help you reach your goals and sharing ideas from those books with friends will increase your confidence and give you opportunities to grow and learn. The emotional impact of learning is overwhelming.

There is also a service, www.audible.com, where, for a fee, you can download a specific number of books every month and add them to your permanent collection An electronic reader is another great idea so you can have access to many books. But if you're like me, I like to add books to my physical, permanent collection so I can hold them in my hands, mark in them, and make them part of my life. Whatever way you find it best to read, make reading part of your life.

Day 26: Deal with Clutter

Today's Key 7 Minute Takeaway:
Physical clutter is a barrier between what you want
to accomplish and how you will get there.

It is time to declutter your space. The stack of paper that is sitting on your desk is actually a to-do list of things that you have simply not decided what to do with yet. Gather up all the loose papers, and schedule a time on your calendar to tend to each one, file it, trash it, or take action on it. If you're an Outlook user, you can create a list of items in your Outlook tasks. You can also add a file to your Unfinished Tasks List and then schedule a time to tend to it.

To declutter your space, you will also want to organize your e-mail and your computer file folders and buy the supplies you need to be efficient: Post-it notes, markers, staplers, paper clips, extra ink for your printer, and a professional file labeler. By having professional labels on your files, you will keep the most important things in the proper order. Decluttering and simplifying your work space will save you a lot of time and make you more efficient. The time spent is well worth the investment.

The 7 Minute Solution Action Step:
Deal with physical clutter. Schedule a time on your calendar to spend several hours decluttering the paper in your office.

Clutter, procrastination, unfinished projects, poorly organized work flow systems, and an overflow of paper are common situations. Creating a clean, organized work space is the goal. The following checklist should merely serve as a starting point for simplifying and improving your daily work environment.

1. ____ Declutter your desk and credenza. Start with the top of your desk. Then move to each drawer and even through the old file folders.
2. ____ Set a goal to reduce the physical amount of paper in your office by 50 percent. If a file or piece of paper is not absolutely necessary for helping you reach your goals, give yourself the freedom to throw it away.
3. ____ Make a decision to touch each piece of paper only once. Do not leave an unfinished task unfinished. Tend to it, delegate it, trash it, or put it into a time slot on your calendar when you will complete the task.
4. ____ Clean up and tend to your e-mail folders: the inbox and sent and deleted folders.

5. _____ Call your computer support hotline and fix any nagging computer issues that have not been fully resolved.

6. _____ Make sure your written correspondence is up to date. Have you written all of the letters and thank-you notes you need to? Make a list, and set a specific time on your calendar to finish those tasks.

7. _____ Throw away all old training materials and binders that are no longer relevant to helping you grow your business.

8. _____ Get rid of everything that does not work. Throw away or destroy old laptops, pens, and any other machines and objects that are out of date or broken.

9. _____ Put together a box of useful items that you sometimes need at the office and never have available: Band-Aids, antibiotic ointment, comb or brush, deodorant, lotion, nails, hammer, screwdriver, and so on. Place them all in one location.

10. _____ Once the clutter has been removed, take the time to deep-clean your entire office, dust the furniture, plants, and picture frames, wipe out the inside of the drawers, vacuum under your desk, wipe down the baseboards, replace any burned-out lightbulbs, dust the bottom of your office furniture, and clean the windows.

The key will be to set a regular time on your calendar to spend one hour per week staying organized and keeping your work space clean.

Day 27: Home Repair and Car Repair

Today's Key 7 Minute Takeaway:
Nonworking items cause unnecessary stress.

How often have you walked into a room and turned on the light only to find that the light fixture is out? Rather than taking the two minutes necessary to fix the lightbulb, have you ever walked across the room to a different lamp and turned on the light?

It's time to make a list of everything in your home that needs repair and everything about your car that needs to be fixed. Make a complete list, prioritize that list, and then schedule the time and people necessary to fix them.

Home and car repairs can be incredibly frustrating. Having a leaky faucet is always on your mind. Call a repairman and get it fixed. Think about how good it will make you feel afterwards.

The 7 Minute Solution Action Step:
Prioritize the items you would like to have repaired,
and schedule a time to do so.

REPAIR NEEDED	WHO TO CALL	PHONE NO.	EST. COST
_____	_____	_____	$ _____
_____	_____	_____	$ _____
_____	_____	_____	$ _____
_____	_____	_____	$ _____
_____	_____	_____	$ _____
_____	_____	_____	$ _____
_____	_____	_____	$ _____
_____	_____	_____	$ _____
_____	_____	_____	$ _____
_____	_____	_____	$ _____

Day 28: Being Accountable

Today's Key 7 Minute Takeaway: You must have someone to help you push through the process of accountability.

To learn and grow, we must constantly challenge ourselves to take on new projects and new priorities. Some of us may find this a lonely process. We find it helpful to find someone to go on the journey with you.

Start a four- to five-person mastermind group for the following ninety days. Have one conference call every month for the next three months. Choose a topic on what you'd like to be mentored on and how you'd like to be held accountable.

A great resource for scheduling free conference calls is www.free conferencecall.com.

The 7 Minute Solution Action Step:
Who will you select to be involved in your mastermind group?

NAME	PHONE NUMBER
1.	
2.	
3.	
4.	
5.	

Day 29: The One-Yard Line

Today's Key 7 Minute Takeaway: Finish what you start.

In my book *The Seven Minute Difference,* there is an entire chapter about what it means to push past the one-yard line of life. Many of you who know me know that I am an enormous football fan. I love to watch football because there are so many tactical decisions that have to be made. I love the competition and everything about it. But as we said at the beginning, it's always amazing to watch the offensive team catch the ball in its own end zone, run the ball ninety-nine yards, and land on the one-yard line right in front of the opposing team's end zone. It just cannot go the final thirty-six inches to score the touchdown. Those guys weigh 300-plus pounds, they're in the best physical shape of their lives, and I want to yell, "Dude, just lean forward! Just lean over, and you'll be in the end zone!" But there is so much pushing against them that they just cannot go that final thirty-six inches.

Then I started looking at my own life and I thought, "You know what? There are years of your life when you did well, but you never really scored that touchdown, you were never really in the end zone."

The best example I can give you of this comes from my book *The Seven Minute Difference*. In that book I talk about the phenomenon of the one-yard line:

> This phenomenon is not limited to football either. Common wisdom in the business community says that although many executives can move a project to 98 percent of completion, only a few actually finish the last 2 percent successfully. I see this 2 percent rule at work all the time; people achieve true success and growth in their business and personal lives only to stop short of fully accomplishing their goals. They do well but they never quite live up to their full potential; they just cannot seem to push past the one-yard line that separates them from peak performance.

By now you've gone through twenty-eight days of this process. Today we want to take you through the last thirty-six inches, to help you push past the one-yard line of life. We want to help you organize your life and bring in some habits that can become repeatable processes and systems. As you think about this, picture the one-yard line in life. Maybe you are not very far from where you want to be. All we want to do is help you move the chaos out of your life so you can push forward, go that last thirty-six inches, and get to where you want to be.

The 7 Minute Solution Action Step:
Write about what is keeping you from leaning forward into life.

_____

_____

_____

_____

_____

_____

_____

_____

_____

_____

Day 30: Serving

Today's Key 7 Minute Takeaway:
Life is not about us, it's about serving others.

Part of the 7 Minute Solution involves serving others. It's about serving, loving, connecting, sharing, and growing. It's about reaching into your heart, understanding your gifts and talents, and finding out what drives you most. You will find that serving others and using your efforts to help make the world a better place will bring meaning, fulfillment, and flow into your life. To create an optimal life, we must reach inside our hearts and souls and live a life that is in congruence with what we most value.

The 7 Minute Solution Action Step: Create a plan to serve others.

WHO WILL YOU SERVE?   HOW WILL YOU SERVE?

_____   _____

_____   _____

_____   _____

_____   _____

_____   _____

_____   _____

Day 31: What have you learned? What will you do?

Today's Key 7 Minute Takeaway:
Think, write, do. Prioritize, organize, simplify.
Change happens in an instant.®
It happens the moment you decide to change.

There's not much left for us to say. Now it's your turn. Now is the time to take what you have learned and decide what you will do with it. Life isn't just in the planning; life is in the doing. We experience life through our thoughts, we enjoy them as we write them down, but we live life by doing.

Your final action step is *do*.

The 7 Minute Solution Action Step: Make a list of what you will do.

1. _____

2. _____

3. _____

4. _____

5. _____

6. _____

7. _____

8. _____

9. _____

10. _____

For More Information

The 7 Minute Solution Fast Start Guide—A 31 Day Action Plan was cowritten by Allyson Lewis and Susan Naylor. Susan is the President of Seven Minutes, Inc. To find out more about the 7 Minute tools, ideas, and concepts and how you can join the 7 Minute Community, visit www.The7MinuteLife.com.

To find out how you can connect with Allyson Lewis and have her speak to your group, please e-mail Susan Naylor at susan@The 7MinuteLife.com or call her at 870-897-0845.

Welcome to the 7 Minute Solution!

The 7 Minute Solution Tools and Worksheets

At Seven Minutes, Inc., we strive to help people prioritize, organize, and simplify their lives at home and at work. In this appendix you will find what we call our 7 Minute Productivity Pack. It is filled with several of our most popular time management and productivity tips, tools, and worksheets.

With proper copyright, all of these forms may be copied and distributed with full permission.

You can also download PDF versions by visiting www.The7Minute Life.com and subscribing to the Member Tools section.

daily progress report
with contacts

S M T W Th F S
○ ○ ○ ○ ○ ○ ○ _____

date

Minute Life

Daily Contacts

1. _____
2. _____
3. _____
4. _____
○ 5. _____
6. _____
7. _____
8. _____
9. _____
○ 10. _____
11. _____
12. _____
13. _____
14. _____
○ 15. _____
16. _____
17. _____
18. _____
19. _____
○ 20. _____
21. _____
22. _____
23. _____
24. _____
○ 25. _____

What I will do... *5 before 11*™

1. _____ ○
2. _____ ○
3. _____ ○
4. _____ ○
5. _____ ○

"7 Minute Life" Connections

1. _____ ○
2. _____ ○
3. _____ ○

Unfinished Tasks

1. _____ ○
2. _____ ○
3. _____ ○
4. _____ ○
5. _____ ○
6. _____ ○
7. _____ ○
8. _____ ○
9. _____ ○
10. _____ ○

What I Spent

item   amount
1. _____ ○
2. _____ ○
3. _____ ○

water: 🥛🥛🥛🥛🥛🥛🥛🥛

sleep in hours | exercise in minutes | reflection in minutes | reading in minutes

breakfast   lunch   dinner

snack   snack

Did I do what I said
I would do today?   Yes   No

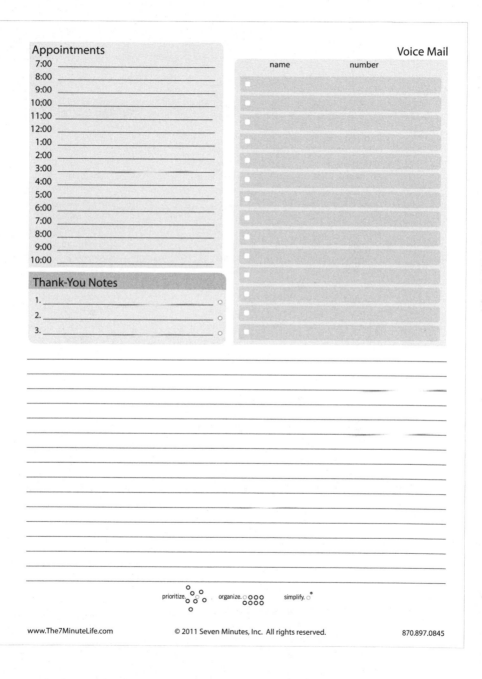

Appointments

7:00	
8:00	
9:00	
10:00	
11:00	
12:00	
1:00	
2:00	
3:00	
4:00	
5:00	
6:00	
7:00	
8:00	
9:00	
10:00	

Voice Mail

name   number

Thank-You Notes

1.
2.
3.

prioritize. organize. simplify.

870.897.0845

Prioritize

What's Important
Define and Prioritize your top 10 Personal Values

7 Minute Life

Rank ✓			Rank ✓			Rank ✓	
○ Love			○ Faith			○ Family	
○ Friendships			○ Change			○ Serving others	
○ Achievement			○ Philanthropy			○ Leading	
○ Excitement			○ Authenticity			○ Solitude	
○ Arts			○ Balance			○ Time	
○ Community			○ Laughter			○ Honesty	
○ Happiness			○ Influencing others			○ Knowledge	
○ Security			○ Compassion			○ Recognition	
○ Meaningful work			○ Money			○ Contributing	
○ Helping			○ Nature			○ Inspire	
○ Choice			○ Sharing			○ Pleasure	
○ Freedom			○ Competence			○ Health	
○ Intimacy			○ Joy			○ Self-respect	
○ Success			○ Efficiency			○ Teaching	
○ Adventure			○ Growing			○ Stability	
○ Independence			○ Adventure			○ Expertise	
○ Power			○ Peace			○ Travel	
○ Learning			○ Integrity			○ Connecting	
○ Fun			○ Creativity			○ Recreation / Play	
○ Passion			○ Belonging			○ Making a difference	
○ Comfort			○ Advancement			○ Competition	
○ Trust			○ Relationships			○ Financial security	
○ Order			○ Intellect			○ Decisiveness	
○ Reach full potential			○ Excellence			○ Taking risk	
○ Wisdom			○ Tradition			○ Leaving a legacy	

Prioritize   We all value different things and our values influence our actions, our attitudes, and the choices we make in life. Please check and rank your top 10 personal values. List what is most important to you below.

1. _____   6. _____

2. _____   7. _____

3. _____   8. _____

4. _____   9. _____

5. _____   10. _____

Discovering Your Purpose

Minute Life

Purpose is what you do for others.
Purpose is how you use your gifts and talents to change the world.
Love is the foundation of purpose.

My purpose in life is.....

_____

What I Love

1. _____
2. _____
3. _____
4. _____
5. _____
6. _____
7. _____

Purpose Words

1. _____
2. _____
3. _____
4. _____
5. _____
6. _____
7. _____

At the age of 85, I will know I have fulfilled my purpose when: _____

_____

Signed _____   Dated _____

90 Day Personal Goals

Minute Life

Date:_____

Goals	Completed By

1. _____   _____

Action:_____
Action:_____   What was the outcome?
Action:_____
Action:_____
Action:_____

2. _____   _____

Action:_____
Action:_____   What was the outcome?
Action:_____
Action:_____
Action:_____

3. _____   _____

Action:_____
Action:_____   What was the outcome?
Action:_____
Action:_____
Action:_____

4. _____   _____

Action:_____
Action:_____   What was the outcome?
Action:_____
Action:_____
Action:_____

5. _____   _____

Action:_____
Action:_____   What was the outcome?
Action:_____
Action:_____
Action:_____

6. _____   _____

Action:_____
Action:_____   What was the outcome?
Action:_____
Action:_____
Action:_____

7. _____   _____

Action:_____
Action:_____   What was the outcome?
Action:_____
Action:_____
Action:_____

90 Day Work Goals

Minute Life

Date:_____

Goals	Completed By

1. _____ _____

    Action:_____

    Action:_____ What was the outcome?

    Action:_____

    Action:_____

    Action:_____

2. _____ _____

    Action:_____

    Action:_____ What was the outcome?

    Action:_____

    Action:_____

    Action:_____

3. _____ _____

    Action:_____

    Action:_____ What was the outcome?

    Action:_____

    Action:_____

    Action:_____

4. _____ _____

    Action:_____

    Action:_____ What was the outcome?

    Action:_____

    Action:_____

    Action:_____

5. _____ _____

    Action:_____

    Action:_____ What was the outcome?

    Action:_____

    Action:_____

    Action:_____

6. _____ _____

    Action:_____

    Action:_____ What was the outcome?

    Action:_____

    Action:_____

    Action:_____

7. _____ _____

    Action:_____

    Action:_____ What was the outcome?

    Action:_____

    Action:_____

    Action:_____

Unfinished Home Tasks

Unfinished tasks cause
stress and chaos in your life

Minute Life

Task	Action
1.	
2.	
3.	
4.	
5.	
6.	
7.	
8.	
9.	
10.	
11.	
12.	
13.	
14.	
15.	
16.	
17.	
18.	
19.	
20.	
21.	
22.	
23.	
24.	
25.	
26.	
27.	
28.	
29.	
30.	

Unfinished Work Tasks

Unfinished tasks cause
stress and chaos in your life

Minute Life

Task	Action
1.	
2.	
3.	
4.	
5.	
6.	
7.	
8.	
9.	
10.	
11.	
12.	
13.	
14.	
15.	
16.	
17.	
18.	
19.	
20.	
21.	
22.	
23.	
24.	
25.	
26.	
27.	
28.	
29.	
30.	

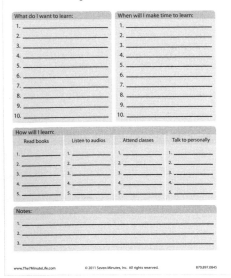

The Learning Worksheet

What do I want to learn:
1.
2.
3.
4.
5.
6.
7.
8.
9.
10.

When will I make time to learn:
1.
2.
3.
4.
5.
6.
7.
8.
9.
10.

How will I learn:

Read books	Listen to audios	Attend classes	Talk to personally
1.	1.	1.	1.
2.	2.	2.	2.
3.	3.	3.	3.
4.	4.	4.	4.
5.	5.	5.	5.

Notes:
1.
2.
3.

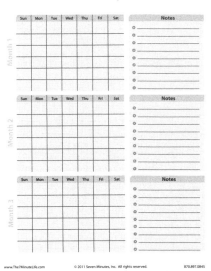

The 7 Minute Life™ 90 Day Calender Worksheet

Month 1

Sun	Mon	Tue	Wed	Thu	Fri	Sat

Notes

Month 2

Sun	Mon	Tue	Wed	Thu	Fri	Sat

Notes

Month 3

Sun	Mon	Tue	Wed	Thu	Fri	Sat

Notes

Connections
personal

Friends . Network . Prospects.
Who do you know that you need to stay in touch with?

Connection	Phone	Comments	Data Contacted
1.			
2.			
3.			
4.			
5.			
6.			
7.			
8.			
9.			
10.			
11.			
12.			
13.			
14.			
15.			
16.			
17.			
18.			
19.			
20.			
21.			
22.			
23.			
24.			
25.			
26.			
27.			
28.			
29.			
30.			

Connections
business

Friends . Network . Prospects.
Who do you know that you need to stay in touch with?

Connection	Phone	Comments	Data Contacted
1.			
2.			
3.			
4.			
5.			
6.			
7.			
8.			
9.			
10.			
11.			
12.			
13.			
14.			
15.			
16.			
17.			
18.			
19.			
20.			
21.			
22.			
23.			
24.			
25.			
26.			
27.			
28.			
29.			
30.			

Your Highest and Best

What is the best use of your time right
Describe what you love to do most, your strengths,
your "highest value activities" & how you want to be rewarded.

What I love to do at work:
1.
2.
3.
4.
5.
6.
7.
8.
9.
10.

My strengths include:
1.
2.
3.
4.
5.
6.
7.
8.
9.
10.

My "Highest Value Activities" are:
1.
2.
3.
4.
5.
6.
7.
8.
9.
10.

I like to be rewarded by:
1.
2.
3.
4.
5.
6.
7.
8.
9.
10.

15 Minute Increment Tracking Sheet

Time	Activity	Time	Activity
5:00		1:00	
:15		:15	
:30		:30	
:45		:45	
6:00		2:00	
:15		:15	
:30		:30	
:45		:45	
7:00		3:00	
:15		:15	
:30		:30	
:45		:45	
8:00		4:00	
:15		:15	
:30		:30	
:45		:45	
9:00		5:00	
:15		:15	
:30		:30	
:45		:45	
10:00		6:00	
:15		:15	
:30		:30	
:45		:45	
11:00		7:00	
:15		:15	
:30		8:00	
:45		9:00	
12:00		10:00	
:15		11:00	
:30		12:00	
:45			

Grocery List

✓ Groceries

PHARMACY
Alcohol
Peroxide
Antibiotic cream
Band-Aids*
Deodorant
Shampoo / Conditioner
Soap
Lotion
Eye drops
Hair gel
Bath soap
Antibacterial hand soap
Multivitamin
Hairspray
Q-tips*
Razors
Shaving cream
Toothbrush / Toothpaste
Mouth rinse
Tylenol* / Ibuprofen
Aspirin
Cold medicine

HARDWARE
Duct Tape
Light bulbs 40-75-100
WD40*
Picture Hangers
Nails

CHILD DEPT.
Baby bath
Baby shampoo
Baby lotion
Baby powder
Diapers / Wipes
Formula
Baby food
Cereal

CLEANING
Detergent
Dryer sheets
Stain remover
Dishwashing liquid
Tilex*
Brillo* Pads
Sponges
Formula 409*
Clean up spray
Clean up wipes
Lysol* kitchen
Lysol* bathroom
Toilet bowl cleaner
Rags
Gloves
Windex*
Mop / Bucket
Furniture polish
Kitchen cleaner

TRASH BAGS/STORAGE
13 gallon
30 gallon
Compactor bags
Foil
Saran* wrap
Ziploc*
Coat hangers

PAPER PRODUCTS
Kleenex*
Paper towels
Toilet paper
Travel Kleenex*
Paper plates
Paper napkins
Plastic cups

SOFT DRINKS
Coke* / Diet Coke*
Pepsi* / Diet Pepsi*
Dr. Pepper*
Sprite*
Root beer
2-liter
Bottled water big/little
Sparkling water

SNACK FOODS
Oreos*
Choc. Chip cookies
Fritos big/ little*
Potato chips
Ruffles*
Pringles*
Tortilla chips
Cheetos* big/little
Goldfish* crackers
Graham crackers
Pretzels
Popcorn
Ritz* crackers
Saltine crackers
Snack mix
Salsa

CEREAL
Apple Jacks*
Total*
Raisin Bran*
Smart Start*
Cheerios*
Pop-tarts*
Fruit Loops*
Cereal bars
Frosted Flakes*
Granola bars
Oatmeal
Syrup
Fruit Snacks

BAKING GOODS
Flour
Baking powder
Baking soda
Chocolate chips
Corn starch
Nuts
Oil / Pam* spray
Salt / Pepper
Sugar
Powdered sugar
Brown sugar
Shortening
Spices
Jell-O* /Pudding
Vanilla
Food coloring / Sprinkles
Brownie mix
Cake mix/ frosting

CANNED FRUIT
Peaches
Pineapples
Applesauce
Fruit cocktail

JUICE
Gatorade* red/green
Kool-Aid*
Cranberry
Grape
Apple juice
Juice boxes

RICE AND PASTA
Bouillon
Beef / Chicken
Spaghetti sauce
Parmesan cheese
Gravy mixes
Brown / White
Kraft Macaroni & Cheese*
Kraft Shells & Cheese*
Elbow noodles
Spaghetti
Other pasta
White rice
Minute Rice*

CANNED VEGETABLES
Creamed corn
Whole Kernel Corn
Green beans
Mushrooms
Spinach
Beets
Peas
Tomatoes 28oz / 14.5oz
Tomato sauce
Jalapeños
Whole new potatoes
Sliced new potatoes
French-fried onions
Whole kernel corn
Lima beans
Kidney beans

SOUP
Chili with beans
Chili no beans
Vegetable soup
Chicken noodle
Beef broth
Chicken broth
French onion soup
Mushroom soup
Cream of chicken

CONDIMENTS
Caesar dressing
Croutons
Oil / Vinegar
Mayonnaise
Mustard
Catsup
Ranch dressing
French-Italian-Thousand
Relish
Pickles
Olives

BREAD
Wheat / white bread
Hotdog buns
Hamburger buns
French bread
Garlic bread
Dinner rolls
Grape jelly
Peanut butter
Honey
Jam

FROZEN FOODS
Frozen pizza
Lean Cuisine*
Chicken nuggets
Frozen lasagna
Frozen corn
Fish sticks
Hash browns
Broccoli spears
Chicken pot pie
Ice cream
Ice cream sandwiches
Juice bars
Orange juice/ lemon juice
Popsicles
Whipped cream
Waffles

DAIRY
Orange Juice
American cheese/slices
Biscuits
Crescent rolls
Cinnamon rolls
Margarine tub
Margarine stick
Butter stick
Cheddar cheese block
Shredded cheese
Cream cheese
Eggs
Whole milk gallon
Skim milk ½ gallons
Mozzarella cheese
Sour cream
Whipped cream
Dips
Choc. Chip Cookie Dough

MISCELLANEOUS
Pictures/ film
Greeting cards
Girl b-day present
Boy b-day present
Gift Cards
Scotch Tape
Ink Pens

PET SUPPLIES
Dog food
Cat food
Bird food
Treats
Toys

DELI
Turkey
Ham
Roast Beef
Chicken Breast
American white
Other sliced cheese
Lunchables*

MEAT
Chicken breasts
Fully cooked chicken
Chicken legs
Chicken nuggets
Hot dogs
Ground beef
Steak
Pot roast
Pork chops
Pork tenderloin
Bacon
Spiral cut ham
Frozen hamburgers
Fajita meat
Chicken
Beef

VEGETABLES
Lettuce
Bag lettuce
Tomatoes
Potatoes
Onions
Cilantro
Celery
Broccoli
Cucumber
Carrots
Baby carrots
Corn
Mushrooms

FRUITS
Apples
Oranges
Bananas
Cantaloupe
Grapes
Lemons
Peaches
Strawberries
Watermelon

CANDY
Chocolates
Licorice
Gum
Mints
Hard candy

Travel Checklist

Name of Event: _____   Date of Event: _____
Contact Person: _____   Cell: _____
City: _____   State: _____
Hotel: _____   Address: _____
Time of Event: _____

○ Flight Reservations
  Airline leaving from [Name of City:
  Airline: _____
  Flight # _____ Departing _____ Arriving _____
  Flight # _____ Departing _____ Arriving _____
○ Hotel Reservations
  Confirmation # _____
○ Ground Transportation
  Confirmation # _____
  _____ Take Shuttle to Hotel _____ Take Taxi to Hotel _____ Take Car Service to Hotel

Expenses:
Mileage: $_____
Air Fare: $_____
Hotel: $_____
Airport Parking: $_____
Tips: $_____ $_____ $_____ $_____
Meals: $_____
        $_____
        $_____
        $_____
Other: $_____
        $_____
        $_____
        $_____
        $_____

Contacts made at event:
Name: Phone #:

Packing Checklist:
○ Work clothes
○ Evening clothes
○ Other clothes
○ Dress Shoes
○ Socks / Hose
○ Belt
○ Underwear
○ Sleepwear
○ Workout Clothes
○ Workout Shoes
○ Toiletries
○ Medicine
○ Cellphone plug
○ Business Cards
○ Airline Ticket
○ Supplies for Event
○ Money for Trip

Mental Clutter
home & work
Avoidance, Procrastination, Distraction, Indecision.
What is causing clutter and stress in my life?

Minute Life

Issue	Action
1.	
2.	
3.	
4.	
5.	
6.	
7.	
8.	
9.	
10.	
11.	
12.	
13.	
14.	
15.	
16.	
17.	
18.	
19.	
20.	
21.	
22.	
23.	
24.	
25.	
26.	
27.	
28.	
29.	
30.	

Annual projects & tasks
Plan ahead for all repeatable events

Minute Life

July
1.
2.
3.
4.
5.
6.

August
1.
2.
3.
4.
5.
6.

Home Repair
Who to contact

Minute Life

Repair	Contact	Phone
1.		
2.		
3.		
4.		
5.		
6.		
7.		
8.		
9.		
10.		
11.		
12.		
13.		
14.		
15.		
16.		
17.		
18.		
19.		
20.		
21.		
22.		
23.		
24.		
25.		
26.		
27.		
28.		
29.		
30.		

Expense Worksheet
Date: _____

Minute Life

Current Expenses	Monthly Avg	Annual Avg
Personal Savings	$	$
Personal Investments		
Retirement Investments		
Education Investments		
Federal, State and Local Taxes		
Mortgage Payments		
Rental Payments		
Homeowners Insurance		
Electric Utilities		
Gas Utilities		
Telephone		
Cell Phone		
Internet Connection		
Water		
Cable TV		
Home Furnishings		
Home Maintenance and Pest Control		
Lawn Maintenance		
Real Estate Taxes		
Personal Property Taxes		
Car Payment		
Car Insurance		
Gasoline		
Car maintenance		
Food		
Toiletries		
Clothing		
Entertainment		
Health Club Dues		
Other Club Dues		
Visa/Amex/MC/Loans		
Vacations		
Childcare/Dependent Care/Alimony		
Tuition		
Health Insurance		
Life Insurance		
Disability Insurance		
Long-term care or other insurance		
Doctors		
Dentists		
Eyeglasses		
Drugs		
Household Help		
Dry Cleaning		
Beauty Salon/Barber		
Pets/Vets		
Subscriptions		
Florists		
Gifts		
Church Donations		
Community Donations		
Hobbies		
CPA		
Professional Dues		
Other		
Other		
Other		
TOTAL EXPENSES	$	$

Current Income	Monthly Avg	Annual Avg
Sources of Income		
Earned Income	$	$
Bonus Income		
Royalties/Rental Income		
Investment Income		
Income from Social Security		
Pension Income		
TOTAL INCOME	$	$
Total Income		
Total Savings		
Total Expenses		
REMAINING INCOME	$	$

Exercise Progress Report

Minute Life

Check off the days you've worked out or exercised

JANUARY

S	M	T	W	Th	F	S

FEBRUARY

S	M	T	W	Th	F	S

MARCH

S	M	T	W	Th	F	S

APRIL

S	M	T	W	Th	F	S

MAY

S	M	T	W	Th	F	S

JUNE

S	M	T	W	Th	F	S

JULY

S	M	T	W	Th	F	S

AUGUST

S	M	T	W	Th	F	S

SEPTEMBER

S	M	T	W	Th	F	S

OCTOBER

S	M	T	W	Th	F	S

NOVEMBER

S	M	T	W	Th	F	S

DECEMBER

S	M	T	W	Th	F	S

Daily Task Checklist

Minute Life

Date: _____

✓	Daily Tasks

Meeting Planner

Minute Life

Strategy. Idea. Project. Campaign. Vision.

Concept/Description

What is the desired outcome?

Who needs to be involved?

Action Steps:

1. _____
2. _____
3. _____
4. _____
5. _____
6. _____
7. _____

Business Assessment

Minute Life

Assessments provide a framework to learn more about yourself. You will find you have natural aptitudes for many areas of your work and your life - typically, these are the areas you find most meaningful in life. You may also find some areas which need improvement. Once you have completed the assessment you can make conscious decisions for how you will spend your time.

Business Assessment	Excellent	Good	Average	Needs Some Work	Needs Improvement
Written Business Plan for the next 90 Days					
Workable Business Plan for the next 90 Days					
Strategic Clarification of your Goals					
Daily Activity Level					
Professional Competency					
Business writing skills (letters, proposals, contracts)					
Knowledge of technology (Outlook, Excel, Word, PowerPoint)					
Marketing strategy (compelling story - crushing offer)					
Distinctive branding					
Indentifiable brand image (brochures, letter head, website)					
Financial understanding (P&L, balance sheet, cashflow)					
One-on-one communication skills					
Public Speaking Skills					
Business etiquette					
Time Management & Organization Assessment					
Do you have a written daily plan of action?					
Are you effectively using repeatable processes & systems?					
Is your work space organized and clutter free?					
Method to prioritize and accomplish Unfinished Tasks					
Planning complex tasks and executing them					
Ability to start and fully finish every task					
Work / Life Balance					
Do you have the appropriate time to accomplish those tasks?					
Personal Assessment					
Understanding of Purpose, Passion and Driving Force					
Defined values and knowlege of what is most important					
Personal goals for life					
Do you have a clear vision of where you will be in 90 days?					
Listening skills					
Emotional Intelligence					
Overall health					
Exercise					
Weight					
Sleep					
Stress level					
Relationships					
Faith					

ACKNOWLEDGMENTS

To be able to think, imagine, and dream and shape ideas into language that can be made into stories and shared in a book is a miracle. Words are a gift from God. All thanks begin there.

Next, I would like to thank my husband, Mark Lewis, and our children, Abby and J. In every page of writing this book I have become more aware of my love for my family. Daily they are showing me how to create a life with meaning.

To my parents, Ann and Al White; for more than half a century their unabashed love has allowed me to thrive.

To my friends and teammates, Susan Naylor and Heather Skinner, so much of our life is experienced during the hours we spend at "work." The two of you have helped me understand how knowing your purpose can make a difference in the lives we serve. Thanks for teaching me about time management, organization, and fun.

A special thanks to Susan Naylor for inspiring many of the 7 Minute ideas and tools shown in this book. She also cowrote The 7 Minute Solution Fast Start Guide: A 31 Day Action Plan.

In the pages of this book you will see yourself in the stories of my family, friends, and mentors—and from amazing authors, scholars, psychologists, professors, and physicians you will begin to discover the depths of the power of the human brain. Special thanks to Shawn Achor; Judy Adair; Daniel Amen, MD; Joseph Annabali, MD; Leslie Banks; Jahnae H. Barnett, PhD; Earl Bell; Karen and Michael Berry, MD; Mimi Bock; Bob Burg; Denise Clompton, PhD; Steve Cox; Mihaly Csikszentmihalyi, PhD; Jennifer and Max Dacus; JoAnn Dahlkoetter, PhD; Colin Daymude; Lyn and Ted Drake; Cozy Dixon; Norman Doidge, MD; Dawn Duca; Mark Duckworth; Donna Evans; Margaret Feurtado, MD; Donna Feyen; Karon and Brad Fields, MD; James N. Flack, MD; John Foley; Terri Fulton; Winifred Gallagher; Hal Gatewood; Lieutenant Colonel (ret.) Dave Grossman; Joe Hardy, PhD; Grant Hinkson; Dan Holmes, PhD; Rhonda Horne; Andy Hudmon, PhD; Debbie Irvin; Susan Ishmael; Jill and Larry James; Seth James; Glen and Sharon Jones; Laurie Beth Jones; Patsy Jones; Steve and Nellon Jones; Guy Kochel; Florence Krause, PhD; Michelle and Alan Lawson; Bobbi Layton; Gloria Lewis; Jill Lewis; Conley Madden; George McLeod; Jessica Miller; Sharon Milligan; Bridget and Mark Newman; Lucy Jo Palladino, PhD; Jean Pamplin; Sean Phillips; Daniel Pink; Joe Puthur; Whit Raymond; Veronica and Dan Reeves; Dan and Debbie Ring; Dave Savage; Mark Schwab; Michael Sears; Brian Shambo; Shelly Shepherd; Esther Silver-Parker; Steve Spencer; Adam Staples; Colin Stewart; Deonne Sullivan; Elizabeth Talbot; Celia and Henry Torres; Joan Townsend; Amy Tyler; Chris Vinyard; John Weller; Al White, III; Kes White; Sam White; Jon Wilbanks; Jason Womack; and Stuart Yudofski, MD.

To my first literary agent, Larry Kirshbaum, you are a wonderful friend and teacher; thank you for believing.

The 7 Minute Solution: Creating a Life with Meaning 7 Minutes at a Time shares the importance of learning how to focus your attention on what is most important. My editor and book coach, Erin Casey, worked with me on this project from the beginning. From rewrite to rewrite she helped me narrow the focus and improve the meaning of each page. Erin, thank you for the structure, the advice, and the belief you brought to this manuscript.

To John Arnold, my chief brainstorming, copywriting, buzzword-creating, right-brained narrator, I am so appreciative of all of the effort you put into this project. You are an inspiration; thank you for adding depth, richness, and color to this book.

To Jenna Lang, thank you for the clarity and the objectivity you added.

To Mimi Bock, someone I have known for almost two decades, who in one moment spoke a single phrase that has made the lives of thousands more meaningful.

To Mark McNabb (www.ChrisMarketing.com), Grant Hinkson, and Sohan Singh for their creativity and talent in helping design many of the 7 Minute images and tools.

Next, working with the men and women at Free Press has been such a joy, thanks to Leslie Meredith, Donna Loffredo, and Phil Metcalf. I especially want to thank Leah Miller, who diligently guided me though every single word on every single page.

My purpose in life is growing and helping others grow. My final acknowledgment is to you, the readers of this book, and the members of the 7 Minute Community. My hope is that you will find more meaning in life. May God bless you.

Allyson Lewis
Jonesboro, Arkansas
2012

ABOUT THE AUTHOR

Allyson Lewis's life changed the moment she discovered her purpose. Since then, she has been on a mission to help others connect with their purpose and consistently accomplish their life goals through her unique, highly effective time and life management system.

Allyson is a time management expert, bestselling author, and speaker. Her enthusiasm is believable and contagious. You will be entertained and enthralled at the same time. Readers and audiences across the country have left with their hearts pumping and their brains full of concrete ideas that can be applied immediately to their daily lives. In as little as "7 Minutes" a day you can clarify your goals, improve your time management, and create repeatable systematic processes to create a life with meaning.

The author of two other books, *The 7 Minute Life™ Daily Planner* and *The 7 Minute Difference*, Allyson has trained thousands of people nationwide and has been a guest on CNN and Bloomberg Information TV. She is a monthly columnist for MorningstarAdvisor.com. She lives in Jonesboro, Arkansas, with her husband, Mark Lewis, and their two children, Abby and J. They have two golden retrievers, Buddy and Vero.